SAVANNAH

JIM MOREKIS

Contents

Maps

SIGHTS

- 7 World War II Memorial
- 13 City Hall
- 14 Chatham Artillery Guns
- 20 Savannah Cotton Exchange
- 21 Rousakis Plaza
- 25 Factor's Walk
- 28 Emmet Park
- 31 The Waving Girl
- 34 First African Baptist Church
- 36 Haitian Monument
- 37 Ships of the Sea Maritime Museum
- 40 American Prohibition Museum
- 44 U.S. Custom House
- 47 Christ Episcopal Church
- 48 Olde Pink House
- 50 Oliver Sturgis House
- 51 Lucas Theatre for the Arts
- 54 Hampton Lillibridge House and Charles Oddingsells House
- 55 Trustees Garden
- 72 Trustees Theater
- 73 Jen Library
- 79 Telfair Academy of Arts and Sciences
- 80 Trinity United Methodist Church
- 81 Federal Courthouse and Post Office
- 83 Evangelical Lutheran Church of the Ascension
- 85 Owens-Thomas House
- 86 Isaiah Davenport House Museum
- 87 Kehoe House
- 91 Second African Baptist Church
- 92 Cunningham House
- 94 Jepson Center for the Arts
- 97 Juliette Gordon Low Birthplace

Tours

- 17 Savannah Riverboat Cruises
- 32 Savannah Belles
- 33 Savannah Slow Ride
- 75 Savannah Bike Tours
- 76 Savannah Taste Experience

RESTAURANTS

- 16 Olympia Café
- 19 Vic's on the River
- 22 Treylor Park
- 29 B. Matthew's Eatery
- 35 Vinnie VanGoGo's
- 38 Lulu's Chocolate Bar
- 43 Co Savannah
- 46 The Lady & Sons
- 49 Olde Pink House
- 56 The Grey
- 59 The Coffee Fox
- 67 Kayak Kafe
- 71 Leopold's Ice Cream
- 77 Tequila's Town
- 82 Wright Square Cafe
- 84 Zunzi's
- 89 17Hundred90 Inn
- 95 Husk Savannah
- 96 The Collins Quarter

NIGHTLIFE

- 3 Chuck's Bar
- 6 Club One Jefferson
- 8 Kevin Barry's Irish Pub
- 9 Rocks on the Roof
- 12 Moon River Brewing Company
- 24 Bayou Cafe
- 39 Rail Pub
- 41 22 Square
- 45 The Jinx
- 53 Abe's on Lincoln
- 60 Circa 1875
- 63 Chive Sea Bar and Lounge
- 70 O'Connell's

World War II Memorial 7

WILLIAMSON ST

3
4
5
8
9 10
11
15 16 17 18 19

Rousakis Plaza 21

E LOWER FACTORS WALK

UPPER FACTORS WK

City Hall 13 14

20 Savannah Cotton Exchange 22

W BAY ST

33
6
W BAY LN
12
Chatham Artillery Guns 44
U.S. Custom House

Franklin Square

35
41 42
43
W BRYAN ST

First African Baptist Church 34

Ellis Square
46
Johnson Square

Olde Pink House 48 49

36 Haitian Monument
40
W CONGRESS ST

47 Christ Episcopal Church

50 Oliver Sturgis House

37
38 39
Ships of the Sea Maritime Museum
W CONGRESS LN
American Prohibition Museum
45
60
70

ZUBLEY ST

W BROUGHTON ST
58 59
61
63 64 65 66
67 68 69

57
W BROUGHTON LN

56
76
77
78

W STATE ST

Telfair Academy of Arts and Sciences 79
Federal Courthouse and Post Office 81

Evangelical Lutheran Church of the Ascension 83

Telfair Square

Wright Square
E PRESIDENT ST

W PRESIDENT ST
Trinity United Methodist Church 80
W YORK ST
84

82

W YORK LN

Jepson Center for the Arts 94
95
96

Juliette Gordon Low Birthplace 97 98

W OGLETHORPE AVE

W OGLETHORPE LN

HISTORIC DISTRICT

© AVALON TRAVEL

SEE MAP 2

W HULL ST

Chippewa Square

ARTS AND CULTURE
52 Lucas Theatre for the Arts
62 Savannah Philharmonic

SPORTS AND ACTIVITIES
2 Savannah Derby Devils

SHOPS
4 Black Dog General Store
5 Jere's Antiques
15 Savannah Bee Company
18 River Street Sweets
23 The Mad Hatter
26 Woof Gang Bakery
27 Harley-Davidson
57 Chocolat by Adam Turoni
58 Savannah Bee Company
61 The Paris Market & Brocante
64 Levy Jewelers
65 Civvies New and Recycled Clothing
66 24e Furnishings at Broughton
68 Half Moon Outfitters
69 Globe Shoe Co.
74 Blick Art Materials

HOTELS
1 Westin Savannah Harbor Golf Resort and Spa
10 Bohemian Hotel Savannah
11 Hyatt Regency Savannah
30 The Brice
42 Andaz Savannah
78 The Marshall House
88 The Kehoe House
90 17Hundred90
93 The Green Palm Inn
98 Ballastone Inn

Savannah

River

Morrell Park

Factor's Walk 25
E RIVER ST
26 27
31
The Waving Girl

23 24
E LOWER FACTORS WALK
FACTORS WALK

WATERFRONT
Emmet Park 28
RIVER ST

32

E BAY ST
29
E BAY LN
30

53

E BRYAN ST

Reynolds Square
Warren Square
E ST JULIAN ST
Washington Square
54
Hampton Lillibridge House and Charles Oddingsells House

Trustees Garden
55

Lucas Theatre for the Arts
51
52
E CONGRESS ST

Trustees Theater
71 72
74 75
E CONGRESS LN

73
Jen Library
E BROUGHTON ST

E BROUGHTON LN

Owens-Thomas House
85
Kehoe House
87
86
Isaiah Davenport House Museum
Cunningham House

88
E STATE ST
91 92
Greene Square
93

Oglethorpe Square
Columbia Square
E PRESIDENT ST

89
90
E YORK ST
Second African Baptist Church

E YORK LN
PRICE ST
BURNEY DR

E OGLETHORPE AVE

Colonial Park Cemetery
E OGLETHORPE LN

SEE MAP 2

0   100 yds
0   100 m
DISTANCE ACROSS MAP
Approximate: 1 mi or 1.6 km

DISTANCE ACROSS MAP
Approximate: 1.1 mi or 1.7 km

SEE MAP 1

SIGHTS

1   SCAD Museum of Art
2   Savannah History Museum
5   Battlefield Park
6   Georgia State Railroad Museum
7   Savannah Children's Museum
8   Independent Presbyterian Church
9   Colonial Cemetery
11   First Baptist Church
12   Historic Savannah Theatre
19   Cathedral of St. John the Baptist
20   Beach Institute
21   Green-Meldrim House
23   Unitarian Universalist Church of Savannah
24   Andrew Low House Museum
25   Hamilton-Turner Inn
26   Flannery O'Connor Childhood Home
27   Scottish Rite Temple
29   Poetter Hall
31   Jones Street
42   Ralph Mark Gilbert Civil Rights Museum
43   Mercer-Williams House Museum
46   Temple Mickve Israel
47   Wesley Monumental United Methodist Church
48   Massie Heritage Center

Tours
3   Savannah Movie Tour
32   Old City Walks
36   Sixth Sense Savannah Ghost Tour
49   Walking Tours Savannah

RESTAURANTS

30   Crystal Beer Parlor
33   Mrs. Wilkes' Dining Room
51   Fork & Dagger

© AVALON TRAVEL

SEE MAP 3

Independent Presbyterian Church **8**

9 E OGLETHORPE AVE

Colonial Cemetery

10

Historic Savannah Theatre **12**
13

11 First Baptist Church

Chippewa Square

W HULL ST

E HULL ST

E MC DONOUGH ST

E MC DONOUGH ST

14

E PERRY ST

E PERRY ST

HISTORIC DISTRICT

E PERRY LN

15

E PERRY LN

E LIBERTY ST

17

16

E LIBERTY LN

Cathedral of St. John the Baptist

Beach Institute **20**

Green-Meldrim House

18

19

23 Unitarian Universalist Church of Savannah

21

Madison Square

22

E MACON ST

Lafayette Square

E MACON ST

24

25 Hamilton-Turner Inn

W CHARLTON ST

Andrew Low House Museum

E CHARLTON ST

Scottish Rite Temple **27** **28**

29 Poetter Hall

26 Flannery O'Connor Childhood Home

E CHARLTON LN

Jones Street **32**

31

33 **34**

35

E JONES ST

36

31

E JONES LN

37

38

39

E TAYLOR ST

40

41

Wesley Monumental United Methodist Church

Monterey Square

E WAYNE ST

47 *Calhoun Square*

Whitefield Square

43

46

Mercer-Williams House Museum

44 **45**

Temple Mickve Israel

E GORDON ST

48

49

Massie Heritage Center

E GORDON LN

E GASTON ST

MARINE MEMORIAL

VICTORIAN DISTRICT

Forsyth Fountain

51

Forsyth Park

CONFEDERATE MEMORIAL

NIGHTLIFE
4 The Distillery
14 McDonough's
18 The Original Pinkie Master's
50 The Chromatic Dragon

ARTS AND CULTURE
13 Historic Savannah Theatre

SHOPS
15 The Book Lady
17 Saints and Shamrocks
22 E. Shaver Bookseller
28 shopSCAD
34 One Fish Two Fish
37 Small Pleasures
38 The Corner Door
39 V&J Duncan
40 Madame Chrysanthemum
41 Custard Boutique
44 Alex Raskin Antiques
45 Folklorico

HOTELS
10 Foley House Inn
16 The DeSoto Savannah
35 Eliza Thompson House

SEE MAP 2

SIGHTS
4 Forsyth Park
9 Carnegie Branch Library
10 Laurel Grove Cemetery

Tour
8 Hearse Ghost Tours

RESTAURANTS
6 The Sentient Bean
11 Cotton & Rye
12 Foxy Loxy
13 Elizabeth on 37th
14 Back in the Day Bakery
17 Green Truck Neighborhood Pub
19 Atlantic

NIGHTLIFE
7 American Legion Bar

SPORTS AND ACTIVITIES
5 Forsyth Park
20 Wilderness Southeast

SHOPS
15 Graveface Records & Curiosities
16 Gypsy World
18 Picker Joe's Antique Mall & Vintage Market

HOTELS
1 The Gastonian Inn
2 Dresser-Palmer House
3 Mansion on Forsyth Park

Laurel Grove Cemetery 10

Laurel Grove Cemetery 10

W WAYNE ST
MONTGOMERY ST
MARTIN LUTHER KING JR BLVD
W GWINNETT ST
EMERALD DR
GWINNETT CT
MAY ST
W ANDERSON ST
W 31ST ST
W 32ND ST
W 35TH ST
W 36TH ST
W 37TH ST
W 38TH ST
W 39TH ST
W 40TH ST
W 41ST ST
W 42ND ST
W VICTORY DR
W 44TH ST
W 45TH ST
W 46TH ST
W 47TH ST
STILES AVE
OGEECHEE RD RD
HOPKINS ST
STEVENS ST
BULLOCH ST
FLORENCE ST
BURROUGHS ST
MARTIN LUTHER KING JR BLVD
MONTGOMERY ST

0 — 250 yds
0 — 250 m
DISTANCE ACROSS MAP
Approximate: 2.2 mi or 3.5 km

Chatham Square

Monterey Square

Calhoun Square

E TAYLOR ST

SEE MAP 2

Mother Matilda Beasley Park

E GORDON LN

1

W GASTON ST

2

MARINE MEMORIAL

E GASTON LN

Forsyth Fountain

E HUNTINGDON ST

E HUNTINGDON LN

E HALL ST

VICTORIAN DISTRICT

CONFEDERATE MEMORIAL

3

E HALL LN

E GWINNETT ST

Forsyth Park

E BOLTON ST

4

E WALDBURG ST

5

THE HIKER

E PARK AVENUE LN

6

E DUFFY ST

8

7

E HENRY ST

E ANDERSON ST

9

Carnegie Branch Library

E 31ST ST

W 32ND ST

W 33RD ST

W 34TH ST

11

E 35TH ST

SOFO

12

E 36TH ST

204

E 37TH ST

13

W 38TH ST

E 38TH ST

W 39TH ST

E 39TH ST

W 40TH ST

E 40TH ST

15 14

204

16

17

W 41ST ST

E 41ST ST

W 42ND ST

E 41ST LN

18

19

E VICTORY DR

80

E 44TH ST

E 45TH ST

E 46TH ST

WASHINGTON AVE

20

© AVALON TRAVEL

BARNARD ST
WHITAKER ST
DRAYTON ST
ABERCORN ST
LINCOLN ST
HABERSHAM ST
PRICE ST
E BROAD ST
EAST BROAD ST
BULL ST
ABERCORN ST
LINCOLN ST
DRAYTON ST
PRICE ST
EAST BROAD ST
REYNOLDS ST
ATLANTIC AVE
PAULSEN ST
HABERSHAM ST
CHATHAM CRES

Savannah River

E PRESIDENT ST

SEE MAP 1

1 Old Fort Jackson

2

80

3
Oatland Island
Wildlife Center

SEE MAP 2

Bonaventure
Cemetery
4
5

80

JOHNNY
MERCER BLVD

9

6

Whitemarsh
Island

7 8
Daffin Park

Thunderbolt
Museum **10**
SEE MAP 3
11

Thunderbolt

Savannah
State University
12

LA ROCHE AVE

13

Wilmington River

Wilmington
Island
14

Dutch
Island

EISENHOWER DR

16

NORWOOD AVE

University of Georgia
Marine Educational
Center and Aquarium
15

Skidaway
Island

MCWHORTER DR

WILMINGTON ISLAND RD

Isle of
Hope
17 **19**

18
Wormsloe
State Historic Site

FERGUSON AVE

Isle of
Hope

Skidaway Island
State Park
23
24

Pin Point
Heritage Museum
20

204

22
21

MCWHORTER DR

SIGHTS
1 Old Fort Jackson
3 Oatland Island Wildlife Center
4 Bonaventure Cemetery
7 Daffin Park
10 Thunderbolt Museum
12 Savannah State University
15 University of Georgia Marine Educational Center and Aquarium
18 Wormsloe State Historic Site
19 Isle of Hope
20 Pin Point Heritage Museum
23 Skidaway Island State Park

RESTAURANTS
6 Desposito's
17 Sandfly BBQ

SPORTS AND ACTIVITIES
2 Savannah Fly Fishing Charters
5 Savannah Canoe & Kayak
8 Daffin Park
9 The Savannah Bananas
11 Telecaster Charters
13 Miss Judy Charters
14 Wilmington Island Club
16 Bacon Park
21 Moon River Kayak Tours
22 Skidaway Narrows
24 Skidaway Island State Park

0   1 mi
0   1 km
DISTANCE ACROSS MAP
Approximate: 6.3 mi or 10.1 km

© AVALON TRAVEL

SOUTH CAROLINA

Savannah River

GEORGIA

Fort Pulaski National Monument

Cockspur Island

Lazaretto

Creek

80

Tybee Island Light Station and Museum

SOLOMON AVE

80

Tybee Post Theater

DAV ISLAND RD

CHATHAM AVE

BUTLER AVE

SEE DETAIL

SIGHTS
1	Fort Pulaski National Monument
11	Tybee Island Light Station and Museum
14	Tybee Post Theater
20	South End
24	Tybee Island Marine Science Center

RESTAURANTS
7	The Crab Shack
8	Huc-a-Poo's Bites & Booze
12	North Beach Grill
21	Tybee Island Social Club
23	The Breakfast Club

SPORTS AND ACTIVITIES
2	Fort Pulaski National Monument
3	McQueen's Island Trail
4	Lazaretto Creek
5	Amick's Deep Sea Fishing
6	North Island Surf and Kayak
9	Sea Kayak Georgia
15	High Tides Surf Shop
16	Tybee Island Memorial Park
17	Sundial Nature Tours
18	Little Tybee Island
19	North Beach

HOTELS
10	River's End Campground
13	Lighthouse Inn
22	The Georgianne Inn
25	Atlantis Inn
26	Beachview Bed & Breakfast

Little Tybee Island

0   750 yds
0   750 m
DISTANCE ACROSS MAP
Approximate: 3.8 mi or 6.1 km

2ND AVE

LOVELL AVE

9TH ST

10TH ST

South End

11TH ST

JONES AVE

12TH ST

BUTLER AVE

13TH ST

14TH ST

Tybee Island Marine Science Center

15TH ST

TABRISA ST

17TH ST

19

20

21   22

23   24

25

26

© AVALON TRAVEL

SIGHTS

2 Jerusalem Evangelical Lutheran Church

3 New Ebenezer Retreat and Conference Center

8 National Museum of the Mighty Eighth Air Force

14 Coastal Georgia Botanical Gardens at the Bamboo Farm

19 Richmond Hill Historical Society and Museum

20 Fort McAllister State Historic Site

21 Wassaw Island National Wildlife Refuge

23 Midway Museum

25 Geechee Kunda

26 Seabrook Village

28 Fort Morris State Historic Site

31 Ossabaw Island

RESTAURANTS

4 Pie Society

5 Molly MacPherson's Scottish Pub and Grill

6 Naan Appetit

16 The Upper Crust Pizzeria

18 Steamers Restaurant & Raw Bar

24 Holton's Seafood

27 Sunbury Crab Company

SPORTS AND ACTIVITIES

1 Ebenezer Creek

9 Laurel Hill Wildlife Drive

10 Savannah National Wildlife Refuge

11 Club at Savannah Harbor

12 Savannah-Ogeechee River Canal

13 Henderson Golf Club

22 LeConte-Woodmanston Botanical Garden

30 Youmans Pond

32 Gray's Reef National Marine Sanctuary

SHOPS

7 Tanger Outlets Savannah

15 Keller's Flea Market

17 Oglethorpe Mall

HOTELS

29 Dunham Farms

To **32** Gray's Reef National Marine Sanctuary ↓

DISCOVER

Savannah

In an increasingly homogenized society, Savannah is one of the last places where eccentricity is celebrated and even encouraged. This outspoken, often stubborn determination to make one's own way in the world is personified by the old Georgia joke about Savannah being the capital of "the state of Chatham," the county in which it resides. In typical contrarian fashion, Savannahians take this nickname as a compliment.

Savannah was built as a series of rectangular "wards," each constructed around a central square. As the city grew, each square took on its own characteristics, depending on who lived on the square and how they made their livelihood. Sounds simple—and it is. That's why its effectiveness has lasted so long.

It is this individuality that is so well documented in John Berendt's *Midnight in the Garden of Good and Evil*. The squares of Savannah's downtown—a National Landmark Historic District since 1965—are also responsible for the city's walkability, another defining characteristic. Just as cars entering a square must yield to traffic already within, pedestrians are obliged to slow down and interact with the surrounding environment, both constructed and natural. You become participant and audience simultaneously, a feat made easier by the local penchant for easy conversation.

Savannah is also known for being able to show you a rowdy good time, and not only during its massive world-famous St. Patrick's Day celebration. Savannahians will use any excuse for a party, exemplified by the city's very liberal open-container law. It is this sort of freedom of merriment that captures Savannah's essence.

So go on, join in the fun—you may even learn something new about yourself.

Clockwise from top left: a Savannah home; "Gracie" sculpture in Bonaventure Cemetery; fountain in front of the Savannah Cotton Exchange; River Street.

8 TOP EXPERIENCES

1 **Historic Tours:** The historic downtown area of Savannah is best experienced on foot or by carriage (page 90).

2 **Southern Cuisine:** Some of America's finest award-winning chefs ply their trade in this city, serving up dishes both homestyle and high style (page 28).

3 **Festival Fever:** St. Patrick's Day is famous in Savannah—come find out why (page 120).

>>>

4 **Cemetery Scenery:** For both intriguing American history and scenic beauty, check out Bonaventure Cemetery (page 75), Laurel Grove Cemetery (page 70), and Colonial Cemetery (page 58).

5 **African American Heritage:** Savannah's history is black history, from the oldest black congregation in North America to the living legacy of the Gullah from the nearby Golden Isles (page 30).

6 **Forsyth Park:** This verdant expanse ringed by old live oaks and chockablock with memorials is the true center of downtown life (page 70).

7 **To-Go Cup Revelry:** Savannah is one of the few cities in the United States where you can stroll the streets enjoying an adult beverage— legally (page 117)!

>>>

8 **A Day at the Beach:** From family-friendly beaches on Hilton Head Island to romantic solitude on Cumberland Island, there's a beach here for everyone (page 31).

>>>

Planning Your Trip

Neighborhoods

WATERFRONT

It's only natural to start one's adventures in Savannah where Oglethorpe's adventures themselves began: on the waterfront, now dominated by scenic and **historic River Street.** Once the **bustling center** of Savannah's thriving cotton and naval stores export industry, the waterfront also includes **Factor's Walk** and **Bay Street.**

CITY MARKET

In local parlance, the phrase "City Market" refers not only to the **refurbished warehouses** that make up this **tourist-friendly** area of shops and restaurants in the historic district's western portion but also to its bookends, **Franklin and Ellis Squares.**

HISTORIC DISTRICT

Life in the bulk of **downtown** revolves around Savannah's many **historic squares,** legacies of the colony's founding. Churches, homes, shops, and businesses abound in this sizable but very **walkable** National Landmark Historic District.

SOFO DISTRICT

The name means "South of Forsyth Park," and this pretty, quiet, but **up-and-coming** area includes Savannah's Victorian district as well as turn-of-the-20th-century "streetcar suburbs." It also has many of Savannah's **foodie gems.**

Old Town Trolley Tours in downtown Savannah

Tybee Island Light Station

VICTORIAN DISTRICT

Boasting 50 blocks of fine **Victorian and Queen Anne frame houses,** Savannah's Victorian district is truly magnificent. The city's first sub-urb, it was built between 1870 and 1910. In addition to the glories of **Forsyth Park,** some key areas for connoisseurs of truly grand **Victorian architecture** are the residential blocks of East Hall Street between Lincoln and Price Streets—one of the few street sections in town with the **original paving.** Some other nice examples are in the 1900-2000 blocks of Bull Street near the large Bull Street Public Library, including the famous "Gingerbread House" at 1917 Bull Street.

EASTSIDE

Eastside includes many areas that are technically **islands,** but you'll sense little difference from the mainland. **Marshland, Spanish moss,** and **outdoor scenery** are the draws.

SOUTHSIDE

To most locals, "Southside" refers to the generic strip-mall sprawl below Derenne Avenue, but for our purposes, the term also includes some **outlying islands.** They are among the **most scenic** areas in Savannah.

TYBEE ISLAND

Its name means "salt" in the old Euchee tongue, indicative of the island's chief export in those days. And Tybee Island—"Tybee" to locals—is indeed one of the **essential seasonings** of life in Savannah. Tybee is part and parcel of the city's social and cultural fabric. Many of the island's 3,000 full-time residents, known for their boozy bonhomie and quirky personal style, commute to work in the city. And those living "in town" often reciprocate by visiting Tybee to dine in its few but **excellent restaurants,** drink in its casual and **crazy watering holes,** and frolic on its wide, **beautiful beaches** lined with rare sea oats waving in the Atlantic breeze.

GREATER SAVANNAH

Outlying areas of Savannah differ in character, ranging from the bustling new growth of **West Chatham County,** featuring the Mighty Eighth National Air Force Museum, to the Henry Ford-related history of the bedroom community of **Richmond Hill,** to the blackwater ecosystem of **New Ebenezer,** to the quaint and quiet **Liberty County,** home of two out of three of Georgia's signers of the Declaration of Independence.

When to Go

Springtime is for lovers, and it's no coincidence that springtime is when most love affairs with the region begin. Unless you have severe pollen allergies—not a trivial concern given the explosion of plant life at this time—you should try to experience this area at its peak of natural beauty during the magical period from **mid-March to mid-May.** Not surprisingly, lodging is the most expensive and most difficult to secure at that time. Hilton Head's busiest time is during the **RBC Heritage golf tournament** in mid-April. While last-minute cancellations are always possible, the only real guarantee is to secure reservations as far in advance as possible (a full year in advance is not unusual for peak times).

Activity here slows down noticeably in **July and August.** But overall, summertime in the South gets a bad rap and is often not appreciably worse than summers north of the Mason-Dixon Line—though it's certainly more humid.

My favorite time of year on the southeastern coast is the **middle of November,** when the tourist crush noticeably subsides. Not only are the days delightful and the nights crisp (but not frigid), but you can get a room at a good price.

What to Take

Unless you're coming in the winter to take advantage of lower rates or to enjoy the copious seasonal cheer, there's not much need for a heavy jacket. A **sweater or windbreaker** will do fine for chillier days. Also note that the ocean and the larger rivers can generate some surprisingly crisp breezes, even on what otherwise might be a warm day.

Because of the area's temperate climate, perspiration is likely to be a constant travel companion; pack accordingly. Whatever you wear, stay with **natural fabrics** such as cotton. The humidity and generally warm weather combine for a miserable experience with polyester and other synthetic fabrics.

Unless you're coming in the hottest days of summer or the coldest part of winter—both unlikely scenarios—plan on a trip to a drugstore or supermarket to buy some **bug spray** or Skin So Soft, an Avon product that also keeps away the gnats.

The Best of Savannah

Downtown Savannah comprises one of the largest historic districts in the country, and is certainly among the most walkable and friendly. This itinerary also takes you to outlying areas around Savannah and down the beautiful Georgia coast, where you can experience the area's natural beauty and pleasant climate.

Day 1

SAVANNAH

Hit downtown Savannah hard today, starting with a walk down **River Street.** Then enjoy the aesthetic charms of the two adjacent museums, one traditional and one modern, composing the **Telfair Museums.** Tour the exquisite **Owens-Thomas House Museum** and then take a walk through the squares, visiting the **Cathedral of St. John the Baptist** in Lafayette Square and the **Mercer-Williams House** on Monterey Square.

Day 2

On your way out to Tybee Island, stop for a walk through amazing **Bonaventure Cemetery**—about 15 minutes outside downtown—and pay your respects to native son Johnny Mercer. A half-hour drive takes you to scenic and historically important **Fort Pulaski National Monument.** Scoot on into Tybee another 10 minutes and climb to the top of the **Tybee Island Light Station** before dinner.

the Telfair Academy of Arts and Sciences

Southern Cooking: High Style and Homestyle

Sandfly BBQ

Fresh Seafood

The best seafood places put a premium on freshly harvested fish and shellfish:

- **Desposito's,** Savannah (page 105): Shrimp and oysters dockside.

- **Red Fish,** Hilton Head Island (page 178): Stylish but always fresh.

- **Speed's Kitchen,** Shellman Bluff (page 208): Delicacies right off the boat.

New Southern

The area is home to some adventurous chefs offering an updated take on Low-country classics:

- **The Grey,** Savannah (page 99): Savannah's new world-class restaurant, competitive with the best in the nation.

Classic Southern

Your best bets for fine old-school Southern cooking:

- **Mrs. Wilkes' Dining Room,** Savannah (page 103): Old-school "pass the plate" community seating in a historic home.

- **17Hundred90,** Savannah (page 100): Enjoy dinner and soothing piano music in one of Savannah's most historic buildings.

Barbecue

The pleasures of the pig are never far away in this region:

- **Sandfly BBQ,** Savannah (page 106): Excellent Memphis-style barbecue on the south side of Savannah.

Savannah in One Day

Savannah's beautiful, walkable historic district makes for a relatively easy way to spend a day.

Begin with a morning stroll through big, scenic **Forsyth Park** and enjoy this jewel of Victorian green-space design. Don't forget the no-brainer selfie stop at the Forsyth Park Fountain!

Next, walk a block northeast to Calhoun Square for a stop at the **Massie Heritage Center,** probably the best one-stop place for a full but digestible Savannah history lesson, via its state-of-the-art displays.

Walk a few blocks north to check out the stunning **Cathedral of St. John the Baptist** on Lafayette Square, the old stomping grounds of Southern author Flannery O'Connor. Another block north is **Colonial Cemetery,** the city's oldest, which you can walk through on your way to **Kayak Kafe** on Broughton Street for a quick and tasty lunch.

After lunch, walk a few blocks to the **Owens-Thomas House** and enjoy a tour of America's best single example of Regency architecture. After your tour, head around the corner and take a stroll on **Broughton Street,** Savannah's main shopping thoroughfare, and maybe enjoy a cone at **Leopold's Ice Cream Shop.**

Either via your own car or a rideshare, spend the rest of the afternoon on a side trip to beautiful and historic **Bonaventure Cemetery** on the city's eastside.

End with an early evening stroll on the ballast stones of **River Street** before heading to **17Hundred90** to dine in a historic building with a great menu. Consider following up with a nightcap on top of the Bohemian Hotel at **Rocks on the Roof,** with great drinks and a gorgeous view of the entire waterfront.

Day 3
THE GOLDEN ISLES

Drive down scenic U.S. 17 through the Altamaha River estuary, about an hour and a half south of Savannah, and stop by historic **Hofwyl-Broadfield Plantation,** near Brunswick, for a glimpse at an authentic old rice plantation. Make the five-minute trip over the causeway and enjoy the afternoon at **The Village** on St. Simons Island, with a visit to historic **Fort Frederica National Monument.**

Day 4

This morning, a 20-minute drive takes you into the **Jekyll Island Historic District.** Tour the grounds and have lunch at any of the great restaurants on-site. Rent a bike and pedal up to the **Clam Creek Picnic Area,** checking out the **Horton House Tabby Ruins** along the way. Ride on the sand to **Driftwood Beach** and relax awhile.

Day 5

This morning, drive an hour south to St. Marys and have a walk around the cute little downtown area before heading out on the ferry to **Cumberland**

Island National Seashore. The 45-minute ferry ride takes you to a full day of biking or hiking the many trails among the ruins and dunes.

Day 6

Make the half-hour drive into Folkston and the Suwanee Canal Recreation Area at **Okefenokee National Wildlife Refuge.** Take a guided tour up and down the blackwater canal, or walk the trails out to the swamp's prairie vistas and drink in this unique natural beauty.

With More Time
HILTON HEAD ISLAND

Drive to **Hilton Head Island,** where you can spend a few hours sunning or biking on the family-friendly beach, shop, or visit the free and informative **Coastal Discovery Museum at Honey Horn.** A half hour away, make a late-afternoon stop in **Old Town Bluffton** to shop for art, see the beautiful **Church of the Cross** on the May River, and have a light dinner. Another half hour's drive puts you into a cute B&B in Savannah to relax for the night, maybe stopping in a pub for a pint or two.

African American Heritage

TOP EXPERIENCE

The cities and Sea Islands of the Georgia coast are integral to a full understanding of the experience of African Americans in the South. More than that, they are living legacies, with a thriving culture—called Gullah in South Carolina and Geechee in Georgia—whose roots can be traced directly back to West Africa.

Waterfront

Check out the **African American Monument** in Rousakis Plaza on River Street.

Historic District

Visit the former center of black life in Savannah, Martin Luther King Jr. Boulevard (once West Broad St.), and see the **Ralph Mark Gilbert Civil Rights Museum.**

The **Second African Baptist Church** is where Sherman announced the famous "40 acres and a mule" field order.

The **Beach Institute** is a repository of African American art, culture, and history. Check out the restored schoolroom at **Massie Heritage Center,** Savannah's first African American school.

A Day at the Beach

Hilton Head Island

Not far from Savannah, there are plenty of beaches, many of them are made even more enjoyable by the fact that they tend to get much less traffic than more touristy areas. Here's a quick guide to match the beach to the trip:

Family-Friendly

- **Hilton Head Island**'s beaches are roomy and spotlessly maintained. And because no alcohol is allowed on them, they're more geared toward families with children.

- A playground for the people of Georgia by order of the state legislature, **Jekyll Island** is a safe, roomy, and friendly getaway.

Sportin' Life

- You can ride your bike for 12 miles on the expansive, hard-packed sand all around **Hilton Head Island,** as well as enjoy more strenuous adventures such as parasailing.

- **Tybee Island** offers kayak adventures, parasailing, and boogie boarding. Enjoy a nice bike ride on a converted railbed that takes you into the grounds of historic Fort Pulaski.

Peace and Quiet

- Romantic and isolated, **Cumberland Island** is virtually the mossy picture of the old Sea Island South.

- Low-traffic **Sapelo Island** offers friendly folks and a really beautiful beach.

Dog-Friendly

- Easily the most dog-friendly beach in the area is **Jekyll Island**. Just keep 'em on a leash and you're fine year-round.

- **Hilton Head** doesn't allow canines 10am-5pm Memorial Day-Labor Day, but you can take them on a leash 10am-5pm April 1 until the day before Memorial Day.

- Sorry, Rover can't come over to Tybee Island at all.

City Market

Tour the **First African Baptist Church** in City Market, the oldest black congregation in North America. Nearby is the **Haitian Monument,** a nod to the volunteers who helped the cause of independence in the Revolutionary War.

Victorian District

Supreme Court Justice Clarence Thomas once studied at the **Carnegie Branch Library,** Savannah's first black library.

Westside

Pay your respects at **Laurel Grove Cemetery South,** a historic African American cemetery with stirring memorials to some of Savannah's most notable black figures.

The Golden Isles

Harris Neck National Wildlife Refuge was once the site of an African American community, displaced for a World War II airfield. Be sure to visit the vernacular **Gould Cemetery** near the landing within the refuge.

If you drive all the way down to little Meridian near Darien and ride the ferry out to **Sapelo Island,** you can take a guided day tour of the island and its rich Gullah/Geechee history, including the community of Hog Hammock.

Hilton Head

On Hilton Head, stop by the **Coastal Discovery Museum at Honey Horn** and take an African American heritage tour, visiting the site of Mitchelville, the first community of freed slaves in the United States.

Laurel Grove Cemetery South

Coastal Cruising

Fans of retro Americana and roadside kitsch will find a treasure trove of down-home sites along the old Coastal Highway, now known as U.S. 17. Before the arrival of the interstate highway system, U.S. 17 was by far the most traveled route in the region. While now just a shadow of its former self, it is still a vital roadway and contains a lot of interesting, little-known history. Here's a look at some of the highlights, beginning just south of Savannah and ending at Brunswick, Georgia. This is a fun road trip you could easily accomplish in a day, just checking out the sights along the way.

Keller's Flea Market

- **Keller's Flea Market:** South of Savannah and about a half-hour from Hardeeville on U.S. 17, at the intersection with Highway 204 (Abercorn Extension), you'll find this classic rambling and friendly Southern flea market. Look for the statue of the hat-wearing cow out front.

- **Midway Church:** Forty-five minutes south of Savannah in the Liberty County town of Midway is this beautiful 1792 church, whose congregation once boasted two of Georgia's signers of the Declaration of Independence. Don't miss the historic cemetery across the street.

- **Smallest Church in North America:** About 15 minutes south of Midway on the side of the road near South Newport is the miniscule and charming Memory Park Christ Chapel. The current building was rebuilt after arson sadly destroyed the original in 2015.

- **Butler Island:** In another 15 minutes or so, just south of Darien, Georgia, on the west side of U.S. 17, you'll find this tall chimney—the only remnant of the Butler plantation. English actress Fanny Kemble, who married a Butler heir, wrote the influential abolitionist work *Journal of a Residence on a Georgian Plantation* after witnessing the miserable life of the enslaved people who worked here. (Strangely, the nearby historical marker makes no mention of this.)

- **Brunswick Stew:** Allegedly the container in which the first batch of Brunswick stew was cooked up, you can find this cast-iron pot in Mary Ross Waterfront Park in downtown Brunswick, Georgia.

Kayaking Southern Swamps

The Savannah area is framed by the largest contiguous salt marsh in the world and is just a short drive from Okefenokee National Wildlife Refuge. These places are not only a kayaker's paradise, but amazing natural habitats for indigenous and migratory birds. This five-day trip hits the green highlights.

Day 1

Head down to Tybee Island outside Savannah for a day trip across the Back River to undeveloped **Little Tybee Island,** where wilderness camping is allowed, or a kayak run at **Skidaway Narrows,** near Skidaway State Park, which also offers great camping. If you opt not to camp out under the stars, enjoy a great dinner in Savannah's historic district.

Day 2

Today, head west of town to the undeveloped blackwater **Ebenezer Creek,** amid the cypress swamps and crisscrossed by old rice paddy field dikes. Later visit the nearby **Savannah National Wildlife Refuge,** with parts in both South Carolina and Georgia and an excellent bird-watching (and gator-watching!) area.

Day 3

Bird-watchers mustn't miss a trip to **Harris Neck National Wildlife Refuge,** world-renowned for its colonies of wood storks and other waterfowl. Have a meal at nearby **Shellman Bluff,** a picturesque shrimping village with a couple of excellent, authentic down-home seafood restaurants.

Day 4

This morning, make a run down the hybrid blackwater **Altamaha River,** Georgia's largest. Amid the remnants of what were once some of America's largest rice and cotton plantations, you'll see a stunning display of waterfowl and migratory birds. Tonight have a nice dinner on relaxing **St. Simons Island,** or make it onto **Jekyll Island** in time to see the birds on the north-side beaches. There's a nifty little campground on Jekyll's north end.

Day 5

This is a full day at **Okefenokee National Wildlife Refuge,** a vast natural wonderland that belies the name "swamp." On its broad

Family Fun

A steady diet of house museums and long-ago history will bore anyone to tears, not just the young folks in your traveling party. Fortunately, there's a range of options here to please children of all ages.

Savannah

- **Ellis Square:** This square's modernist renovation includes a large wading fountain—a great spot to cool off when it gets hot.

- **Georgia State Railroad Museum:** Climb aboard and take a short train ride complete with old-fashioned steam whistle. As a bonus, also located within the complex is the small but growing **Savannah Children's Museum.**

- **Jepson Center for the Arts:** You'll find a neat children's section, the **Artzeum,** inside this shiny new arts center.

- **Oatland Island Educational Center:** To view wildlife up close and personal, head a few minutes east of town to this facility, which houses cougars and an entire wolf pack along its winding marsh-side nature trail.

- **Fort Pulaski National Monument:** Kids can climb on the parapets, earthworks, and cannons, and explore the great nature trail nearby. They'll no doubt learn a few things as well.

Hilton Head and the Golden Isles

- **Coastal Discovery Museum at Honey Horn:** This museum comes with acres of peaceful green space containing a plethora of artifacts, livestock, and historic re-creations and outbuildings.

- **Summer Waves:** This water park on the south end of Jekyll Island offers a great respite from the summer heat.

- **Georgia Sea Turtle Center:** This rescue and research facility is also a high quality, hands-on museum. Don't miss the tour of the area where the turtles are kept while they rehabilitate.

- **Driftwood Beach:** Kids can climb for hours on the driftwood found on this Jekyll Island beach.

- **Neptune Park:** A kid-friendly play area is a key feature of this beachfront area next to the St. Simons Island Pier.

"prairies" bird-watchers will see a nearly unmatched variety of species for this region, and kayakers can paddle down several blackwater runs amid the cypress. Extend your trip an extra night by camping out in the middle of the swamp on one of the refuge's special raised platforms, or at one of two great state parks east and west of the Okefenokee. Look out for the alligators!

Seaside Romance

Spanish moss, friendly beaches, sunsets over the water, sultry weather, moonlit carriage rides—what more could you ask for? The Lowcountry and Georgia coast pretty much wrote the book on romantic getaways. Here's a starter list of the most romantic spots.

Savannah

- Relax on the grass at vast, scenic **Forsyth Park,** surrounded by Victorian architecture.

- Yes, cemeteries can be romantic, especially gorgeous **Bonaventure Cemetery.**

- Avoid the lines at The Lady & Sons and instead have a delightful dinner at **The Grey** or **Elizabeth on 37th.** Share a coffee, sweet treat, or perhaps a signature martini at **Lulu's Chocolate Bar.**

- Have a nightcap at **Rocks on the Roof** on top of the Bohemian Hotel Savannah and watch the big cargo ships roll in and out on the river.

- Up for a crazy night of dancing? **Club One Jefferson** is the ticket.

The Golden Isles

- Stay at the **Jekyll Island Club,** former stomping ground of the world's richest people. Rent a bike and crisscross the whole island in the late afternoon, coming back to the club to enjoy a romantic dinner

Bonaventure Cemetery

by the fireplace at the **Courtyard at Crane.**

- Take the ferry to **Cumberland Island National Seashore,** surely one of the most romantic locations on earth. Rent a bike on arrival and take your time pedaling among the ruins of the old mansions, making sure to visit the chapel at the **First African Baptist Church,** site of the wedding of John F. Kennedy Jr. and Carolyn Bessette. Before you board the ferry to conclude your journey, maybe you'll get lucky and encounter some of the island's famous wild horses, fitting symbols of passion and romance.

Sights

Look for ★ to find
recommended sights

Highlights

★ **Best Place to See Enormous Ships Up Close:** There's still nothing like strolling the cobblestones of **River Street** amid the old cotton warehouses, enjoying the cool breeze off the river, and watching the huge cargo ships on their way to and from the bustling port (page 40).

★ **Most Unusual Church:** The oldest black congregation in the United States, **First African Baptist Church** still meets in its historic sanctuary, a key stop on the Underground Railroad (page 46).

★ **Oldest Public Art Museum in the South:** Old school meets new school in a museum complex that comprises the traditional collection of the ultramodern **Jepson Center for the Arts** and the **Telfair Academy of Arts and Sciences,** located within a stone's throw of each other (page 54).

★ **If There's Only Time for One House Museum Tour:** Possibly the country's best example of Regency architecture and definitely an example of state-of-the-art historic preservation in action, **Owens-Thomas House** is Savannah's single greatest historic home (page 56).

★ **Most Inspirational Sight:** The soaring Gothic Revival edifice of the **Cathedral of St. John the Baptist** is complemented by its ornate interior and its matchless location on verdant Lafayette Square, stomping ground of the young Flannery O'Connor (page 61).

★ **Most Iconic Square:** Quintessential **Monterey Square** has some of the best examples of local architecture and world-class ironwork all around its periphery (page 64).

★ **Savannah's Version of Central Park:** A verdant expanse ringed by old live oaks and chockablock with memorials, **Forsyth Park** is the true center of downtown life. It is also Savannah's backyard (page 70).

★ **Most Oddly Romantic Burial Ground:** The moss-draped **Bonaventure Cemetery** is the final resting place for some of Savannah's favorite citizens, including the great Johnny Mercer, and makes great use of its setting on the banks of the Wilmington River (page 75).

★ **Best History Site for the Whole Family:** The well-run **Fort Pulaski National Monument,** built with the help of a young Robert E. Lee, is not only historically significant, its beautiful setting makes it a great place for the entire family (page 78).

Assigned by King George II of England to buffer Charleston from the Spanish, General James Edward Oglethorpe laid out his settlement in a deceptively simple plan that is still studied the world over as a model of nearly perfect urban design.

Savannah was built as a series of rectangular "wards," each constructed around a central square. As the city grew, each square took on its own characteristics, depending on who lived on the square and how they made their livelihood.

It's best to introduce yourself to the sights of Savannah by traveling from the river southward. It's no small task to navigate the nation's largest contiguous historic district, but when in doubt it's best to follow James Oglethorpe's original plan of using the five "monumental" squares on Bull Street (Johnson, Wright, Chippewa, Madison, and Monterey) as focal points.

Originally known as West Broad Street (you'll still hear old-timers refer to it that way), Martin Luther King Jr. Boulevard is the spiritual home of Savannah's African American community, though it has gone through several transformations. In the early 1800s, West Broad was a fashionable address, but during the middle of that century its north end got a bad reputation for crime and blight as thousands of Irish immigrants packed in right beside the area's poor black population.

Several important sites are clustered together on MLK Jr. Boulevard under the auspices of the Coastal Heritage Society: the Savannah History Museum, the Georgia State Railroad Museum, the Savannah Children's Museum, and Battlefield Park.

Previous: Bonaventure Cemetery; horse-drawn carriage.

Savannah's outlying areas still bear the indelible marks of the plantation era. While history is no less prominent, it is more subtle in these largely semirural areas, and the tourist infrastructure is much less developed than in Savannah proper.

This area contains some of the most impoverished communities in Georgia, so keep in mind that the locals may have more on their minds than keeping you entertained—though certainly at no point will their Southern manners fail them. And also keep in mind that you are traveling in one of the most unique ecosystems in the country, and natural beauty is never far away.

In Savannah, you don't need a car to have a great time and see most sights worth enjoying. A strong walker can easily traverse the length and breadth of downtown in a day, although less energetic travelers should consider a central location or make use of the free downtown shuttle. To fully enjoy the city, however, you'll need access to a vehicle so you can go east to Tybee Island and south to various historic sites with spottier public transportation. You'll appreciate downtown all the more when you can get away and smell the salt air.

Waterfront Map 1

★ River Street

It's much tamer than it was 30 years ago—when muscle cars cruised its cobblestones and a volatile mix of local teenagers, sailors on shore leave, and soldiers on liberty made things less than family-friendly after dark—but River Street still has more than enough edginess to keep things interesting. Families are safe and welcome here, but energetic pub crawling remains a favorite pastime for locals and visitors alike.

If you have a car, park it somewhere else and walk. The cobblestones—actually old ballast stones from some of the innumerable ships that docked here over the years—are tough on the suspension, and much of River Street is dedicated to pedestrian traffic anyway.

FACTOR'S WALK

One level up from River Street, Factor's Walk has nothing to do with math, though a lot of money has been counted here. In arcane usage, a "factor" was a broker, i.e. a middleman for the sale of cotton, Savannah's chief export during most of the 1800s. Factors mostly worked in Factor's Row, the traditional phrase for the actual buildings on River Street, most all of which were used in various import-export activities before their current transformation into a mélange of shops, hotels, restaurants, and taverns. Factor's Walk is divided into Lower Factor's Walk, comprising the alleys and back entrances behind Factor's Row, and Upper Factor's Walk, the

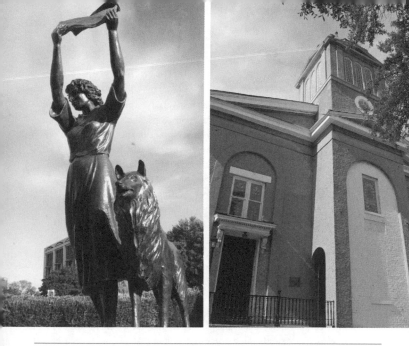

Clockwise from top left: *The Waving Girl;* First African Baptist Church; cargo ships off River Street.

system of crosswalks at the upper levels of Factor's Row that lead directly to Bay Street.

MAP 1: E. River St. between Bull St. and Lincoln St.

ROUSAKIS PLAZA

Rousakis Plaza is a focal point for local festivals. It's a great place to sit, feed the pigeons, and watch the huge container ships go back and forth from the Georgia Ports Authority's sprawling complex farther upriver (you can see the huge Panamax cranes in the distance). The **African American Monument** at the edge of Rousakis Plaza was erected in 2002 to controversy for its stark tableau of a dazed-looking African American family with broken shackles around their feet. Adding to the controversy was the graphic content of the inscription at the base of the 12-foot statue, written especially for the monument by famed poet Maya Angelou. It reads:

> We were stolen, sold and bought together from the African continent.
> We got on the slave ships together. We lay back to belly in the holds of
> the slave ships in each other's excrement and urine together, some-
> times died together, and our lifeless bodies thrown overboard together.
> Today, we are standing up together, with faith and even some joy.

Nearby you can't miss the huge, vaguely cubist Hyatt Regency Savannah, another controversial local landmark. The modern architecture of the Hyatt caused quite a stir when it was first built in 1981, not only because it's so contrary to the area's historic architecture but because its superstructure effectively cuts off one end of River Street from the other. "Underneath" the Hyatt—actually still River Street—you'll find elevators to the hotel lobby, the best way to get up off the waterfront if you're not up for a walk up the cobblestones. Immediately outside the west side of the Hyatt up toward Bay Street is another exit and entry point, a steep and solid set of antebellum stairs that, despite its decidedly pre-Americans with Disabilities Act aspect, is nonetheless one of the quicker ways to leave River Street for those with strong legs and good knees.

MAP 1: E. River St., behind City Hall

THE WAVING GIRL

At the east end of River Street is the statue of Florence Martus, a.k.a. *The Waving Girl,* set in the emerald-green expanse of little Morrell Park. Beginning in 1887 at the age of 19, Martus—who actually lived several miles downriver on Elba Island—took to greeting every passing ship with a wave of a handkerchief by day and a lantern at night, without fail for the next 40 years. Ship captains returned the greeting with a salute of their own on the ship's whistle, and word spread all over the world of the beguiling woman who waited on the balcony of that lonely house. Martus was a lifelong spinster who lived with her brother, the lighthouse keeper, and was by most accounts an eccentric, delightful person. After her brother died, Martus moved into a house on the Wilmington River, whiling away the hours by—you guessed it—waving at passing cars. Martus became such

an enduring symbol of the personality and spirit of Savannah that a U.S.
Liberty ship was named for her in 1943. She died at the age of 75, a few
months after the ship's christening.

MAP 1: Morrell Park, E. River St. and E. Broad St.

WORLD WAR II MEMORIAL

Near the foot of the Bohemian Hotel Savannah Riverfront on River Street
is a 21st-century addition to Savannah's public monuments. Installed in
2010, the World War II Memorial—fairly modernist by local standards—
features a copper-and-bronze globe torn in half to represent the European
and Pacific theaters of the war. The more than 500 local people who gave
their lives in that conflict are memorialized by name.

MAP 1: W. River St., near Bohemian Hotel Savannah Riverfront, 102 W. Bay St.

BAY STREET

Because so few downtown streets can accommodate 18-wheelers, Bay Street
unfortunately has become the default route for industrial traffic in the
area on its way to and from the industrial west side of town. In front of the
Hyatt Regency Savannah is a concrete bench marking the spot on which
Oglethorpe pitched his first tent.

CITY HALL

Dominating Bay Street is City Hall, with its gold-leaf dome. The 1907 building was designed by acclaimed architect Hyman Witcover and erected on
the site of Savannah's first town hall.

MAP 1: 2 E. Bay St.

CHATHAM ARTILLERY GUNS

Directly adjacent to City Hall on the east is a small canopy sheltering two
cannons, which together compose the oldest monument in Savannah.
These are the Chatham Artillery Guns, presented to the local militia group
of the same name by President George Washington during his one and only
visit to town in 1791. Today, locals use the phrase "Chatham Artillery"
differently, to refer to a particularly potent local punch recipe that mixes
several hard liquors.

MAP 1: Adjacent to City Hall, 2 E. Bay St.

SAVANNAH COTTON EXCHANGE

Directly behind the Chatham Artillery Guns is the ornate Savannah Cotton
Exchange, built in 1886 to facilitate the city's huge cotton export business.
Once nicknamed "King Cotton's Palace" but now a Masonic lodge, this delightful building by William Gibbons Preston is one of Savannah's many
great examples of the Romanesque style.

MAP 1: 100 E. Bay St.

A Visionary Aristocrat

One of the greatest products of the Enlightenment, **James Edward Oglethorpe** was a study in contrasts, embodying all the vitality, contradiction, and ambiguity of that turbulent age. A stern moralist yet an avowed liberal, an aristocrat with a populist streak, an abolitionist and an anti-Roman Catholic, a man of war who sought peace—the founder of Georgia would put his own inimitable stamp on the new nation to follow, a legacy personified to this day in the city he designed.

After making a name for himself fighting the Turks, the young London native and Oxford graduate would return home only to serve a two-year prison sentence for killing a man in a brawl. The experience was a formative one for Oglethorpe, scion of a large and upwardly mobile family, as he was now forced to see how England's underbelly really lived. Upon his release, the 25-year-old Oglethorpe ran for the "family" House of Commons seat once occupied by his father and two brothers, and won. He distinguished himself as a campaigner for human rights and an opponent of slavery. Another jail-related epiphany came when Oglethorpe saw a friend die of smallpox in debtors prison. More than ever, Oglethorpe was determined to right what he saw as a colossal wrong in the draconian English justice system. His crusade took the form of establishing a sanctuary for debtors in North America.

To that end, he and his friend Lord Perceval established the Trustees, a 21-member group who lobbied King George for permission to establish such a colony. The grant from the king—who was more interested in containing the Spanish than in any humanitarian concerns—would include all land between the Altamaha and Savannah Rivers and from the headwaters of these rivers to the "south seas." Ironically, there were no debtors among Savannah's original colonists. Nonetheless, the new settlement was indeed a reflection of its founder's core values, banning rum as a bad influence (though beer and wine were allowed), prohibiting slavery, and eschewing lawyers on the theory that a gentleman should always be able to defend himself.

Nearing 40 and distracted by war with the Spanish, Oglethorpe's agenda gradually eroded in the face of opposition from settlers, who craved not only the more hedonistic lifestyle of their neighbors to the north in Charleston but the economic advantage that city enjoyed through the use of slave labor. In nearly the same hour as his greatest military victory, crushing the Spanish at the Battle of Bloody Marsh on St. Simons Island, Oglethorpe also suffered an ignominious defeat: being replaced as head of the 13th colony, which he had founded.

He went back to England, never to see the New World again. But his heart was always with the colonists. After successfully fending off a political attack and a court-martial, Oglethorpe married and commenced a healthy retirement. He supported independence for the American colonies, making a point to enthusiastically receive the new ambassador from the United States, one John Adams. The old general died on June 30, 1785, at age 88. Fittingly for this lifelong philanthropist and humanitarian, his childhood home in Godalming, Surrey, is now a nursing home.

The large gray Greek Revival building directly across from City Hall is the U.S. Custom House (not "customs," regardless of what the tour guides may say). Built on the spot of Georgia's first public building in 1852, the Custom House was also Georgia's first federal building and was the first local commission for renowned New York architect John Norris, who went on to design 22 other buildings in Savannah. Within its walls was held the trial of the captain and crew of the notorious slave ship *Wanderer,* which illegally plied its trade after a national ban on the importation of slaves. Local newspaper publisher and educator John H. DeVeaux worked here after his appointment as the first African American U.S. Collector of Customs. MAP 1: 1 E. Bay St.

City Market

Map 1

ELLIS SQUARE

Ellis Square's history as Savannah's main open-air marketplace goes back to 1755, when there was a single City Market building in the square itself. The fourth City Market was built in 1872, an ornate Romanesque affair with a 50-foot roofline. In 1954, the city decided to build a parking garage in the square. So the magnificent City Market building—and Ellis Square—simply ceased to exist.

Several large warehouses surrounding City Market survived. Now a hub of tourism, City Market encompasses working art studios, hip bars, cute cafés, live music in the east end of the courtyard, cutting-edge art galleries, gift shops, and restaurants.

The eyesore that was the Ellis Square parking garage is gone, and the square has been rebuilt as a pedestrian hangout, complete with a fountain, all atop a huge underground parking garage. Be sure to check out the smallish bronze of native Savannahian and Oscar-winning lyricist Johnny Mercer on the square's western edge.

There is a small staffed visitors center (Aug.-Oct. daily 10am-9pm, Mar.-July daily 10am-10pm, Feb. and Nov. daily 10am-8pm, Dec.-Jan. daily 10am-6pm) with public restrooms on the northwest corner of the square.

AMERICAN PROHIBITION MUSEUM

During the Prohibition era, Savannah was a major rum-running point on the bootlegging circuit. That scofflaw history is commemorated in the new American Prohibition Museum, a collection of artifacts and fun living history from costumed docents. The museum is organized and run by a local trolley tour company, so don't expect Smithsonian-level standards of scholarship, though it is fun. Of course there is a "speakeasy" on-site where those 21 and over can enjoy adult beverages.

MAP 1: City Market, 209 W. St. Julian St., 855/245-8892, www.trolleytours.com; daily 10am-5 pm.; $12 adults, $9 students and seniors

FRANKLIN SQUARE

Until recently, Franklin Square was, like Ellis Square, a victim of "prog-ress," this time in the form of a highway going right through the middle of it. But as part of the city's effort to reclaim its history, Franklin Square was returned to its original state in the mid-1980s.

★ FIRST AFRICAN BAPTIST CHURCH

The premier historical attraction on Franklin Square is the First African Baptist Church, the oldest black congregation in North America, dating from 1777. The church also hosted the first African American Sunday school, begun in 1826. The church's founding pastor, George Liele, was the first black Baptist in Georgia and perhaps the first black missionary in the country. The present building dates from 1859 and was built almost entirely by members of the congregation themselves, some of whom redi-rected savings intended to purchase their freedom toward the building of the church. A key staging area for the Underground Railroad, First African Baptist still bears the scars of that turbulent time. In the floor of the fel-lowship hall—where many civil rights meetings were held, because it was safer for white citizens to go there instead of black activists going outside the church—you'll see breathing holes, drilled for use by escaped enslaved people hiding in a cramped crawlspace.

MAP 1: 23 Montgomery St., 912/233-2244, http://firstafricanbc.com; tours Tues.-Sat. 11am, 2pm, and 4pm, Sun. 1pm; $10 adults, $9 students and seniors

HAITIAN MONUMENT

The Haitian Monument in the center of the square commemorates the sac-rifice and service of "Les Chasseurs Volontaires de Saint-Domingue," the 750 Haitian volunteers who fought for American independence and lost many of their number during the unsuccessful attempt to wrest Savannah back from the British in 1779.

MAP 1: Franklin Square

Top: Ellis Square. **Bottom:** the Haitian Monument in Franklin Square.

JOHNSON SQUARE

Due east of City Market, Johnson Square, Oglethorpe's very first square, is named for Robert Johnson, governor of South Carolina at the time of Georgia's founding. The roomy, shaded square, ringed with major bank branches and insurance firms, is dominated by the **Nathanael Greene Monument** in honor of George Washington's second-in-command, who was granted nearby Mulberry Grove plantation for his efforts. The Marquis de Lafayette himself laid the cornerstone for the monument during his famous Southern tour in 1825. In typically maddening Savannah fashion, there is a separate square named for Greene, which has no monument to him at all.

CHRIST EPISCOPAL CHURCH

The southeast corner of Johnson Square is dominated by Christ Episcopal Church, a.k.a. Christ Church, a historic house of worship also known as the "Mother Church of Georgia" because its congregation traces its roots to that first Anglican service in Savannah, held the same day Oglethorpe landed. While this spot on Johnson Square was reserved for the congregation from the very beginning, this is actually the third building on the site, dating from 1838. Much of the interior is more recent than that, however, since a fire gutted the inside of the church in 1895. In the northeast bell tower is a bell forged in 1919 by Revere and Sons of Boston.

MAP 1: 28 Bull St., 912/236-2500, www.christchurchsavannah.org

REYNOLDS SQUARE

Walk directly east of Johnson Square to find yourself at Reynolds Square, named for John Reynolds, the first (and exceedingly unpopular) royal governor of Georgia. First called "Lower New Square," Reynolds Square originally served as site of the filature, or cocoon storage warehouse, during the fledgling colony's ill-fated flirtation with the silk industry (a federal building now occupies the site). As with Johnson Square, the monument in Reynolds Square has nothing to do with its namesake, but is instead a likeness of John Wesley dedicated in 1969 near the spot believed to have been his home.

OLDE PINK HOUSE

A Reynolds Square landmark, the Olde Pink House is not only one of Savannah's most romantic restaurants but quite a historic site as well. It's the oldest Savannah mansion from the 18th century still standing as well as the first place in Savannah where the Declaration of Independence was read aloud. The Georgian mansion was built in 1771 for rice planter James Habersham Jr., one of America's richest men at the time and a member of the notorious "Liberty Boys" who plotted revolution. The building's pink

How to Pronounce Savannah Names

With so many visitors to town also comes plenty of opportunities to mispronounce local place names. Don't sound like a tourist—here's how to say it the way locals do:

- **Broughton Street:** BRAW-ton. What's now Savannah's main shopping thoroughfare is named for Thomas Broughton, a colonial governor of South Carolina.

- **Tybee Island:** TIE-bee. The name supposedly means "salt" in a Native American language.

- **Chatham County:** CHAT-um. The second "h" is silent, in the British fashion.

- **Houston Street:** HOUSE-ton. You're not in Texas! Houston Street in New York City is pronounced the same as Savannah's. Both streets are actually named for the same person, William Houstoun of Georgia, a member of the Continental Congress and an original Trustee of the University of Georgia.

- **Abercorn Street:** No, it's not "Abercrombie." That's a clothing brand. It's pronounced "Abber-corn."

- **Habersham Street:** HAB-er-shum, again clipped short in the British fashion.

- **Barnard Street:** BAR-nerd. Not barnyard, nor Bernard.

- **DeRenne Avenue:** duh-REN. The traditional, if somewhat inaccurate, dividing line between "old" Savannah and suburban Savannah.

exterior was a matter of serendipity, resulting from its core redbrick seeping through the formerly white stucco outer covering.

MAP 1: 23 Abercorn St.

LUCAS THEATRE FOR THE ARTS

Built in 1921 as part of Arthur Lucas's regional chain of movie houses, the wonderfully ornate Lucas Theatre for the Arts also featured a stage for road shows. In 1976, the Lucas closed after a screening of *The Exorcist*. When the building faced demolition in 1986, a group of citizens created a nonprofit to save it and its expert craftsmanship. Despite numerous starts and stops, the 14-year campaign finally paid off in a grand reopening in 2000, an event helped by timely donations from the cast and crew of the locally shot *Midnight in the Garden of Good and Evil* and *Forrest Gump*.

The theater's schedule stays pretty busy, so it should be easy to check out a show while you're in town.

MAP 1: 32 Abercorn St., 912/525-5040, www.lucastheatre.com

OLIVER STURGIS HOUSE

At the southwest corner of Reynolds Square is the understated Oliver Sturgis House, former home of the partner with William Scarbrough in the launching of the SS *Savannah*. This is one of the few Savannah buildings to feature the stabilizing earthquake rods that are much more common in Charleston. Don't miss the dolphin downpour spouts at ground level.

MAP 1: 27 Abercorn St.

COLUMBIA SQUARE

Named for the mythical patroness of America, Columbia Square features at its center not an expected portrait of that female warrior figure but the original fountain from Noble Jones's Wormsloe Plantation, placed there in 1970.

ISAIAH DAVENPORT HOUSE MUSEUM

Columbia Square is primarily known as the home of the Isaiah Davenport House Museum. The house museum is a delightful stop in and of itself because of its elegant simplicity, sweeping double staircase, and near-perfect representation of the Federalist style. But the Davenport House occupies an exalted place in Savannah history as well, because the fight to save it began the preservation movement in the city. In 1955 the Davenport House, then a tenement, was to be demolished for a parking lot. But Emma Adler and six other Savannah women, angered by the recent destruction of Ellis Square, refused to let it go down quietly. Together they formed the Historic Savannah Foundation in order to raise the $22,500 needed to purchase the Davenport House.

Most Octobers, the Davenport House hosts living history dramatizations based on Savannah's yellow fever plague of the 1820s. Despite the grim subject matter, the little playlets are usually quite entertaining. Other special seasonal tours include a madeira wine tour and "Tea with Mrs. Davenport."

MAP 1: 324 E. State St., 912/236-8097, www.davenporthousemuseum.org; Mon.-Sat. 10am-4pm, Sun. 1pm-4pm; $9 adults, $5 children

KEHOE HOUSE

Across the corner from the Davenport House is the Classical Revival masterpiece Kehoe House, designed for local ironworks owner William Kehoe in 1892 by DeWitt Bruyn. Sadly, the proof of Kehoe's self-described "weakness for cupolas" no longer exists, the cupola having rotted away. Once a funeral home, the Kehoe House is now one of Savannah's premier bed-and-breakfasts. It's unique not only in its exuberantly Victorian architecture but in its twin fireplaces and ubiquitous rococo ironwork, courtesy of the irrepressible Kehoe himself.

MAP 1: 123 Habersham St.

Warren Square and its neighbor Washington Square formed the first extension of Oglethorpe's original four squares, and they boast some of the oldest houses in the historic district. Both squares are lovely little garden spots, ideal for a picnic in the shade.

HAMPTON LILLIBRIDGE HOUSE AND CHARLES ODDINGSELLS HOUSE

Two houses near Washington Square were restored by the late Jim Williams of *Midnight* fame: the Hampton Lillibridge House, which once hosted an Episcopal exorcism, and the Charles Oddingsells House.

MAP 1: 507 E. St. Julian St. and 510 E. St. Julian St.

GREENE SQUARE

Named for Revolutionary War hero Nathanael Greene, but bearing no monument to him whatsoever, Greene Square is of particular importance to local African American history. In 1818, the residence at 542 East State Street was constructed for free blacks Charlotte and William Wall. The property at 513 East York Street was built for Catherine DeVeaux, part of a prominent African American family.

CUNNINGHAM HOUSE

At the corner of Houston (pronounced "HOUSE-ton") and East State Streets is the 1810 Cunningham House, built for Henry Cunningham, the formerly enslaved founding pastor of the Second African Baptist Church.

MAP 1: Houston St. and State St.

SECOND AFRICAN BAPTIST CHURCH

The Second African Baptist Church, on the west side of the square, is where General Sherman made his famous promise of "40 acres and a mule." The founding pastor of the church was Henry Cunningham, whose home is also on Green Square.

MAP 1: 124 Houston St., 912/233-6163, www.secondafrican.org

OLD FORT

One of the lesser-known aspects of Savannah history is this well-trod neighborhood at the east end of Bay Street, once the site of groundbreaking experiments and piratical intrigue, and then a diverse melting pot of Savannah citizenry.

EMMET PARK

Just north of Reynolds Square on the north side of Bay Street you'll come to Emmet Park, first a Native American burial ground and then known as "the Strand" or "Irish Green" because of its proximity to the Irish slums of the Old Fort. In 1902 the park was named for Robert Emmet, an Irish patriot of the early 1800s, who was executed by the British for treason. Within it is the eight-foot **Celtic Cross,** erected in 1983 and carved of Irish limestone. The Celtic Cross is at the center of a key ceremony for local Irish Catholics during the week prior to St. Patrick's Day.

Close by is one of Savannah's more recent monuments, the **Vietnam War Memorial** at East Bay Street and Rossiter Lane. The reflecting pool is in the shape of Vietnam itself, and the names of all 106 Savannahians killed in the conflict are carved into an adjacent marble tablet.

Walk a little farther east and you'll find my favorite little chapter of Bay Street history, the **Beacon Range Light,** tucked into a shady corner. Few visitors bother to check out this masterfully crafted 1858 navigation aid, intended to warn approaching ships of the old wrecks sunk in the river as a defense during the Revolutionary War.

MAP 1: E. Bay St. west of E. Broad St.

TRUSTEES' GARDEN

At the east end of Bay Street where it meets East Broad Street rises a bluff behind a masonry wall—at 40 feet off the river, still the highest point in Chatham County. This is Trustees' Garden, the nation's first experimental garden. Trustees' Garden became the site of Fort Wayne, named after General "Mad Anthony" Wayne of Revolutionary War fame, who retired to a plantation near Savannah. The Fort Wayne area—still called the "Old Fort" neighborhood by old-timers—fell from grace and became associated with the "lowest elements" of Savannah society, which in the 19th and early 20th centuries were Irish and African Americans. It also became known for its illegal activity and as the haunt of sea salts such as the ones who frequented what is now the delightfully schlocky **Pirates' House** restaurant. That building began life in 1753 as a seamen's inn and was later chronicled by Robert Louis Stevenson in *Treasure Island* as a rogue's gallery of pirates and nautical ne'er-do-wells.

Find the **Herb House** on East Broad Street, the older-looking clapboard structure next to the Pirates' House entrance. You're looking at what is considered the single oldest building in Georgia and one of the oldest in the United States. Constructed in 1734, it was originally the home of Trustees' Garden's chief gardener.

To the rear of Trustees' Garden is the 1881 Hillyer building, now the **Charles H. Morris Center,** a mixed-use performing arts and meeting space that is heavily used during the springtime Savannah Music Festival. Adjacent to this space is the newly renovated Kehoe Iron Works, including an outdoor event space and a restored historic ironworks building, also a multiuse space.

MAP 1: 10 E. Broad St., 912/443-3277, http://trusteesgarden.com

BROUGHTON STREET

Downtown's main shopping district for most of the 20th century was Broughton Street. Postwar suburbs and white flight brought neglect to the area by the 1960s, and many thought Broughton was gone for good. But

College of Art and Design (SCAD), Broughton was able not only to get back
on its feet, but also to thrive as a commercial center once again.

JEN LIBRARY

The Savannah College of Art and Design's Jen Library is a state-of-the-art
facility set in the circa-1890 Levy and Maas Brothers department stores.
MAP 1: 201 E. Broughton St.

TRUSTEES THEATER

Around the corner from the Lucas Theatre on Reynolds Square is the art
moderne Trustees Theater, a Savannah College of Art and Design (SCAD)
operation that seats 1,200 and hosts concerts, film screenings, and the
school's much-anticipated spring fashion show. It began life in the postwar
boom of 1946 as the Weis Theatre, another one of those ornate Southern
movie houses that took full commercial advantage of being the only buildings at the time to have air-conditioning. But by the end of the 1970s it had
followed the fate of Broughton Street, lying dormant and neglected until
its purchase and renovation by SCAD in 1989.

This block of Broughton in front of Trustees Theater is usually blocked
off to mark the gala opening of the SCAD Savannah Film Festival each fall.
Searchlights crisscross the sky, limos idle in wait, and Hollywood guests
strike poses for the photographers.
MAP 1: 216 E. Broughton St., 912/525-5051, www.trusteestheater.com

WRIGHT SQUARE

The big monument in Wright Square, Oglethorpe's second square, has
nothing to do with James Wright, royal governor of Georgia before the
Revolution, for whom it's named. Instead the monument honors William
Gordon, former mayor and founder of the Central of Georgia Railway.
More importantly, Wright Square is the final resting place for the great
Yamacraw chief Tomochichi, buried in 1737 in an elaborate state funeral
at James Oglethorpe's insistence. A huge boulder of North Georgia granite
honoring the chief was placed in a corner of the square in 1899 under the
auspices of William Gordon's daughter-in-law. Tomochichi is not buried
under the boulder but somewhere underneath the Gordon monument.

EVANGELICAL LUTHERAN CHURCH OF THE ASCENSION

Next to the old courthouse is the historic Evangelical Lutheran Church of
the Ascension, built in the 1870s for a congregation that traced its roots
to some of the first Austrian Salzburgers to come to Savannah in 1734.
MAP 1: 120 Bull St., 912/232-4151, www.elcota.org

FEDERAL COURTHOUSE AND POST OFFICE

On the west side of Wright Square is the Federal Courthouse and Post
Office, built in 1898 out of Georgia marble. The building's stately facade

makes an appearance in several films, including the original *Cape Fear* and *Midnight in the Garden of Good and Evil*.
MAP 1: 125-127 Bull St.

TELFAIR SQUARE

Telfair Square was named for Mary Telfair, last heir of a family that was one of the most important in Savannah history. Mary bequeathed the family mansion to the Georgia Historical Society upon her death in 1875 to serve as a museum. Originally called St. James Square after a similar square in London, Telfair was the last of Oglethorpe's original four squares.

Telfair Square hosts two of the three buildings operated by **Telfair Museums,** an umbrella organization that relies on a combination of private and public funding and has driven much of the arts agenda in Savannah for the last 125 years. The third building operated by Telfair Museums is the Owens-Thomas House on Oglethorpe Square.

Get a triple-site pass to the Jepson Center, the Telfair Academy, and the Owens-Thomas House for $20 pp.

★ JEPSON CENTER FOR THE ARTS

The proudest addition to the Telfair Museums group is the striking, 64,000-square-foot Jepson Center for the Arts, whose ultramodern exterior sits catty-corner from the Telfair Academy of Arts and Sciences. Promoting a massive, daringly designed new facility devoted to nothing but modern art was a hard sell in this traditional town, especially when renowned architect Moshe Safdie insisted on building a glassed-in flyover across a lane between two buildings. After a few delays in construction, the Jepson opened its doors in 2006 and has since wowed locals and visitors alike with its cutting-edge traveling exhibits and rotating assortment of late 20th-century and 21st-century modern art. If you get hungry, you can enjoy lunch in the expansive atrium café, and, of course, there's a nice gift shop.

Each late January-early February, the Jepson Center hosts most events of the unique Pulse Art + Technology Festival, a celebration of the intersection of cutting-edge technology and performing and visual arts.
MAP 1: 207 W. York Lane, 912/790-8800, www.telfair.org; Sun.-Mon. noon-5pm, Tues.-Sat. 10am-5pm; $12 adults, $5 students

★ TELFAIR ACADEMY OF ARTS AND SCIENCES

The oldest public art museum in the South, the Telfair Academy of Arts and Sciences was built in 1821 by the great William Jay for Alexander Telfair, scion of that famous Georgia family. The five statues in front are of Phidias, Raphael, Rubens, Michelangelo, and Rembrandt. As well as displaying Sylvia Judson Shaw's now-famous *Bird Girl* sculpture, which originally stood in Bonaventure Cemetery (actually the third of four casts by the sculptor), the Telfair Academy features an outstanding collection of primarily 18th- and 20th-century works, most notably the largest public collection of visual art by Khalil Gibran. Major paintings include works by

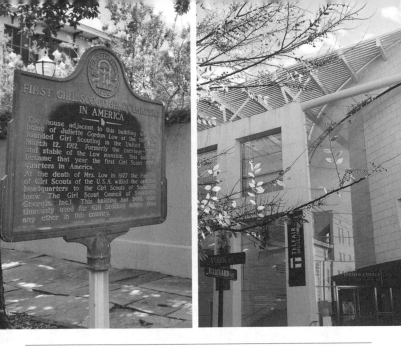

Clockwise from top left: plaque at Juliette Gordon Low Birthplace; Jepson Center for the Arts; the Telfair Academy of Arts and Sciences.

Childe Hassam, Frederick Frieseke, Gari Melchers, and the massive *Black Prince of Crécy* by Julian Story.

MAP 1: 121 Barnard St., 912/790-8800, www.telfair.org; Sun.-Mon. noon-5pm, Tues.-Sat. 10am-5pm; $12 adults, $5 students

TRINITY UNITED METHODIST CHURCH

Directly between the Telfair and the Jepson stands Trinity United Methodist Church, Savannah's first Methodist church. Built in 1848 on the site of the Telfair family garden, its masonry walls are of famous "Savannah Gray" bricks—a lighter, more porous, and elegant variety—under stucco. Virgin longleaf pine was used for most of the interior, fully restored in 1969. The sanctuary occasionally hosts secular concerts, which are well-attended. Call ahead for a tour.

MAP 1: 225 W. President St., 912/233-4766, www.trinitychurch1848.org; sanctuary daily 9am-5pm, services Sun. 8:45am and 11am

OGLETHORPE SQUARE

Don't look for a monument to Georgia's founder in the square named for him. His monument is in Chippewa Square. Originally called "Upper New Square," Oglethorpe Square was created in 1742.

JULIETTE GORDON LOW BIRTHPLACE

Around the corner from Wright Square at Oglethorpe and Bull is the Juliette Gordon Low Birthplace, declared the city's very first National Historic Landmark in 1965, and fresh off a significant restoration effort. The founder of the Girl Scouts of the USA lived here from her birth in 1860 until her marriage. The house was completed in 1821 for Mayor James Moore Wayne, future Supreme Court justice, but the current furnishings, many original, are intended to reflect the home during the 1880s.

Also called the Girl Scout National Center, the Low birthplace is probably Savannah's most festive historic site because of the heavy traffic of Girl Scout troops from across the United States. They flock here year-round to take part in programs and learn more about their organization's founder, whose family sold the house to the Girl Scouts in 1953. You don't have to be affiliated with the Girl Scouts to tour the home. Tours are given every 15 minutes, and tickets are available at the Oglethorpe Avenue entrance.

MAP 1: 10 E. Oglethorpe Ave., 912/233-4501, www.juliettegordonlowbirthplace.org; Mar.-Oct. Mon.-Sat. 10am-4pm; $15 adults, $12 children, $10 Girl Scouts

TOP EXPERIENCE

★ OWENS-THOMAS HOUSE

The square's main claim to fame, the Owens-Thomas House, lies on the northeast corner. Widely known as the finest example of Regency architecture in the United States, the Owens-Thomas House was designed by

Scout's Honor

Known as "Daisy" to family and friends, **Juliette Magill Kinzie Gordon** was born to be a pioneer. Her father's family took part in the original settlement of Georgia, and her mother's kin were among the founders of Chicago. Mostly known as the founder of the **Girl Scouts of the USA,** Daisy was also an artist, adventurer, and healer. Born and raised in the house on Oglethorpe Avenue in Savannah known to Girl Scouts across the nation as simply "the Birthplace," she was an animal lover with an early penchant for theater, drawing, and poetry.

In 1911 while in England, Daisy met Robert Baden-Powell, founder of the Boy Scouts and Girl Guides in Britain. Struck by the simplicity and usefulness of his project, she carried the seeds of a similar idea back with her to the United States. "I've got something for the girls of Savannah, and all of America, and all the world, and we're going to start it tonight," were her famous words in a phone call to a cousin after meeting Baden-Powell. So on March 12, 1912, Daisy gathered 18 girls to register the first troop of American Girl Guides, later the Girl Scouts of the USA.

Juliette "Daisy" Gordon Low died of breast cancer in her bed in the Andrew Low House on January 17, 1927. She was buried in Laurel Grove Cemetery. Girl Scout troops from all over the United States visit her birthplace, the Andrew Low House, and her gravesite to this day, often leaving flowers and small personal objects near her tombstone as tokens of respect and gratitude.

brilliant young English architect William Jay. One of the first professionally trained architects in the United States, Jay was only 24 when he designed the home for cotton merchant or "factor" Richard Richardson, who lost the house in the depression of 1820 (all that remains of Richardson's tenure are three marble-top tables). The house's current name is derived from Savannah mayor George Owens, who bought the house in 1830.

Perhaps most interestingly, a complex plumbing system features rain-fed cisterns, flushing toilets, sinks, bathtubs, and a shower. When built, the Owens-Thomas House in fact had the first indoor plumbing in Savannah. On the south facade is a beautiful cast-iron veranda from which Revolutionary War hero Marquis de Lafayette addressed a crowd of starstruck Savannahians during his visit in 1825. The associated slave quarters are in a surprisingly intact state, including the original "haint blue" paint. The carriage house, where all tours begin, is now the home's gift shop.

The Owens-Thomas House is owned and operated by the Telfair Museums. Get a combination pass to all Telfair sites—the Jepson Center for the Arts, the Telfair Academy of Arts and Sciences, and the Owens-Thomas House—for $20 pp.

MAP 1: 124 Abercorn St., 912/233-9743, www.telfair.org; Sun.-Mon. noon-5pm, Tues.-Sat. 10am-5pm, last tour 4:30pm; $20 adults, $15 students, ticket includes Jepson Center and Telfair Academy

MARTIN LUTHER KING JR. BOULEVARD

SHIPS OF THE SEA MARITIME MUSEUM

One of Savannah's more unique museums is the quirky Ships of the Sea Maritime Museum. The stunning Greek Revival building in which it resides is known as the Scarbrough House because it was initially built in 1819 by the great William Jay for local shipping merchant William Scarbrough, co-owner of the SS *Savannah*, the first steamship to cross the Atlantic. After the Scarbroughs sold the property, it became the West Broad School for African Americans from Reconstruction through integration.

Inside, children, maritime buffs, and crafts connoisseurs can find intricate and detailed scale models of various historic vessels, such as Oglethorpe's *Anne*, the SS *Savannah*, and the NS *Savannah*, the world's first nuclear-powered surface vessel. There's even a model of the *Titanic*.

MAP 1: 41 MLK Jr. Blvd., 912/232-1511, http://shipsofthesea.org; Tues.-Sun. 10am-5pm; $9 adults, $7 students

Historic District South   Map 2

CHIPPEWA SQUARE

Named for a battle in the War of 1812, Chippewa Square has a large monument not to the battle, natch, but to James Oglethorpe, clad in full soldier's regalia. Notice the general is still facing south, toward the Spanish.

Yes, the bench on the square's north side is in the same location as the one Tom Hanks occupied in *Forrest Gump*, but it's not the same bench that hosted the two-time Oscar winner's backside—that one was donated by Paramount Pictures to be displayed in the Savannah History Museum on MLK Jr. Boulevard.

TOP EXPERIENCE

COLONIAL CEMETERY

Just north of Chippewa Square is Oglethorpe Avenue, originally called South Broad and the southern boundary of the original colony. At Oglethorpe and Abercorn Streets is Colonial Cemetery, first active in 1750. You'd be forgiven for assuming it's the "DAR" cemetery; the Daughters of the American Revolution contributed the ornate iron entranceway in 1913, thoughtfully dedicating it to themselves instead of the cemetery itself.

Unlike the picturesque beauty of Bonaventure and Laurel Grove Cemeteries, Colonial Cemetery has a morbid feel. The fact that burials stopped here in 1853 plays into that desolation, but maybe another reason is because it's the final resting ground of many of Savannah's yellow fever victims. Famous people buried here include Button Gwinnett, one of Georgia's three signers of the Declaration of Independence. The man who reluctantly killed Gwinnett in a duel, General Lachlan McIntosh, is also buried here. The original burial vault of Nathanael Greene is in the cemetery, although the Revolutionary War hero's remains were moved to Johnson Square over a century ago.

MAP 2: Oglethorpe St. and Abercorn St., www.savannahga.gov; daily 8am-dusk; free

FIRST BAPTIST CHURCH

The nearby First Baptist Church—not to be confused with the more famous First African Baptist Church on Franklin Square—claims to be the oldest original church building in Savannah, with a cornerstone dating from 1830. Services were held here throughout the Civil War, with Union troops attending during the occupation. The church was renovated by renowned local architect Henrik Wallin in 1922. Call ahead for a tour.

MAP 2: 223 Bull St., 912/234-2671; service Sun. 11am

HISTORIC SAVANNAH THEATRE

At the square's northeast corner is the Historic Savannah Theatre, which claims to be the oldest continuously operating theater in the United States. Designed by William Jay, it opened in 1818 with a production of *The Soldier's Daughter.* In the glory days of gaslight theater in the 1800s, some of the nation's best actors, including Edwin Booth, brother to Lincoln's assassin, regularly trod the boards of its stage. Due to a fire in 1948, little remains of Jay's original design except a small section of exterior wall. The building is currently home to a semiprofessional revue company specializing in oldies shows.

MAP 2: 222 Bull St., 912/233-7764, www.savannahtheatre.com

INDEPENDENT PRESBYTERIAN CHURCH

Built in 1818, possibly by William Jay—scholars are unsure of the scope of his involvement—Independent Presbyterian Church is called the "mother of Georgia Presbyterianism." A fire destroyed most of Independent Presbyterian's original structure in 1889, but the subsequent rebuilding was a very faithful rendering of the original design, based on London's St. Martin-in-the-Fields. The church's steeple made a cameo appearance in *Forrest Gump* as a white feather floated by. Lowell Mason, composer of the hymn "Nearer My God to Thee," was organist at Independent Presbyterian. In 1885 Woodrow Wilson married local parishioner Ellen Louise Axson in the manse to the rear of the church. During the Great Awakening in 1896, almost 3,000 people jammed the sanctuary to hear famous evangelist D. L. Moody preach. Call ahead for a tour.

MAP 2: 207 Bull St., 912/236-3346, www.ipcsav.org; services Sun. 11am, Wed. noon

MADISON SQUARE

Named for the nation's fourth president, Madison Square memorializes a local hero who gave his life for his city during the American Revolution. Irish immigrant Sergeant William Jasper, hero of the Battle of Fort Moultrie in Charleston three years earlier, was killed leading the American charge during the 1779 Siege of Savannah, when an allied army failed to retake the city from the British. The monument in the square honors Jasper, but he isn't buried here; his body was interred in a mass grave near the battlefield along with other colonists and soldier-immigrants killed in the one-sided battle.

The two small, suitably warlike cannons in the square have nothing to do with the Siege of Savannah. They commemorate the first two highways in Georgia, today known as Augusta Road and Ogeechee Road.

GREEN-MELDRIM HOUSE

Given the house's beauty and history, visitors will be forgiven for not immediately realizing that the Green-Meldrim House is also the rectory of the adjacent St. John's Episcopal Church, which acquired it in 1892. This is the place where Sherman formulated his ill-fated "40 acres and a mule" Field Order No. 15, giving most of the Sea Islands of Georgia and South Carolina to freed blacks. A tasteful example of Gothic Revival architecture, this 1850 design by John Norris features a beautiful external gallery of filigree ironwork.

MAP 2: 1 W. Macon St., 912/232-1251, www.stjohnssav.org; tours every 30 minutes Tues. and Thurs.-Fri. 10am-4pm, Sat. 10am-1pm; $10 adults, $5 students and children

POETTER HALL

The Savannah College of Art and Design's first building, Poetter Hall, known to old-timers as the Savannah Volunteer Guards Armory, is directly across from the Scottish Rite Temple. With its imposing but somewhat whimsical facade right out of a Harry Potter movie, this brick and terracotta gem of a Romanesque Revival building was built in 1893 by William Gibbons Preston. It housed National Guard units (as well as a high school) until World War II, when the USO occupied the building during its tenant unit's service in Europe.

MAP 2: 342 Bull St., www.scad.edu

SCOTTISH RITE TEMPLE

The old Scottish Rite Temple at Charlton and Bull Streets was designed by Hyman Witcover, who also designed City Hall. A popular drugstore with a soda fountain for many years, it currently houses the **Gryphon Tea Room,** run by the Savannah College of Art and Design.

MAP 2: Charlton St. and Bull St., 912/525-5880; Mon.-Sat. 11am-6pm, Sun. 11am-3pm

LAFAYETTE SQUARE

One of Savannah's favorite squares, especially on St. Patrick's Day, verdant Lafayette Square boasts a number of important sights and attractions.

ANDREW LOW HOUSE MUSEUM

A major landmark on Lafayette Square is the Andrew Low House Museum, once the home of Juliette "Daisy" Gordon Low, the founder of the Girl

Scouts of the USA, who was married to cotton heir William "Billow" Low, Andrew Low's son. Despite their happy-go-lucky nicknames, the union of Daisy and Billow was a notably unhappy one. Still, divorce was out of the question, so the couple lived separate lives until William's death in 1905. The one good thing that came out of the marriage was the germ for the idea for the Girl Scouts, which Juliette got from England's Girl Guides while living there with her husband, Savannah being the couple's winter residence. Designed by the great New York architect John Norris, the Low House is a magnificent example of the Italianate style. Check out the cast-iron balconies on the long porch, a fairly rare feature in historic Savannah homes. Antiques junkies will go nuts over the furnishings, especially the massive secretary in the parlor, one of only four of this type in existence (a sibling is in New York's Metropolitan Museum of Art). Author William Makepeace Thackeray ate in the dining room, now sporting full French porcelain service, and slept in an upstairs room; he also wrote at the desk by the bed. Also on the 2nd floor you'll see the room where Robert E. Lee stayed during his visit and the bed where Juliette Gordon Low died.

MAP 2: 329 Abercorn St., 912/233-6854, www.andrewlowhouse.com; Mon.-Sat. 10am-4pm, Sun. noon-4pm; $10 adults, $9 children

★ CATHEDRAL OF ST. JOHN THE BAPTIST

Spiritual home to Savannah's Irish community and the oldest Roman Catholic church in Georgia, the Cathedral of St. John the Baptist was initially known as Our Lady of Perpetual Help. It's the place to be for mass the morning of March 17 at 8am, as the clans gather in their green jackets and white dresses to take a sip of communion wine before moving on to harder stuff in honor of St. Patrick.

Despite its overt Celtic character today, the parish was originally founded by French émigrés from Haiti who arrived after the successful overthrow of the colonial government by a slave uprising on the island in the late 1700s. The first sanctuary on the site was built in 1873. Fire swept through the edifice in 1898, leaving only two spires and the external walls, but the cathedral was completely rebuilt within a year and a half. In the years since, many renovations have been undertaken. The most recent, from 1998 to 2000, involved the intricate removal, cleaning, and releading of more than 50 of the cathedral's stained-glass windows, a roof replacement, and an interior makeover, introducing a 9,000-pound altar and an 8,000-pound baptismal font, both made of Italian marble.

MAP 2: 222 E. Harris St., 912/233-4709, www.savannahcathedral.org; daily 9am-noon and 12:30pm-5pm, mass Sun. 8am, 10am, 11:30am, Mon.-Sat. noon, Latin mass Sun. 1pm

FLANNERY O'CONNOR CHILDHOOD HOME

On a corner of Lafayette Square stands the rather Spartan facade of the Flannery O'Connor Childhood Home. The Savannah-born novelist lived in this three-story townhome from her birth in 1925 until 1938 and attended church at the cathedral across the square. Once a fairly nondescript attraction for so favorite a native daughter, a recent round of renovations has returned the two main floors to the state Flannery would have known, including an extensive library. A nonprofit association sponsors O'Connor-related readings and signings. While the current backyard garden dates to 1993, it's the place where five-year-old Flannery is said to have taught a chicken to walk backward, foreshadowing the eccentric, Gothic flavor of her writing.

MAP 2: 207 E. Charlton St., 912/233-6014, www.flanneryoconnorhome.org; Fri.-Wed. 1pm-4pm; $6 adults, $5 students, free under age 15

HAMILTON-TURNER INN

Across from the O'Connor house is the Hamilton-Turner Inn. Now a privately owned bed-and-breakfast, this 1873 Second Empire mansion is best known for the showmanship of its over-the-top Victorian appointments and its role in *Midnight in the Garden of Good and Evil* as the home of Joe Odom's girlfriend, "Mandy Nichols" (real name Nancy Hillis). In 1883 it was reportedly the first house in Savannah to have electricity.

MAP 2: 330 Abercorn St., 912/233-1833, www.hamilton-turnerinn.com

TROUP SQUARE

Low-key Troup Square boasts the most modern-looking monument downtown, the **Armillary Sphere.** Essentially an elaborate sundial, the sphere is a series of astrologically themed rings with an arrow that marks the time by shadow. It is supported by six tortoises.

BEACH INSTITUTE

Just east of Troup Square, near the intersection of Harris and Price Streets, is the Beach Institute. Built as a school by the Freedmen's Bureau soon after the Civil War, it was named after its prime benefactor, Alfred Beach, editor of *Scientific American*. It served as an African American school through 1919. Restored by SCAD and given back to the city to serve as a museum, the Beach Institute houses the permanent Ulysses Davis collection and a rotating calendar of art events with a connection to black history.

MAP 2: 502 E. Harris St., 912/234-8000; Tues.-Sun. noon-5pm; $4

JONES STREET

There aren't a lot of individual attractions on Jones Street, the east-west avenue between Taylor and Charlton Streets just north of Monterey Square. Rather, it's the small-scale, throwback feel of the place and its tasteful, dignified homes, including the former home of **Joe Odom** (16 E. Jones St.), that are the attraction. The **Eliza Thompson House** (5 W. Jones St.), now a bed-and-breakfast, was the first home on Jones Street.

MAP 2: Jones St. between Taylor St. and Charlton St.

The Story of "Jingle Bells"

James Pierpont wrote "Jingle Bells" while in the congregation of the Unitarian Universalist Church.

Boston and Savannah vie over bragging rights as to where the classic Christmas song "Jingle Bells" was written. The song's composer, James L. Pierpont, led a life at times as carefree as the song itself. Born in Boston, Pierpont ventured from his wife and young children in 1849 to follow the gold rush to San Francisco. When his brother John was named minister of the new Unitarian congregation in Savannah in 1853, Pierpont followed him, becoming music director and organist, again leaving behind his wife and children in Boston. During this time Pierpont became a prolific composer of secular tunes, including polkas, ballads, and minstrel songs.

In August 1857, a Boston-based publisher, Oliver Ditson and Co., published Pierpont's song "One Horse Open Sleigh." Two years later it was re-released with the current title, "Jingle Bells." At neither time, however, was the song a popular hit. It took action by his son Juriah in 1880 to renew the copyright to what would become one of the most famous songs of all time.

In Massachusetts, they swear Pierpont wrote the song while at the home of one Mrs. Otis Waterman. In Georgia, scholars assure us a homesick Pierpont wrote the tune during a winter at a house at Oglethorpe and Whitaker Streets, long since demolished. The Savannah contingent's ace in the hole is the fact that "Jingle Bells" was first performed in public at a Thanksgiving program at the local Unitarian Universalist Church in 1857. And despite persistent claims in Massachusetts that he wrote the song there in 1850, Southern scholars point out that Pierpont was actually in California in 1850.

UNITARIAN UNIVERSALIST CHURCH OF SAVANNAH

Troup Square is the home of the historic Unitarian Universalist Church of Savannah. This original home of Savannah's Unitarians, who sold the church when the Civil War came, was recently reacquired by the congregation. It is where James L. Pierpont first performed his immortal tune "Jingle Bells." When he did so, however, the church was actually on Oglethorpe Square. The entire building was moved to Troup Square in the mid-1800s.

MAP 2: 313 E. Harris St., 912/234-0980, www.jinglebellschurch.org; service Sun. 11am

★ Monterey Square

Originally named "Monterrey Square" to commemorate the local Irish Jasper Greens' participation in a victorious Mexican-American War battle in 1846, the spelling morphed into its current version somewhere along the way. But Monterey Square remains one of the most visually beautiful and serene spots in all of Savannah. At the center of the square is a monument not to the victory for which it is named but to Count Casimir Pulaski, killed while attempting to retake the city from the British, and whose remains supposedly lie under the 55-foot monument. As early as 1912, people began noticing the disintegration of the monument due to substandard marble used in some key parts, but it wasn't until the 1990s that a full restoration was accomplished. The restoration company discovered that one of the monument's 34 sections had been accidentally installed upside down. In the true spirit of preservation, they dutifully put the section back—upside down. The *Goddess of Liberty* atop the monument, however, is not original; you can see her in the Savannah History Museum. Fans of ironwork will enjoy the ornate masterpieces in wrought iron featured at many houses on the periphery of the square.

MERCER-WILLIAMS HOUSE MUSEUM

The Mercer-Williams House Museum sees a lot of visitors due to its role in the hugely popular *Midnight in the Garden of Good and Evil*. While this grand John Norris building is now primarily known as a crime scene involving late antiques dealer Jim Williams and his lover, if you take a tour of the home, you might hear less about "The Book" than you may have expected. Now proudly owned by Jim Williams's sister Dorothy Kingery, an established academic in her own right, the Mercer-Williams House deliberately concentrates on the early history of the home and Jim Williams's prodigious talent as a collector and conservator of fine art and antiques. Tours are worth it for art aficionados even though the upstairs, Dr. Kingery's residence, is off-limits.

The house was built for General Hugh W. Mercer, Johnny Mercer's great-grandfather, in 1860, but the war interrupted construction. General Mercer—descendant of the Revolutionary War general and George Washington's close friend Hugh Mercer—survived the war, in which he was charged with the defense of Savannah. But he soon fell on hard times and was forced to sell the house to John Wilder, who moved in after completion in 1868. Despite what any tour guide might tell you, no member of the Mercer family—including the great Johnny Mercer himself—ever lived in the house.

MAP 2: 429 Bull St., 912/236-6352, www.mercerhouse.com; Mon.-Sat. 10:30am-4pm, Sun. noon-4pm; $12.50 adults, $8 students

TEMPLE MICKVE ISRAEL

Directly across Monterey Square from the Mercer House is Temple Mickve Israel, a notable structure for many reasons: It's Georgia's first synagogue;

Clockwise from top left: inside the Massie Heritage Center; building on Monterey Square; Mercer-Williams House Museum.

it's the only Gothic synagogue in the country; and it's the third-oldest Jewish congregation in North America, following those in New York and Newport, Rhode Island. Notable congregants have included Dr. Samuel Nunes Ribeiro, who helped stop an epidemic in 1733, and his descendant Raphael Moses, considered the father of the peach industry in the Peach State.

Mickve Israel offers 30- to 45-minute tours of the sanctuary and museum. No reservations are necessary for tours.

MAP 2: 20 E. Gordon St., 912/233-1547, www.mickveisrael.org; Mon.-Fri. 10am-1pm and 2pm-4pm, closed Jewish holidays; $4 suggested donation

CALHOUN SQUARE

The last of the 24 squares in Savannah's original grid, Calhoun Square is also the only square with all its original buildings intact.

MASSIE HERITAGE CENTER

Dominating the south side of Calhoun Square is Savannah's first public elementary school and the spiritual home of Savannah educators, the Massie Heritage Center. In 1841, Peter Massie, a Scots planter with a populist streak, endowed the school to give poor children as good an education as the children of rich families (like Massie's own) received. Another of Savannah's masterpieces by John Norris—whose impressive oeuvre includes the Andrew Low House, the Mercer-Williams House, and the Green-Meldrim House—the central portion of the trifold building was completed in 1856. After the Civil War, the "Massie School," as it's known locally, was designated as the area's African American public school. Classes ceased in 1974, and it now operates as a living-history museum, centering on the period-appointed one-room "heritage classroom" but with several other exhibit spaces of note.

A million-dollar renovation in 2012 added an interactive model of Oglethorpe's urban design and several interesting exhibits on aspects of Savannah architecture and history. In all, Massie provides possibly the best one-stop tour for an all-encompassing look at Savannah history and culture. You can either do a self-guided tour or take the very informative guided tour at 11am or 2pm for the same admission price.

MAP 2: 207 E. Gordon St., 912/201-5070, www.massieschool.com; Mon.-Sat. 10am-4pm, Sun. noon-4pm; $9 adults, $7 youth

WESLEY MONUMENTAL UNITED METHODIST CHURCH

The Wesley Monumental United Methodist Church, named not only for movement founder John Wesley but also for his musical younger brother Charles, is home to Savannah's first Methodist parish. Built in 1875 on the model of Queen's Kirk in Amsterdam and the fourth incarnation of the parish home, this is another great example of Savannah's Gothic churches. Its acoustically wonderful sanctuary features a magnificent Noack organ, which would no doubt please the picky ears of Charles Wesley himself, author of the lyrics to "Hark! The Herald Angels Sing."

67

MAP 2: 429 Abercorn St., 912/232-0191, www.wesleymonumental.org; sanctuary daily 9am-5pm, services Sun. 8:45am and 11am

MARTIN LUTHER KING JR. BOULEVARD
BATTLEFIELD PARK
Right off MLK Jr. Boulevard is Battlefield Park, a.k.a. the Spring Hill Redoubt, a reconstruction of the British fortifications at the Siege of Savannah, with an interpretive site. Recent archaeology discovered the actual location of the original redoubt, and it is also recreated about 100 yards west. Eight hundred granite markers signify the battle's casualties, most of whom were buried in mass graves soon afterward. Sadly, most of the remains of these brave men were simply bulldozed up and discarded without ceremony during later construction projects.

MAP 2: Corner of MLK Jr. Blvd. and Louisville Rd.; dawn-dusk; free

GEORGIA STATE RAILROAD MUSEUM
The Georgia State Railroad Museum, a.k.a. "The Roundhouse," is an ongoing homage to the deep and strangely underreported influence of the railroad industry on Savannah. Constructed in 1830 for the brand-new Central of Georgia line, the Roundhouse's design was cutting-edge for the time, the first building to put all the railroad's key facilities in one place. Spared by Sherman, the site saw its heyday after the Civil War. The highlight of the Roundhouse is the thing in the middle that gave the structure its name, a huge central turntable for positioning rolling stock for repair and maintenance. Frequent demonstrations occur with an actual steam locomotive firing up and taking a spin on the turntable.

MAP 2: 601 W. Harris St., 912/651-6823, www.chsgeorgia.org; daily 9am-5pm; $10 adults, $6 students

SAVANNAH CHILDREN'S MUSEUM
Next to the Railroad Museum is the Savannah Children's Museum, open since 2012. The children's museum is a work in progress that currently has an outdoor "Exploration Station" and a pending larger facility.

MAP 2: 655 Louisville Rd., 912/651-6823, www.savannahchildrensmuseum.org; summer Mon.-Sat. 9am-2pm, school year Wed.-Sat. 10am-4pm; $7.50

RALPH MARK GILBERT CIVIL RIGHTS MUSEUM
One of the former black-owned bank buildings on MLK Jr. Boulevard is now home to the Ralph Mark Gilbert Civil Rights Museum. Named for a pastor of the First African Baptist Church and a key early civil rights organizer, the building was also the local NAACP headquarters for a time. Three floors of exhibits here include photos and interactive displays, the highlight for historians being a fiber-optic map of nearly 100 significant civil rights sites. The first floor features a re-creation of the Azalea Room

Walking Tour of Forsyth Park

As you approach the park, don't miss the ornate ironwork on the west side of Bull Street marking the **Armstrong House,** designed by Henrik Wallin. Featured in the 1962 film *Cape Fear* as well as 1997's *Midnight in the Garden of Good and Evil,* this Italianate mansion was once home to Armstrong Junior College before its move to the city's south side. Directly across Bull Street is another site of *Midnight* fame, the **Oglethorpe Club,** one of the many brick and terra-cotta designs by local architect Alfred Eichberg.

It's easy to miss, but as you enter the park's north side, you encounter the **Marine Memorial,** erected in 1947 to honor the 24 Chatham County Marines killed in World War II. Subsequently, the names of Marines killed in Korea and Vietnam were added. Look west at the corner of Whitaker and Gaston Streets; that's **Hodgson Hall,** home of the Georgia Historical Society. This 1876 building was commissioned by Margaret Telfair to honor her late husband, William Hodgson.

Looking east at the corner of Drayton and Gaston Streets, you'll see the old **Poor House and Hospital,** in use until 1854, when it was converted to serve as the headquarters for the Medical College of Georgia. During the Civil War, General Sherman used the hospital to treat Federal soldiers. From 1930 to 1980 the building was the site of Candler Hospital. Behind the old hospital's cast-iron fence is Savannah's most famous tree, the 300-year-old **Candler Oak.** During Sherman's occupation, wounded Confederate prisoners were treated within a barricade around the oak. The tree is in the National Register of Historic Trees and was the maiden preservation project of the Savannah Tree Foundation, which secured the country's first-ever conservation easement on a single tree.

Walking south into the park proper, you can't miss the world-famous **Forsyth Fountain,** an iconic Savannah sight. Cast in iron on a French model, the fountain was dedicated in 1858. Two other versions of this fountain exist—one in Poughkeepsie, New York, and the other in, of all places, the central plaza in Cusco, Peru.

Continuing south, you'll encounter two low buildings in the center of the

---

of the local Levy's department store, an early boycott diner where blacks were not allowed to eat, though they could buy goods from the store. The second floor is more for hands-on education, with classrooms, a computer room, and a video and reading room. A film chronicles mass meetings, voter registration drives, boycotts, sit-ins, kneel-ins (the integration of churches), and wade-ins (the integration of beaches).

MAP 2: 460 MLK Jr. Blvd., 912/231-8900; Tues.-Sat. 10am-4pm; $10

SAVANNAH HISTORY MUSEUM

The Savannah History Museum is the first stop for many a visitor to town because it's in the same restored Central of Georgia passenger shed as the visitors center. It contains many interesting exhibits on local history, concentrating mostly on colonial times. Toward the rear of the museum is a room for rotating exhibits, as well as one of Johnny Mercer's four Oscars, park. The one on the east side is the so-called "Dummy Fort," circa 1909, formerly a training ground for local militia. Now it's the **Forsyth Park Café** (daily 7am-dusk). To the west is the charming **Fragrant Garden for the Blind.** One of those precious little Savannah gems that is too often overlooked, the Fragrant Garden was initially sponsored by the local Garden Club and based on others of its type throughout the United States.

The tall monument dominating Forsyth Park's central mall is the **Confederate Memorial.** Dedicated in 1875, it wasn't finished until several years later. A New York sculptor carved the Confederate soldier atop the monument. In the wake of national controversies involving such memorials, more inclusive and descriptive signage will be added to expand the historical story told at the site.

My favorite Forsyth Park landmark is at the extreme southern end. It's the Memorial to Georgia Veterans of the Spanish-American War, more commonly known as *The Hiker* because of the subject's casual demeanor and confident stride. Savannah was a major staging area for the 1898 conflict, and many troops were bivouacked in the park. Sculpted in 1902 by Alice Ruggles Kitson, more than 50 replicas of *The Hiker* were made and put up all over the United States.

and, of course, the historic "Forrest Gump bench" that Tom Hanks sat on during his scenes in Chippewa Square.

MAP 2: 303 MLK Jr. Blvd., 912/651-6825, www.chsgeorgia.org; daily 9am-5:30pm; $7 adults, $4 children

SCAD MUSEUM OF ART

In 2011, the Savannah College of Art and Design Museum of Art expanded this handsome building into an old railroad facility immediately behind it, more than doubling its exhibition space and adding the impressive Walter O. Evans Collection of African American Art. The SCAD Museum of Art now hosts a rotating series of exhibits, from standard painting to video installations, many of them commissioned by the school itself.

MAP 2: 601 Turner Blvd., 912/525-5220, www.scadmoa.org; Tues.-Wed. and Fri.-Sat. 10am-5pm, Thurs. 10am-8pm, Sun. noon-5pm; $10 adults, $5 students

CARNEGIE BRANCH LIBRARY

The Carnegie Branch Library is the only example of prairie architecture in town, designed by Savannah architect Julian de Bruyn Kops and built, as the name implies, with funding from tycoon-philanthropist Andrew Carnegie in 1914. But more importantly, the Carnegie Library was for decades the only public library for African Americans in Savannah. One of its patrons was a young Clarence Thomas, who would grow up to be a U.S. Supreme Court justice.

MAP 3: 537 E. Henry St., 912/652-3600, www.liveoakpl.org; Mon. 10am-8pm, Tues.-Thurs. 10am-6pm, Fri. 2pm-6pm, Sat. 10am-6pm

TOP EXPERIENCE

★ FORSYTH PARK

A favorite with locals and visitors alike, the vast, lush expanse of Forsyth Park is a center of local life. Deeply influenced by the then-trendy design of green-space areas in France, Forsyth Park's landscape design by William Bischoff dates to 1851. Named for Georgia governor John Forsyth, the park covers 30 acres, and its perimeter is about a mile.

Near the center of the park is the "fort," actually a revitalized version of an old dummy fort used for military drills in the early 20th century, except these days there is a public restroom.

The park is a center of activities all year long, from free festivals to concerts to Ultimate Frisbee games to the constant circuit around the periphery of walkers, joggers, dog owners, and bicyclists. The only time you shouldn't venture into the park is late at night; otherwise, enjoy.

MAP 3: Bordered by Drayton St., Gaston St., Whitaker St., and Park Ave., 912/351-3850; daily 8am-dusk

SoFo District Map 3

TOP EXPERIENCE

LAUREL GROVE CEMETERY

Its natural vista isn't as alluring as Bonaventure Cemetery's, but Laurel Grove Cemetery boasts its own exquisitely carved memorials and a distinctly Victorian type of surreal beauty that not even Bonaventure can match. In keeping with the racial apartheid of Savannah's early days, there are actually two cemeteries: **Laurel Grove North** (802 W. Anderson St.) for whites, and **Laurel Grove South** (2101 Kollock St.) for blacks. Both are well worth visiting.

By far the most high-profile plot in the North Cemetery is that of Juliette Gordon Low, founder of the Girl Scouts of the USA. Other historically significant sites there include the graves of 8th Air Force founder Frank O. Hunter, Central of Georgia Railway founder William Gordon, and "Jingle Bells" composer James Pierpont. But it's the graves of the anonymous and near-anonymous that are the most poignant sights. The various sections for infants, known as "babylands," cannot fail to move. "Mr. Bones," a former Savannah police dog, is the only animal buried at Laurel Grove. There's an entire site reserved for victims of the great yellow fever epidemic. And don't blink or you'll miss the small rock pile, or cairn, near Governor James Jackson's tomb, the origin and purpose of which remains a mystery. Make sure to view the otherworldly display of Victorian statuary, originally from the grand Greenwich Plantation, which burned in the early 20th century. As with Bonaventure, throughout Laurel Grove you'll find examples of so-called "slave tiles," actually Victorian garden tiles, lining gravesites.

Laurel Grove South features the graves of Savannah's early black Baptist ministers, such as Andrew Bryan and Andrew Cox Marshall. Some of the most evocative gravesites are those of African Americans who obtained their freedom and built prosperous lives for themselves and their families. The vast majority of local firefighters in the 1800s were African Americans, and their simple graves are among the most touching, such as the headstone for one known simply as "August," who died fighting a fire.

To get to Laurel Grove North, take MLK Jr. Boulevard to Anderson Street and turn west. To get to Laurel Grove South, take Victory Drive (U.S. 80) west to Ogeechee Road. Take a right onto Ogeechee, then a right onto West 36th Street. Continue on to Kollock Street.

MAP 3: 802 W. Anderson St. and 2101 Kollock St.; daily 8am-5pm; free

Southside

Map 4

ISLE OF HOPE

A charming, friendly seaside community and National Historic District, Isle of Hope is one of a dwindling number of places where parents still let their kids ride around all day on bikes, calling them in at dinnertime. It doesn't boast many shops or restaurants—indeed, the marina is the only real business—but the row of waterfront cottages on Bluff Drive should not be missed. You might recognize some of them from movies such as *Forrest Gump* and *Glory*. Built from 1880 to 1920, they reflect Isle of Hope's reputation as a healing area and serene Wilmington River getaway from Savannah's capitalist hustle.

To get to Isle of Hope, take Victory Drive (U.S. 80) east and take a right on Skidaway Road. Continue south on Skidaway Road and take a left on Laroche Avenue. Continue until you hit Bluff Drive.

MAP 4: 10 miles south of Savannah

The one-of-a-kind Wormsloe State Historic Site was first settled by Noble Jones, who landed with Oglethorpe on the *Anne* and fought beside him in the War of Jenkins' Ear. One of the great renaissance men of history, this soldier was also an accomplished carpenter, surveyor, forester, botanist, and physician. Wormsloe became famous for its bountiful gardens, so much so that the famed naturalist William Bartram mentioned them in his diary after a visit in 1765 with father John Bartram. After his death, Noble Jones was originally buried in the family plot on the waterfront, but now his remains are at Bonaventure Cemetery. Jones's descendants donated 822 acres of Wormsloe to the Nature Conservancy, which transferred the property to the state. The house, dating from 1828, and 65.5 acres of land are still owned by his family.

The stunning entrance canopy of 400 live oaks, Spanish moss dripping down the entire length, is one of those iconic images of Savannah that will stay with you forever. A small interpretive museum, a one-mile nature walk, and occasional living-history demonstrations make this a great site for the entire family. Walk all the way to the Jones Narrows to see the ruins of the site's original 1739 fortification, one of the oldest and finest examples of tabby construction in the United States. No doubt the area's abundance of Native American shell middens, where early inhabitants discarded their oyster shells, came in handy for its construction. You can see one nearby.

To get to Wormsloe, take Victory Drive (U.S. 80) to Skidaway Road. Go south on Skidaway Road for about 10 miles and follow the signs; you'll see the grand entrance on the right.

MAP 4: 7601 Skidaway Rd., 912/353-3023, www.gastateparks.org/wormsloe; Tues.-Sun. 9am-5pm; $10 adults, $4.50 children

PIN POINT

Off Whitefield Avenue (Diamond Causeway) on the route to Skidaway Island is tiny Pin Point, a predominantly African American township better known as the boyhood home of Supreme Court justice Clarence Thomas. Pin Point traces its roots to a community of formerly enslaved people on Ossabaw Island. Displaced by a hurricane, they settled at this idyllic site overlooking the Moon River, itself a former plantation.

PIN POINT HERITAGE MUSEUM

Many Pin Point residents made their living by shucking oysters at the Varn Oyster Company, the central shed of which still remains and forms the basis of the Pin Point Heritage Museum, opened in 2012. The museum tells the story of the Pin Point community through exhibits, a film, and demonstrations of some of the maritime activities at the Varn Oyster Company through the decades, such as crabbing, canning, shucking, and shrimp-net making.

MAP 4: 9924 Pin Point Ave., http://chsgeorgia.org/PHM; Thurs.-Sat. 9am-5pm; $8 adults, $4 children

Pin Point on the Moon River

On Ossabaw Island, formerly enslaved people had settled into freedom as subsistence farmers after the Civil War. But when a massive hurricane devastated the island in 1893, many moved to the mainland, south of Savannah along what would later be known as Moon River, to a place called Pin Point. While many continued farming, plenty gained employment at local factories, where crabs and oysters were packed and sold. The largest and longest-lived of those factories was A. S. Varn & Son, which employed nearly 100 Pin Point residents—about half of the adult population.

Because so many local people worked at the same place, Pin Point developed a strong community bond, one that was instrumental in forging the life and career of future Supreme Court justice Clarence Thomas, who was born at Pin Point in 1948. Until he was seven, Thomas lived in a tiny house there with his parents, one without plumbing and insulated with newspapers. After a house fire, Thomas moved to Savannah with his grandparents.

While times have certainly changed here—paved roads finally came in the 1970s, and most of the old shotgun shacks have been replaced with mobile homes—Pin Point remains a small, close-knit community of about 300 people, with most property still owned by descendants of the freedmen who bought it after Reconstruction. The Varn factory remained the economic heart of Pin Point until it shut down in 1985. Today, the old factory forms the heart of an ambitious new project, the **Pin Point Heritage Museum** (www.pinpointheritagemuseum.com), which conveys the spirit and history of that community, including its most famous native son, through a series of exhibits and demonstrations.

SKIDAWAY ISLAND

Skidaway Island is notable for two beautiful and educational nature-oriented sites.

SKIDAWAY ISLAND STATE PARK

A site of interest to visitors is Skidaway Island State Park. You can camp here ($25-28), but the awesome nature trails leading out to the marsh—featuring an ancient Native American shell midden and an old whiskey still—are worth a trip on their own, especially when combined with the Marine Educational Center and Aquarium. To get here, take Victory Drive (U.S. 80) until you get to Waters Avenue and continue south as it turns into Whitefield Avenue and then the Diamond Causeway. The park is on your left after the drawbridge. An alternative route from downtown is to take the Truman Parkway all the way to its dead end at Whitefield Avenue; then take a left on Whitefield and continue as it turns into Diamond Causeway where it enters Skidaway.

MAP 4: 52 Diamond Causeway, 912/598-2300, www.gastateparks.org; daily 7am-10pm; parking $5

Clockwise from top left: Forsyth Fountain; Bonaventure Cemetery; Wormsloe State Historic Site.

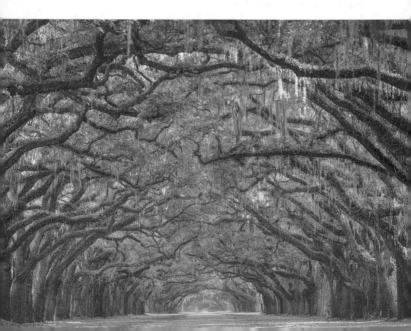

The University of Georgia Marine Educational Center and Aquarium shares a picturesque 700-acre campus on the scenic Skidaway River with the research-oriented Skidaway Institute of Oceanography, also University of Georgia (UGA) affiliated. It hosts scientists and grad students from around the nation, often for trips on its research vessel, the RV *Sea Dawg*. The main attraction of the Marine Center is the small but well-done and recently upgraded aquarium featuring 14 tanks with 200 live animals.

MAP 4: 30 Ocean Science Circle, 912/598-3474, http://gacoast.uga.edu; Mon.-Fri. 9am-4pm, Sat. 10am-5pm; $6 adults, $4 children, cash only

Eastside

Map 4

★ BONAVENTURE CEMETERY

On the banks of the Wilmington River just east of town lies one of Savannah's most distinctive sights, Bonaventure Cemetery. John Muir wrote of Bonaventure's Spanish moss-bedecked beauty in his 1867 book *A Thousand-mile Walk to the Gulf*. While its pedigree as Savannah's premier public cemetery goes back 100 years, it was used as a burial ground as early as 1794. In the years since, this achingly poignant vista of live oaks and azaleas has been the final resting place of such local and national luminaries as Johnny Mercer, Conrad Aiken, Noble Jones, and, of course, the Trosdal plot, former home of the famous *Bird Girl* statue (the original is now in the Telfair Academy of Arts and Sciences). Fittingly, the late great Jack Leigh, who took the *Bird Girl* photo for the cover of *Midnight in the Garden of Good and Evil*, is interred here as well.

If you're doing a self-guided tour, go by the small visitors center at the entrance and pick up one of the free guides to the cemetery, assembled by the Bonaventure Historical Society. By all means, do the tourist thing and pay your respects at Johnny Mercer's final resting place, and go visit beautiful little "Gracie" in Section E, Lot 99. But I also suggest doing as the locals do: Bring a picnic lunch and a blanket and set yourself beside the breezy banks of the Wilmington River, taking in all the lazy beauty and evocative bygone history surrounding you.

To get here from downtown, take the President Street Extension east and take a right on Pennsylvania Avenue, then a left on Bonaventure Road. Alternatively, go east on Victory Drive (U.S. 80) and take a left on Whatley Road in the town of Thunderbolt. Veer left onto Bonaventure Road. The cemetery is one mile ahead on the right.

MAP 4: 330 Bonaventure Rd., 912/651-6843; daily 8am-5pm; free

Johnny Mercer's Black Magic

The great Johnny Mercer is not only without a doubt Savannah's most noteworthy progeny, he is also one of the greatest lyricists music has ever known. Born in 1909, he grew up in Southside Savannah on a small river then called the Back River but since renamed Moon River in honor of his best-known song.

Armed with an innate talent for rhythm and a curious ear for dialogue—both qualities honed by his frequent boyhood contact with Savannah African American culture

Johnny Mercer statue at Ellis Square, by Susie Chisholm

and musicians during the Jazz Age—Mercer wrote what is arguably his greatest song, "Moon River," in 1961. The song, debuted by Audrey Hepburn in the film *Breakfast at Tiffany's,* won an Academy Award for Best Original Song. In addition to "Moon River," Mercer won three other Oscars, for "On the Atchison, Topeka and the Santa Fe" (1946), "In the Cool, Cool, Cool of the Evening" (1951), and "Days of Wine and Roses" (1962).

Today you can pay your respects to Mercer in three places: his boyhood home (509 E. Gwinnett St., look for the historical marker in front of this private residence); the bronze sculpture of Mercer in the revitalized Ellis Square near City Market; and at his gravesite in beautiful Bonaventure Cemetery. And regardless of what anyone tells you, neither Johnny Mercer nor any member of his family ever lived in the Mercer-Williams House on Monterey Square, of *Midnight in the Garden of Good and Evil* fame. Although it was built for his great-grandfather, the home was sold to someone else before it was completed.

DAFFIN PARK

A century spent in Forsyth Park's more genteel shadow doesn't diminish the importance of Daffin Park as Savannah's second major green space. Daffin not only hosts a large variety of local athletes on its fields and courts, but the park's east end is the setting for Historic Grayson Stadium, home of the Savannah Bananas college summer league team. One of the great old ballparks of America, this venue dates from 1941 and has hosted greats such as Babe Ruth, Jackie Robinson, and Mickey Mantle.

Most picturesque for the visitor, however, is the massive fountain set in the middle of the expansive central pond on the park's west side. Originally built in the shape of the continental United States, the pond was the backdrop for a presidential visit by Franklin D. Roosevelt in 1933 that included a speech to an African American crowd. On the far west end of Daffin Park

MAP 4: 1500 F. Victory Dr., daily dawn-dusk

OATLAND ISLAND WILDLIFE CENTER

The closest thing to a zoo in Savannah is the vast, multipurpose Oatland Island Wildlife Center. Set on a former Centers for Disease Control site, it has undergone an extensive environmental cleanup and is now owned by the local school system, although supported purely by donations. Families by the hundreds come here for a number of special Saturdays throughout the year, including an old-fashioned cane grinding in November and a day of sheep shearing in April.

The main attractions here are the critters, located at various points along a meandering two-mile nature trail through the woods and along the marsh. All animals at Oatland are there because they're somehow unable to return to the wild. Highlights include a tight-knit pack of eastern wolves, a pair of bison, cougars (once indigenous to the region), some really cute foxes, and an extensive raptor aviary. Kids will love the petting zoo of farm animals, some of which are free to roam the grounds at will.

MAP 4: 711 Sandtown Rd., 912/898-3980, www.oatlandisland.org; daily 10am-5pm; $5 adults, $3 children

OLD FORT JACKSON

The oldest standing brick fort in Georgia, Old Fort Jackson, named for Georgia governor James Jackson (1798-1801), is also one of eight remaining examples of the so-called Second System of American forts built prior to the War of 1812. Its main claim to fame is its supporting role in the saga of the CSS *Georgia*, a Confederate ironclad now resting under 40 feet of water directly in front of the fort. The *Georgia*, wrapped in an armor girdle of rails, proved too heavy for its engine, so it was simply anchored in the channel opposite Fort Jackson as a floating battery. With General Sherman's arrival in 1864, Confederate forces evacuating to South Carolina scuttled the vessel where it lay to keep it out of Yankee hands.

Operated by the nonprofit Coastal Heritage Society, Fort Jackson is in an excellent state of preservation and provides loads of information for history buffs as well as for kids, who will enjoy climbing the parapets and running on the large parade ground (this area was once a rice field). Inside the fort's casemates underneath the ramparts you'll find well-organized exhibits on the fort's construction and history. Most visitors especially love the daily cannon firings during the summer. If you're really lucky, you'll be around when Fort Jackson fires a salute to passing military vessels on the river—the only historic fort in the United States that does so.

To get to Fort Jackson, take the President Street Extension (Islands

Expressway) east out of downtown. The entrance is several miles down on the left.

MAP 4: Fort Jackson Rd., 912/232-3945, http://chsgeorgia.org; daily 9am-5pm; $8 adults, $4 children

THUNDERBOLT

Near the Bonaventure Cemetery is the little fishing village of Thunderbolt, almost as old as Savannah itself. According to Oglethorpe, the town was named after "a rock which was here shattered by a thunderbolt, causing a spring to gush from the ground, which continued ever afterward to emit the odor of brimstone."

SAVANNAH STATE UNIVERSITY

Continue on River Road and you'll soon be at the entrance to Savannah State University. This historically black university began life in 1890 as the Georgia State Industrial College for Colored Youth. Famous graduates include NFL great Shannon Sharpe. The main landmark is the newly restored Hill Hall, a 1901 building featured in the film *The General's Daughter*.

MAP 4: 3219 College St., 912/356-2186, www.savstate.edu

THUNDERBOLT MUSEUM

Just off Victory Drive is the Thunderbolt Museum, housed in the humble former town hall. Cross Victory Drive onto River Road and notice how the road is built around the live oak tree in the middle of it. Most of the nice views of the river have been obscured by high-rise condos, but there's a cute public fishing pier.

MAP 4: Victory Dr. and Mechanics Ave., 912/351-0836, http://thunderboltmuseum.org; Wed.-Thurs. 9am-4pm, Sat. 1pm-5pm; free

Tybee Island   Map 5

Its name means "salt" in the old Euchee tongue, indicative of the island's chief export in those days. Eighteen miles and about a half-hour drive from Savannah, in truth Tybee is part and parcel of the city's social and cultural fabric. Many of the island's 3,000 full-time residents, known for their boozy bonhomie and quirky personal style, commute to work in the city.

Its wide, beautiful beaches are lined with rare sea oats waving in the Atlantic breeze. The entire island has become a focal point of Georgia's booming film industry. The 2017 reboot of *Baywatch* with Dwayne "the Rock" Johnson was filmed on Tybee's beach, as was the Miley Cyrus film *The Last Song*.

★ FORT PULASKI NATIONAL MONUMENT

There's one must-see before you get to Tybee Island proper. On Cockspur Island you'll find Fort Pulaski National Monument, a delight for any

The Siege of Fort Pulaski

Fort Pulaski's construction was part of a broader initiative by President James Madison in the wake of the War of 1812, which dramatically revealed the shortcomings of U.S. coastal defense. Based on state-of-the-art European design forged in the cauldron of the Napoleonic Wars, Fort Pulaski's thick masonry construction used 25 million bricks, many of them of the famous "Savannah Gray" variety handmade at the nearby Hermitage Plantation.

When Georgia seceded from the Union in January 1861, a small force of Confederates immediately took control of Fort Pulaski and Fort Jackson. In early 1862 a Union sea-land force came to covertly lay the groundwork for a siege of Fort Pulaski. The siege would rely on several batteries secretly set up across the Savannah River. Some of the Union guns utilized new rifled-chamber technology, which dramatically increased the accuracy, muzzle velocity, and penetrating power of their shells. The Union barrage began at 8:15am on April 10, 1862, and Fort Pulaski's walls crumbled under the withering fire. At least one shell struck a powder magazine, igniting an enormous explosion. After 30 hours, Confederate general Charles Olmstead surrendered the fortress.

It was not only Fort Pulaski that was rendered obsolete—it was the whole concept of masonry fortification. From that point forward, military forts would rely on earthwork rather than brick. The section of earthwork you see as you enter Fort Pulaski, the "demilune," was added after the Civil War.

history buff. The pleasure starts when you cross the drawbridge over the moat and see a cannon pointed at you from a narrow gun port. Enter the inside of the fort and take in just how big it is—Union occupiers regularly played baseball on the huge, grassy parade ground. Take a walk around the perimeter, underneath the ramparts. This is where the soldiers lived and worked, and you'll see re-creations of officers' quarters, meeting areas, sick rooms, and prisoners' bunks among the cannons, where Confederate prisoners of war were held after the fort's surrender. Cannon firings happen most Saturdays.

And now for the pièce de résistance: Take the steep corkscrew staircase up to the ramparts themselves and take in the jaw-dropping view of the lush marsh, with the Savannah River and Tybee Island spreading out in the distance. (Warning: There's no railing of any kind on the inboard side of the ramparts. Keep the kids well back from the edge.) Afterward, take a stroll all the way around the walls and see the power of those Yankee guns. Though much of the devastation was soon repaired, some sections of the wall remain in their damaged state. You can even pick out a few cannonballs still stuck in the masonry.

Save some time and energy for the extensive palmetto-lined nature trail through the sandy upland of Cockspur Island on which the fort is located. There are informative markers, a picnic area, and, as a bonus, a coastal defense facility from the Spanish-American War, Battery Hambright.

Continue east on U.S. 80, passing over Lazaretto Creek, named for the quarantine, or "lazaretto," built in the late 1700s to make sure newcomers, mostly enslaved people, were free of disease. As you cross, look to your left over the river's wide south channel. On a tiny oyster shell islet, find the little **Cockspur Beacon** lighthouse, in use from 1848 to 1909, when major shipping was routed through the deeper north channel of the river. The site is now preserved by the National Park Service and is accessible only by boat or kayak. You have to time your arrival with the right tide; check with a local rental place for advice.

MAP 5: U.S. 80 E., 912/786-5787, www.nps.gov/fopu; daily 9am-5pm; $7, free under age 16

SOUTH END

Butler Avenue is Tybee's main drag, the beach fully public and accessible from any of the numbered side streets on the left. Go all the way down to **Tybrisa Street** (formerly 16th St.) to get a flavor of old Tybee. Here's where you'll find the old five-and-dimes like T. S. Chu's, still a staple of local life, and little diners, ice cream spots, and taverns. The new pride of the island is the large, long pier structure called the **Tybrisa Pavilion II,** built in 1996 in an attempt to recreate the lost glory of the Tybrisa Pavilion, social and spiritual center of the island's gregarious resort days. Built in 1891 by the Central of Georgia Railway, the Tybrisa hosted name entertainers and big bands on its expansive dance floor. Sadly, fire destroyed it in 1967, an enormous blow to area morale.

MAP 5: Butler Ave.

TYBEE ISLAND MARINE SCIENCE CENTER

At the foot of the Tybrisa Pavilion is the little Tybee Island Marine Science Center, with nine aquariums and a touch tank featuring native species. Here is the nerve center for the Tybee Island Sea Turtle Project, an ongoing effort to document and preserve the local comings and goings of the island's most beloved inhabitant and unofficial mascot, the endangered sea turtle.

MAP 5: 1510 Strand Ave., 912/786-5917, www.tybeemarinescience.org; daily 10am-5pm; $4 adults, $3 children

TYBEE ISLAND LIGHT STATION AND MUSEUM

At North Campbell Avenue is the entrance to the less-populated, more historically significant north end of Tybee Island, once almost entirely taken up by Fort Screven, a coastal defense fortification of the early 1900s. Rebuilt several times in its history, the Tybee Island Light Station traces its construction to the first year of the colony, based on a design by the multi-talented Noble Jones. At its completion in 1736, it was the tallest structure in the United States. One of a handful of working 18th-century lighthouses today, the facility has been restored to its 1916-1964 incarnation, featuring a nine-foot-tall first-order Fresnel lens installed in 1867.

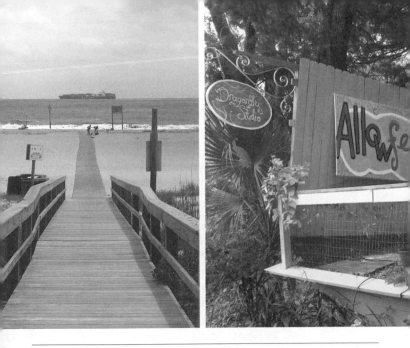

Clockwise from top left: the beach at Tybee Island; an art gallery on the South End of Tybee Island; Inside Fort Pulaski National Monument.

The Tybee Bomb

On a dark night in 1958, at the height of the Cold War, a USAF B-47 Stratojet bomber made a simulated nuclear bombing run over southeast Georgia. A Charleston-based F-86 fighter on a mock intercept came too close, clipping the bomber's wing. Before bringing down the wounded B-47 at Savannah's Hunter Airfield, Commander Howard Richardson decided to jettison his lethal cargo: a 7,000-pound Mark 15 hydrogen bomb, serial number 47782. Richardson, who won the Distinguished Flying Cross for his efforts that night, jettisoned the bomb over water. What no one knows is exactly where. And thus began the legend of "the Tybee Bomb." Speculation ran wild, with some locals fearing a nuclear explosion, radioactive contamination, or even that a team of scuba-diving terrorists would secretly retrieve the weapon.

Commander Richardson, now retired, says the bomb wasn't armed when he jettisoned it. Environmentalists say that doesn't matter, because the enriched uranium the Air Force admits was in the bomb is toxic whether or not there's the risk of a nuclear detonation. People who work in the fishing industry on Tybee say the fact that the bomb also had 400 pounds of high explosive "nuclear trigger" is reason enough to get it out of the waterways.

The Air Force has made several attempts to locate the weapon. In 2000 it sent a team to Savannah to find the bomb, concluding it was buried somewhere off the coast in 5 to 15 feet of mud. In 2005, in another attempt to find the weapon, it sent another team of experts down to look one last time. Their verdict: The bomb's still lost.

All the outbuildings on the lighthouse grounds are original, including the residence of the lighthouse keeper, also the oldest building on the island. If you've got the legs and the lungs, definitely take all 178 steps up to the top of the lighthouse for a stunning view of Tybee, the Atlantic, and Hilton Head Island.

All around the area of the north end around the lighthouse complex you'll see low-lying concrete bunkers. These are remains of Fort Screven's coastal defense batteries, and many are in private hands. Battery Garland is open to tours, and also houses the Tybee Island Museum, a charming, almost whimsical little collection of exhibits from various eras of local history.

One entrance fee gives you admission to the lighthouse, the lighthouse museum, and the Tybee Island Museum.

MAP 5: 30 Meddin Ave., 912/786-5801, www.tybeelighthouse.org; Wed.-Mon. 9am-5:30pm, last ticket sold 4:30pm; $9 adults, $7 children

TYBEE POST THEATER

The new pride of the north end is the Tybee Post Theater, a fully restored performing arts venue that was once, as the name implies, the theater for the Fort Screven military facility. The small but cozy 200-seat space now offers a range of programming from live music to live theater to film

MAP 5: 10 Van Horne Ave., 912/472-4790, www.tybeeposttheater.org; prices vary

Greater Savannah Map 6

MIDWAY AND LIBERTY COUNTY

Locals will tell you that Midway is named because it's equidistant from
the Savannah and Altamaha Rivers on Oglethorpe's old "river road,"
which it certainly is, but others say the small but very historic town is
actually named after the Medway River in England. In seeking to pacify
the local Creek people, the Council of Georgia in 1752 granted a group
of Massachusetts Puritans then residing in Dorchester, South Carolina,
a 32,000-acre land grant as incentive to move south. After moving into
Georgia and establishing New Dorchester, they soon founded a nearby settlement that would later take on the modern spelling of Midway. Midway's
citizens were very aggressive early on in the cause for American independence, which is why the area's three original parishes were combined and
named Liberty County in 1777—the only Georgia county named for a concept rather than a person. Two of Georgia's three signers of the Declaration
of Independence, Lyman Hall and Button Gwinnett, resided primarily in
Midway, and both attended the historic Midway Church. A key part of
Liberty County history is no more: The once-thriving seaport of Sunbury,
which formerly challenged Savannah for economic supremacy in the region, no longer exists.

Tourism in this area has been made much more user-friendly by the
liberal addition of signage for the "Liberty Trail," a collection of key attractions. When in doubt, follow the signs. The main highways in Midway are
I-95, U.S. 17, and U.S. 84, also called Oglethorpe Highway, which becomes
Highway 38 (Islands Hwy.) east of I-95.

FORT MORRIS STATE HISTORIC SITE

Built to defend the once-proud port of Sunbury, Fort Morris State Historic
Site was reconstructed during the War of 1812 and was an encampment
during the Civil War. It was here that Colonel John McIntosh gave his famous reply to the British demand for his surrender: "Come and take it." The
museum has displays of military and everyday life of the era. Reenactments
and cannon firings are highlights. There's a visitors center and a nature
trail. The site is about 50 minutes from Savannah. To get here, take exit 76
off I-95 south. Go east on Islands Highway and take a left on Fort Morris
Road; the site is two miles down.

MAP 6: 2559 Ft. Morris Rd., 912/884-5999, www.gastateparks.org/fortmorris; Thurs.-Sat.
9am-5pm; $4.50 adults, $3 children

GEECHEE KUNDA

A little way south of Midway on the Liberty Trail in tiny Riceboro is Geechee Kunda, a combination museum-outreach center on the site of the former Retreat rice and indigo plantation. It's now dedicated to explaining and exploring the culture of Sea Island African Americans on the Georgia coast. (Don't be confused: *Geechee* is the Georgia word for the Gullah people. Both groups share similar folkways and history, and the terms are virtually interchangeable.) There are artifacts from slavery and Reconstruction, including authentic Geechee relics. Geechee Kunda is about 40 minutes from Savannah. Take exit 67 off I-95 and head north about two miles on U.S. 17.

MAP 6: 622 Ways Temple Rd., Riceboro, 912/884-4440, www.geecheekunda.com; Tues.-Sat. 11am-5pm; free

MIDWAY MUSEUM

In Midway proper is the charming Midway Museum and the adjacent **Midway Church,** sometimes called the Midway Meetinghouse. The museum contains a variety of artifacts, most from the 18th and 19th centuries, and an extensive genealogy collection. The Midway Church, built in 1756, was burned during the Revolution but rebuilt in 1792. Both Button Gwinnett and Lyman Hall attended services here, and during the Civil War some of Sherman's cavalry set up camp on the grounds. The cemetery across the street is wonderfully poignant and is the final resting place of two Revolutionary War generals; Union cavalry kept horses within its walls. The museum, church, and cemetery are 30 miles from Savannah and easy to find: take exit 76 from I-95 south, and take a right on U.S. 84 (Oglethorpe Hwy.). Turn right on U.S. 17, and they're just ahead on the right.

MAP 6: 491 N. Coastal Hwy., 912/884-5837, www.themidwaymuseum.org; Tues.-Sat. 10am-4pm; adults $10, students $5

SEABROOK VILLAGE

West off Islands Highway is Seabrook Village, a unique living-history museum chronicling the everyday life of Liberty County's African Americans, with a direct link to Sherman's famous "40 acres and a mule" Field Order No. 15. There are eight restored buildings on the 100-acre site, including the simple but sublime one-room Seabrook School. From Savannah, take exit 76 off I-95, and then a left onto U.S. 84. After about two miles, take a left onto Trade Hill Road.

MAP 6: 660 Trade Hill Rd., 912/884-7008; Tues. and Thurs. 10:30am-1:30pm; $3

OSSABAW ISLAND

OSSABAW ISLAND

Owned and operated by Georgia as a heritage and wildlife preserve, the island was a gift to the state in 1978 from Eleanor Torrey-West and family, who still retain some property on the island. All public use of the island is managed by the **Ossabaw Island Foundation** (www.ossabawisland.org).

Sunbury: Gone but Not Forgotten

If you spend much time in Liberty County, you'll probably hear someone mention that a certain place or person is "over near Sunbury." Such is the legacy of this long-gone piece of Georgia history that locals still refer to it in the present tense, though the old town itself is no more.

Founded soon after Midway in 1758, Sunbury rivaled Savannah as Georgia's main commercial port by 1761, with a thriving trade in lumber, rice, indigo, corn, and, unfortunately, enslaved people. At one time, seven square-rigged vessels called on the port in a single day.

At various times, all three of Georgia's signers of the Declaration of Independence—Button Gwinnett, Lyman Hall, and George Walton—had connections to Sunbury. The beginning of the end came with those heady days of revolution, however, when Sunbury was the scene of much fighting between colonists and the British army. A British siege in 1778 culminated in this immortal reply from the colonial commander, Colonel John McIntosh, to a redcoat demand for surrender: "Come and take it." By the beginning of 1779, a separate British assault did so.

After U.S. independence, Sunbury remained the Liberty County seat until 1797, but it was never the same, beset by decay, hurricanes, and yellow fever outbreaks. By 1848, nothing of the town remained but the old cemetery, which you can find a short drive from the Fort Morris State Historic Site; ask a park employee for directions.

The 12,000-acre island is much older than Wassaw Island to its north and so has traces of human habitation back to 2000 BC. The island's name comes from an old Muskogean word referring to yaupon holly, found in abundance on the island and used by Native Americans in purification rituals to induce vomiting. There are several tabby ruins on the island, along with many miles of walking trails. Unlike the much-younger Wassaw, Ossabaw Island was not only timbered extensively but hosted several rice and cotton plantations.

Descendants of the island's enslaved workers moved to the Savannah area after the Civil War, founding the community of Pin Point. Similarly to Jekyll Island to the south, Ossabaw was a hunting preserve for wealthy families in the Roaring '20s. Even today, hunting is an important activity on the island, with lotteries choosing who gets a chance to pursue its overly large populations of deer and wild hogs, the latter of which are descended from pigs brought by the Spanish.

Now reserved exclusively for educational and scientific purposes, the island is accessible only by boat. Georgia law ensures public access to all beaches up to the high-tide mark—which simply means that the public can ride out to Ossabaw and go on the beach for day use, but any travel to the interior is restricted and you must have permission first. Contact the Ossabaw Island Foundation for information. Boat trips take about 1.5

hours and vary in price. Day trips can be arranged with charter operators at the marinas in Savannah.

MAP 6: Ossabaw Island, www.ossabawisland.org

WASSAW ISLAND
WASSAW ISLAND NATIONAL WILDLIFE REFUGE

Unique in that it's the only Georgia barrier island never cleared for agriculture or development, the 10,000-acre Wassaw Island National Wildlife Refuge is accessible only by boat. There are striking driftwood-strewn beaches, and the interior of the island has some beautiful old-growth stands of longleaf pine and live oak. Wassaw is a veritable paradise for nature lovers and bird-watchers, with migratory activity in the spring and fall, waterfowl in abundance in the summer, and manatee and loggerhead turtle activity (about 10 percent of Georgia's transient loggerhead population makes use of Wassaw for nesting). There are also about 20 miles of trails and a decaying Spanish-American War-era battery, Fort Morgan, on the north end. National Wildlife Refuge Week is celebrated in October.

Because of its comparatively young status—it was formed only about 1,600 years ago—Wassaw Island also has some unique geographical features. You can still make out the parallel ridge features, vestiges of successive ancient shorelines. A central ridge forms the backbone of the island, reaching an amazing (for this area) elevation of 45 feet above sea level at the south end. Native Americans first settled the island, whose name comes from an ancient word for sassafras, which was found in abundance here. During the Civil War, both Confederate and Union troops occupied the island successively. In 1866 the wealthy New England businessman George Parsons bought the island, which stayed in that family's hands until it was sold to the Nature Conservancy in 1969 for $1 million. The Conservancy in turn sold Wassaw to the U.S. government for $1 to be managed as a wildlife refuge.

It's easiest to get to Wassaw Island from Savannah. Boat rides take roughly 30 minutes and cost around $50 round-trip. Charters and scheduled trips are available from **Captain Walt's Charters** (Thunderbolt Marina, 3124 River Dr., 912/507-3811, www.waltsadventure.com/charters), the **Bull River Marina** (8005 E. U.S. 80, 912/897-7300), **Delegal Marina** (1 Marina Dr., 912/598-0023), **Captain Joe Dobbs** (Delegal Marina, 1 Marina Dr., 912/598-0090, www.captjdobbs.com), and **Isle of Hope Marina** (50 Bluff Dr., 912/354-8187, www.isleofhopemarina.com). Most docking is either at the beaches on the north and south ends or in Wassaw Creek, where the U.S. Fish and Wildlife Service dock is also located (temporary mooring only). There's no camping allowed on Wassaw Island; it's for day use only.

MAP 6: Wassaw Island, www.fws.gov/wassaw; daily dawn-dusk

The Salzburgers of New Ebenezer

Perhaps the most unsung chapter in Europe's great spiritual diaspora of the 1700s, the Salzburgers of New Ebenezer—a thrifty, peaceful, and hard-working people—were Georgia's first religious refugees and perhaps the most progressive as well. The year after Oglethorpe's arrival, a contingent of devout Lutherans from Salzburg in present-day Austria arrived after being expelled from their home country for their beliefs. Oglethorpe, mindful of Georgia's mission to provide sanctuary for persecuted Protestants and wishing for a military buffer to the west, eagerly welcomed them. Given land about 25 miles west of Savannah, the Salzburgers named their first settlement Ebenezer ("stone of help" in Hebrew). They later moved the site to better land nearer to the river and called it New Ebenezer, and so it remains to this day.

Because the settlers spoke German instead of English, the upriver colony maintained its isolation. Still, the Salzburgers were among Oglethorpe's most ardent and loyal supporters. Their pastor and de facto political leader, Johann Martin Boltzius, seeking to build an enlightened agrarian utopia, was an outspoken foe of slavery and the exploitative plantation system. The fragile silk industry thrived in New Ebenezer while it had failed miserably in Savannah, and the nation's first rice mill was built here.

The Trustees' turnover of Georgia to the crown in 1750 signaled the final victory of pro-slavery forces—even Pastor Boltzius acquired a couple of enslaved people as domestic servants. New Ebenezer's influence began a decline that accelerated when British forces pillaged much of the town in the Revolution. Fifty years later, nothing at all remained except the old Jerusalem Church, now the **Jerusalem Evangelical Lutheran Church.**

Although New Ebenezer is often called a "ghost town," this is a misnomer. Extensive archaeological work continues in the area, and the Georgia Salzburger Society works hard to maintain several historic buildings and keep the legacy alive through special events.

WEST CHATHAM
COASTAL GEORGIA BOTANICAL GARDENS AT THE HISTORIC BAMBOO FARM

A joint project of the University of Georgia and Chatham County, this farm is an education and demonstration center featuring a wide array of native species in addition to the garden's eponymous Asian "wonder weed," which has its roots in a private collection dating from the late 1800s. Many of the mature trees were planted in the 1930s. The garden also periodically holds you-pick-'em harvest days for berries. To get here, take exit 94 off of I-95 and take Highway 204 east toward Savannah. Turn right on East Gateway Boulevard, then left on Canebrake Road. Enter at the Canebrake gate. No pets are allowed on-site, even on a leash.

MAP 6: 2 Canebrake Rd., 912/921-5460, www.coastalgeorgiabg.org; Mon.-Fri. 8am-5pm, Sat. 10am-5pm, Sun. noon-5pm; $5 adults, $3 children

POOLER

NATIONAL MUSEUM OF THE MIGHTY EIGHTH AIR FORCE

Military and aviation buffs should not miss the **National Museum of the Mighty Eighth Air Force** (175 Bourne Ave., Pooler, 912/748-8888, www.mightyeighth.org, daily 9am-5pm, $10 adults, $6 children and active-duty military) in Pooler, Georgia, right off I-95. The 8th Air Force was born at Hunter Field in Savannah as the 8th Bomber Command in 1942, becoming the 8th Air Force in 1944; it is now based in Louisiana.

A moving testament to the men and machines that conducted those strategic bombing campaigns over Europe in World War II, the museum also features later 8th Air Force history such as the Korean War, the Linebacker II bombing campaigns over North Vietnam, and the Persian Gulf. Inside you'll find airplanes like the P-51 Mustang and the German ME-109. The centerpiece, however, is the restored B-17 bomber *City of Savannah,* the newest jewel of the collection, acquired from the National Air and Space Museum in Washington DC.

MAP 6: 175 Bourne Ave., Pooler, 912/748-8888, www.mightyeighth.org; daily 9am-5pm; $12 adults, $8 children and active-duty military

RICHMOND HILL AND BRYAN COUNTY

Known as the "town that Henry Ford built," Richmond Hill is a growing bedroom community of Savannah in adjacent Bryan County. Sherman's March to the Sea ended here with much destruction, so little history before that time is left. Most of what remains is due to Ford's philanthropic influence, still felt in many place-names around the area, including the main drag, Highway 144, known as Ford Avenue. After the auto magnate and his wife Clara made the area, then called Ways Station, a summer home, they were struck by the area's incredible poverty and determined to help improve living conditions, building hospitals, schools, churches, and homes. The Fords eventually acquired over 85,000 acres in Bryan County, including the former Richmond plantation. What is now known as Ford Plantation—currently a private luxury resort—was built in the 1930s and centered on the main house, once the central building of the famous Hermitage Plantation on the Savannah River, purchased and moved by Ford south to Bryan County.

FORT MCALLISTER STATE HISTORIC SITE

Perhaps the main attraction in Richmond Hill, especially for Civil War buffs, is Fort McAllister State Historic Site. Unlike the masonry forts of Savannah, Fort McAllister is an all-earthwork fortification on the Ogeechee River, the site of a short but savage assault by Sherman's troops in December 1864 in which 5,000 Union soldiers quickly overwhelmed the skeleton garrison of 230 Confederate defenders. After the war, the site fell into disrepair until Henry Ford funded and spearheaded restoration in the 1930s, as he did with so many historic sites in Bryan County. The fort, which

(Mon.-Sat. 9am-5pm, Sun. 2pm-5pm, $5). An adjacent recreational site features a beautiful oak-lined picnic ground, a nature trail, and the nearby 65-site Savage Island Campground. Bryan County is just 15 minutes from Savannah. Take I-95 south and then exit 90. From there, head east about six miles on Highway 144 (Ford Dr.).

MAP 6: 3894 Ft. McAllister Rd., Richmond Hill, 912/727-2339, www.gastateparks.org; daily 7am-10pm; $7.50 adults, $4.50 children

RICHMOND HILL HISTORICAL SOCIETY AND MUSEUM

The little Richmond Hill Historical Society and Museum is housed in a former kindergarten built by Henry Ford.

MAP 6: Ford Ave. and Timber Trail Rd., Richmond Hill, 912/756-3697; daily 10am-4pm; donation

NEW EBENEZER

JERUSALEM EVANGELICAL LUTHERAN CHURCH

Few people visit New Ebenezer today, west of Savannah in Effingham County. Truth is there's not much there anymore except for one old church, but, oh, what a church. The Jerusalem Evangelical Lutheran Church hosts the oldest continuous congregation in the United States. Built of local clay brick in 1769, its walls are 21 inches thick. Some original panes of glass remain, and its European bells are still rung before each service. Several surrounding structures are also heirs to New Ebenezer's Salzburg legacy.

MAP 6: 2966 Ebenezer Rd., Rincon, 912/754-3915, http://jerusalematebenezer.org; service Sun. 11am

NEW EBENEZER RETREAT AND CONFERENCE CENTER

Around the corner from the Jerusalem Evangelical Lutheran Church is a much newer spiritually themed site, the New Ebenezer Retreat and Conference Center. Built in 1977, the retreat provides acres of calm surroundings, lodging, and meals in an ecumenical Christian setting.

The New Ebenezer Retreat and Conference Center offers a range of very reasonably priced lodgings, most including meals, in a beautiful setting. The extremely fast-growing town of Rincon, through which you will most likely drive on your way to New Ebenezer, offers an assortment of the usual chain food and lodging establishments.

While most facilities are for guests of the retreat, you can tour the grounds on your own. It's scenic and peaceful, and the cottages are charming.

MAP 6: 2887 Ebenezer Rd., Rincon, 912/754-9242, www.newebenezer.org

Carriage Tours

Ah, yes—what could be more romantic than enjoying downtown Savannah the way it was originally intended to be traveled, by horse-drawn carriage? Indeed, this is one of the most fun ways to see the city, for couples as well as for those with horse-enamored children.

There are three main purveyors of equine tourism in town: Carriage Tours of Savannah (912/236-6756, www.carriagetoursofsavannah.com), Historic Savannah Carriage Tours (888/837-1011, www.savannahcarriage.com), and Plantation Carriage Company (912/201-0001, http://plantationcarriagecompany.com). The length of the basic tour and the price are about the same for all—45-60 minutes, about $25 adults, $15 children. All offer specialty tours as well, from ghost tours to evening romantic rides with champagne. Embarkation points vary; check company websites for pickup points. Some will pick you up at your hotel. The City of Savannah does regulate these tours in times of extreme heat or icy road conditions for the animals' safety.

Tours

Savannah's tourism boom has resulted in an explosion of well over 50 separate tour services, ranging from simple guided trolley journeys to horse-drawn carriage rides to specialty tours to ecotourism adventures. Fair warning: Although local tour guides technically must pass a competency test demonstrating their knowledge of Savannah history, in practice facts are often thrown out the window in favor of whatever sounds good at the time. Keep in mind that not everything you hear from a tour guide may be true.

WALKING TOURS
OLD CITY WALKS
The premium tour option is Old City Walks, explorations of well-known and of little-known Savannah attractions, guided by longtime local experts. These aren't budget tours, but they are the state of the art locally. There are several tours and many times; they also offer privately scheduled tours.
MAP 2: E. Jones Lane, 912/358-0700, www.oldcitywalks.com; $48

SPECIALTY TOURS
SAVANNAH SLOW RIDE
For a unique tour experience, take a seat on the Savannah Slow Ride, a sort of combination bar, bicycle, and carriage ride. You get on with a group and everyone helps pedal around the squares on about a two-hour ride at five mph or less. You can even bring your to-go cup with you, as many of the

tour; call for details.

MAP 1: 420 W. Bryan St., 912/414-5634, www.savannahslowride.com; $30

SAVANNAH TASTE EXPERIENCE

Consistently one of the highest-quality tours in town, Savannah Taste Experience takes you on several foodie stops to taste, sip, and learn about Savannah's culinary scene. The basic tour is "First Squares" ($49 adults, $37 children), which focuses on spots within easy walking distance of the waterfront; it meets on River Street. The "Famous and Secret East Side Tour" ($57 adults, $47 children) takes you to more off-the-beaten-path spots; it meets on Liberty Street. Food and drink is of course included, so come hungry and thirsty!

MAP 1: meeting points vary, 912/221-4439, www.savannahtasteexperience.com; prices vary

SAVANNAH MOVIE TOUR

To learn about Savannah's history of filmmaking, try a Savannah Movie Tour, which will take you to various film locations in town. The company also offers an enormous, three-hour Foody Tour ($62 adults) featuring several local eateries, and they offer several other non-movie-related specialty tours.

MAP 2: meeting point at Savannah Visitors Center, 301 MLK Jr. Blvd., 912/234-3440, www.savannahmovietours.com; $30 adults, $18 children

WALKING TOURS SAVANNAH

Longtime tour guide and raconteur Greg Proffit and his staff offer fun walking "pub crawls," wherein the point is to meet your guide at some local tavern, ramble around, learn a little bit, and imbibe a lot—though not necessarily in that order. The adult tour is the "Creepy Crawl" ($25), whereas the tour suitable for kids is the "Creepy Stroll" ($16 adults, $10 children). You may not want to believe everything you hear, but you're sure to have a lot of fun. The tours book up early, so make arrangements in advance.

MAP 2: 527 E. Gordon St., 912/238-3843, www.walkingtourssavannah.com; $10-18 adults

WATER TOURS

SAVANNAH BELLES

If you've just *got* to get out on the river for a short time, by far the best bargain is to take one of the nifty water ferries of the Savannah Belles, named after famous women in Savannah history, which shuttle passengers from River Street to Hutchinson Island and back every 15-20 minutes. Pick one up on River Street in front of City Hall or at the Waving Girl Landing a few blocks east. The watercraft are ADA accessible.

MAP 1: River St. at City Hall and Waving Girl Landing, www.catchacat.org; daily 7am-midnight; free

Trolley Tours

Old Town Trolley Tours

The vehicles of choice for the bulk of the masses visiting Savannah, trolleys allow you to sit back and enjoy the views in reasonable comfort. As in other cities, the guides provide commentary while attempting, with various degrees of success, to navigate the cramped downtown traffic environment. The main trolley companies in town are **Old Savannah Tours** (912/234-8128, www.oldsavannahtours.com, basic on-off tour $28 adults, $12 children) and **Old Town Trolley Tours** (800/213-2474, www.trolleytours.com, basic on-off tour $30 adults, $11 children). Both embark from the Savannah Visitors Center on Martin Luther King Jr. Boulevard about every 15-30 minutes on the same schedule, daily 9am-4:30pm.

Frankly there's not much difference between them, as they all offer a very similar range of services for similar prices. While the common "on-off privileges" allow trolley riders to disembark for a while and pick up another of the same company's trolleys at marked stops, be aware there's no guarantee the next trolley—or the one after that—will have enough room to take you on board.

SAVANNAH RIVERBOAT CRUISES

The heavy industrial buildup on the Savannah River means that the main river tours, all departing from the docks in front of the Hyatt Regency Savannah, tend to be disappointing in their unrelenting views of cranes, docks, and smokestacks. Still, for those into that kind of thing, narrated trips up and down the river on the *Georgia Queen* and the *Savannah River Queen* are offered by Savannah Riverboat Cruises. You can opt for just sightseeing, or an added dinner cruise.

MAP 1: 9 E. River St., 912/232-6404, www.savannahriverboat.com; from $25 adults, $16 ages 4-12

BIKING TOURS

SAVANNAH BIKE TOURS

To see downtown Savannah by bicycle—quite a refreshing experience—let Savannah Bike Tours take you on a two-hour trip through 19 squares and Forsyth Park. Pedaling around the squares and stopping to explore certain sights is a unique pleasure. Tours leave at 9am, 12:30pm, and 4pm daily, plus 6pm in summer. Rent bikes or ride your own.

MAP 1: 41 Habersham St., 912/704-4043, www.savannahbiketours.com; $25 adults, $10 under age 12

GHOST TOURS

SIXTH SENSE SAVANNAH GHOST TOUR

For those who take their paranormal activity *very* seriously, there's Shannon Scott's Sixth Sense Savannah Ghost Tour, an uncensored, straightforward look at Savannah's poltergeist population.

MAP 2: Meeting point Clary's Cafe, 404 Abercorn St., 866/666-3323, www. sixthsensesavannah.com; $20, midnight tour $39

HEARSE GHOST TOURS

The many ghost tours, offered by all the companies, can be fun for the casual visitor who wants entertainment rather than actual history. Students of the paranormal are likely to be disappointed by the cartoonish, Halloween aspect of some of the tours. A standout in the ghost field is Hearse Ghost Tours, a unique company that also operates tours in New Orleans and St. Augustine, Florida. Up to eight guests at a time ride around in the open top of a converted hearse—painted all black, of course—and get a 75-minute, suitably over-the-top narration from the driver-guide. It's still pretty cheesy, but a hip kind of cheesy.

MAP 3: 412 E. Duffy St., 912/695-1578, www.hearseghosttours.com; $17

Restaurants

PRICE KEY

$ Entrées less than $10

$$ Entrées $10–20

$$$ Entrées more than $20

*S*avannah is a fun food town, with a selection of cuisine concocted by a cast of executive chefs who, despite their many personal idiosyncrasies, tend to go with what works rather than experiment for the sake of experimentation.

Note that there isn't a cuisine category for seafood listed in this chapter—that's because seafood is an intrinsic part of most restaurant fare in Savannah, whether through regular menu offerings or through specials. For the freshest seafood, consider a trip to Tybee Island or Thunderbolt, on the way to Tybee.

Highlights

★ **Best Breakfast Downtown:** Hands down, it's **B. Matthew's Eatery** on Bay Street, where you can't go wrong with the omelets or the pancakes (page 97).

★ **Best for Chocoholics:** From choc-olate-chip cheesecake to specialty martinis, **Lulu's Chocolate Bar** can satisfy your sweet tooth (page 98).

★ **Best Repurpose:** Dine on James Beard Award-winning soul food in a former bus depot at **The Grey** (page 99).

★ **Most Luscious Lunch:** The dishes at **Kayak Kafe** are light and adventurous and make for a perfect pit stop during a day of shopping on Broughton Street (page 99).

★ **Tastiest Brush with Hollywood:** Movie producer and Savannah native Stratton Leopold is often seen behind the counter at **Leopold's Ice Cream,** help-ing dish out scoops of his old family recipe ice cream flavors among Hollywood memo-rabilia (page 102).

★ **Most Authentic Southern Experience:** Eat around a communal table in a convivial atmosphere at **Mrs. Wilkes' Dining Room** and enjoy what many consider the finest fried chicken in the South, among other classic dishes (page 103).

★ **Most Romantic Date Night:** One of Savannah's original fine-dining restaurants, **Elizabeth on 37th** remains the local gold standard for a wonderful evening with wonderful food and service (page 104).

★ **Most Bodacious Burger:** The made-to-order patties at **Green Truck Neighborhood Pub** come with tasty toppings, from Greek style to pimento cheese. Wash down your burger with a selection from their great craft brew list. (page 104).

★ **Best Memphis BBQ: Sandfly BBQ** serves the best Memphis-style brisket in Georgia. (page 106).

Leopold's Ice Cream

CLASSIC SOUTHERN

TREYLOR PARK ⑤⑤

The bustling, friendly interior of this popular Bay Street spot plays up the shabby chic undertone of Savannah life, with tasty gourmet takes on downmarket Southern classics like the chicken biscuit, pot pie, and sloppy joe. Don't miss the signature starter dish, the PB&J Wings. A particularly tasteful cocktail menu and a well-curated craft beer list round out the experience.

MAP 1: 115 E. Bay St., 912/495-5557, www.treylorpark.com; Mon.-Fri. noon-1am, Sat. 10am-2am, Sun. 10am-1am

VIC'S ON THE RIVER ⑤⑤⑤

Very few restaurants on River Street rise above tourist schlock, but a standout is Vic's on the River. With dishes like wild Georgia shrimp, stone-ground grits, and blue crab cakes with a three-pepper relish, Vic's combines a romantic old Savannah atmosphere with an adventurous take on Lowcountry cuisine. Note the entrance to the dining room is not on River Street but on the Bay Street level on Upper Factor's Walk.

MAP 1: 16 E. River St., 912/721-1000, www.vicsontheriver.com; Sun.-Thurs. 11am-10pm, Fri.-Sat. 11am-11pm

BREAKFAST

★ B. MATTHEW'S EATERY ⑤⑤

If you're downtown and need something more than your hotel breakfast—and you will!—go to B. Matthew's Eatery, widely considered the best breakfast in the entire Savannah historic district. The omelets—most under $10—are uniformly wonderful, and the sausage and bacon are excellent and not greasy. There are healthier selections as well, and you can actually get a decent bowl of oatmeal. Sunday brunch is incredible, but lunch and dinner here are great as well. Lunch sandwiches and salads are of similarly high quality, and dinner entrées (from $17) include killer osso buco, lamb, and seafood.

MAP 1: 325 E. Bay St., 912/233-1319, www.bmatthewseatery.com; Mon.-Thurs. 8am-9pm, Fri.-Sat. 8am-10pm, Sun. 9am-3pm

ASIAN

CO SAVANNAH ⑤⑤

The newest and most widely regarded as best Asian fusion cuisine in town is at CO Savannah, a block off the waterfront. This regional chain has a menu particularly strong in *bánh mì* and specialty sushi rolls, with a cocktail and beer menu superior to most similar places in town. It's a fun place to get plates to share. Speaking of beverages, upstairs you'll find the affiliated **Savannah Cocktail Co.** (www.savannahcocktailco.com, daily 5pm-1am), which offers a great Sunday brunch.

MAP 1: 10 Whitaker St., 912/234-5375, www.eatatco.com, Sun.-Thurs. 11am-10pm, Fri.-Sat. 11am-11pm

GREEK
OLYMPIA CAFÉ $$

A worthwhile place to stop for a relaxing and tasty meal on River Street is Olympia Café, which serves a variety of Greek dishes such as dolmas, spanakopita, seafood, and lemon chicken in a friendly atmosphere. The standard menu items aren't particularly cheap, but the daily specials often offer a surprisingly good deal for the money.

MAP 1: 5 E. River St., 912/233-3131, www.olympiacafe.net; daily 11am-10pm

City Market

Map 1

CLASSIC SOUTHERN
THE LADY & SONS $$

Every year, thousands of visitors come to Savannah to wait for hours for a chance to sample some of local celebrity Paula Deen's "home" cooking at the Lady & Sons. There's actually a fairly typical Southern buffet with some decent fried chicken, collard greens, and mac and cheese. You must begin waiting in line as early as 9:30am for lunch and as early as 3:30pm for dinner in order to be assigned a dining time.

MAP 1: 102 W. Congress St., 912/233-2600, www.ladyandsons.com; Mon.-Sat. 11am-3pm and 5pm-close, Sun. 11am-5pm

COFFEE, TEA, AND SWEETS
★ LULU'S CHOCOLATE BAR $

Combine a hip bar with outrageously tasty dessert items and you get Lulu's Chocolate Bar. While the whole family is welcome before 10pm to enjoy chocolate-chip cheesecake and the like, after that it's 21-and-over. The late crowd is younger and trendier and comes mostly for the unique specialty martinis, like the pineapple upside-down martini. The prices are quite reasonable all around, and this remains one of the most fun places in town.

MAP 1: 42 MLK Jr. Blvd., 912/238-2012, www.luluschocolatebar.net; Sun.-Thurs. noon-midnight, Fri.-Sat. 2pm-2am

ITALIAN
VINNIE VANGOGO'S $

One would never call Savannah a great pizza town, but the best pizza here is Vinnie VanGoGo's, at the west end of City Market on Franklin Square. The pizza is a thin-crust Neapolitan style—although the menu claims it to be

New York style—with a delightful tangy sauce and fresh cheese. Individual slices are huge, so don't feel obliged to order a whole pie. The waiting list for a table can get pretty long.

MAP 1: 317 W. Bryan St., 912/233-6394, www.vinnievangogos.com; Mon.-Thurs. 4pm-11:30pm, Fri. 4pm-1am, Sat. noon-1am, Sun. noon-11:30pm; cash only

Historic District North Map 1

CLASSIC SOUTHERN

★ THE GREY $$$

Savannah's most dramatic restaurant success story is the Grey, located in a stunningly restored former bus depot. It has taken the national foodie world by storm with beloved regional vernacular and soul food cuisine classics like seafood boudin, veal sweetbreads, roasted yardbird, fisherman's stew, and more, depending on seasonal whim and sourcing availabilities. A James Beard Award finalist in 2015, the Grey features the talents of standout executive chef Mashama Bailey, who grew up in Savannah and has a close eye for what makes the South tick food-wise. At the entrance is the "Diner Bar," a smaller offset bar area offering a punchy bar-food menu strong on sandwiches.

MAP 1: 109 MLK Jr. Blvd., 912/662-5999, www.thegreyrestaurant.com; Sun. and Tues.-Thurs. 5:30pm-10pm, Fri.-Sat. 5:30pm-11pm, supper every 3rd Sun. of the month

★ KAYAK KAFE $$

The best lunch on Broughton Street is at Kayak Kafe, where you can get a killer fresh salad or a fish taco to refresh your energy level during a busy day of shopping or sightseeing. Vegetarians, vegans, and those on a gluten-free diet will be especially pleased by the available options. As one of the very few Broughton Street places with outdoor sidewalk tables, this is also a great people-watching spot.

MAP 1: 1 E. Broughton St., 912/233-6044, www.eatkayak.com; Mon.-Thurs. 11am-10pm, Fri.-Sat. 11am-11pm, Sun. 11am-5pm

OLDE PINK HOUSE $$

Once the home of General James Habersham and the first place the Declaration of Independence was read aloud in Savannah, the Olde Pink House is still a hub of activity, as visitors and locals alike frequent the classic interior of the dining room and the downstairs Planter's Tavern. Olde Pink House is known for its savvy (and often sassy) service and the uniquely regional flair it adds to traditional dishes, with liberal doses of pecans, Vidalia onions, shrimp, and crab. The she-crab soup and lamb chops in particular are crowd-pleasers, and the scored crispy flounder stacks up to similar versions of this dish at several other spots in town. Reservations are recommended.

MAP 1: 23 Abercorn St., 912/232-4286; Sun.-Thurs. 5:30pm-10:30pm, Fri.-Sat. 5:30pm-11pm

HUSK SAVANNAH $$$

The latest reiteration of Southern celebrity chef Sean Brock's devotion to regional food culture, Husk Savannah operates on the now tried-and-true format of all-local farm-to-table food with a rotating seasonal menu. Highlights include inspired seafood dishes with an emphasis on freshness. The restaurant occupies a historic building, with an extensive, modernist interior complete with swanky bar.

MAP 1: 12 W. Oglethorpe St., 912/349-2600; Sun.-Thurs. 5pm-10pm, Fri.-Sat. 5pm-11pm

17HUNDRED90 $$

One of Savannah's oldest continuously operating culinary institutions and lodgings, 17Hundred90 Inn and Restaurant has recently vaulted itself into the upper echelon of Savannah cuisine with the addition of a dynamic menu by executive chef Jim Deja. Expect strong showings on the usual Southern classics—the crab stew is a must-have starter—but some unique takes, which you won't find anywhere else in town, such as a mouthwatering brisket ciabatta. Even the honey butter rolls brought to each table are delectable. The dining room is nostalgically no-frills and straight out of the historic namesake era; there's live piano accompaniment in the main dining room in the evenings. The attached bar area is a popular local watering hole; you can order from the full menu at the bar if you prefer.

MAP 1: 307 E. President St., 912/236-7122, www.17hundred90.com; daily 5pm-9pm

AUSTRALIAN

THE COLLINS QUARTER $$

The prime location of The Collins Quarter on a central corner in downtown Savannah is a big reason for its success. Other reasons include their amazing brunches and upscale sandwich offerings. The main claim to fame, however, might be an exquisite mastery of coffee and tea. Australian owner Anthony Debreceny—the restaurant's name is inspired by a street in Melbourne—says he started his establishment because he wanted to offer a place for truly great coffee. Indeed, their coffee service opens before their kitchen in the mornings.

MAP 1: 151 Bull St., 912/777-4147, www.thecollinsquarter.com; coffee service from 6:30am daily, brunch Mon. 8am-3pm, Wed.-Sat. 8am-3pm, dinner Wed.-Sat. 5:30pm-10pm

COFFEE, TEA, AND SWEETS

THE COFFEE FOX $

The best coffee on Broughton is at the Coffee Fox, a locally owned joint that expertly treads the fine line between hipster hangout and accessible

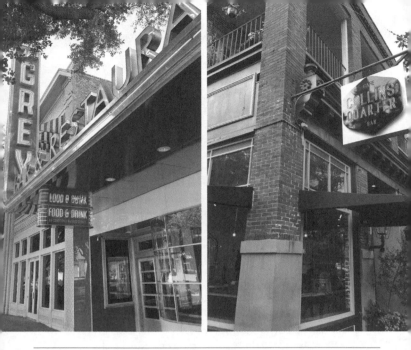

Clockwise from top left: The Grey; The Collins Quarter; the Olde Pink House on Reynolds Square.

hot spot. The freshly baked goodies are nearly as good as the freshly brewed java, which includes cold-brew and pour-over offerings.

MAP 1: 102 W. Broughton St., 912/401-0399, www.thecoffeefox.com; Mon.-Sat. 7am-11pm, Sun. 8am-4pm

★ LEOPOLD'S ICE CREAM $

He helped produce *Mission Impossible III* and other movies, but Savannah native Stratton Leopold's other claim to fame is running the 100-year-old family business at Leopold's Ice Cream. Leopold's also offers soup and sandwiches to go with its delicious sweet treats. Memorabilia from Stratton's various movies is all around the shop, which stays open after every evening performance at the Lucas Theatre around the corner. You can occasionally find Stratton himself behind the counter doling out scoops.

MAP 1: 212 E. Broughton St., 912/234-4442, www.leopoldsicecream.com; Sun.-Thurs. 11am-10pm, Fri.-Sat. 11am-11pm

WRIGHT SQUARE CAFE $

For a more upscale take on sweets, check out the chocolate goodies at Wright Square Cafe. While they do offer tasty wraps and sandwiches, let's not kid ourselves; the draw here is the outrageous assortment of high-quality European-style brownies, cookies, cakes, and other sweet treats.

MAP 1: 21 W. York St., 912/238-1150, www.wrightsquarecafe.com; Mon.-Fri. 7:30am-5:30pm, Sat. 9am-5:30pm

MEXICAN
TEQUILA'S TOWN $$

The best Mexican spot downtown is Tequila's Town, filling an oft-noted void in the Savannah foodie scene. The menu is comprehensive and authentic, a clear step above the usual gringo-oriented fat-fest. Highlights include the chiles rellenos and the seafood, not to mention the guacamole prepared table-side.

MAP 1: 109 Whitaker St., 912/236-3222, www.tequilastown.com; Mon.-Thurs. 11am-10pm, Fri.-Sat. 11am-11pm, Sun. noon-10pm

SOUTH AFRICAN
ZUNZI'S $

Look for the long lunchtime line outside the tiny storefront. This takeout joint is one of Savannah's favorite lunch spots, and it's gotten a lot of national attention for its robust, rich dishes like the exquisite South African-style sausage.

MAP 1: 108 E. York St., 912/443-9555, http://zunzis.com; Mon.-Sat. 11am-6pm

CLASSIC SOUTHERN
CRYSTAL BEER PARLOR ⑤

A very popular spot with locals and tourists alike, the Crystal Beer Parlor offers one of the best burgers downtown. With a history going back to the 1930s, this has been a friendly family tradition for generations of Savannahians. The lively bar area has a very wide range of craft brews, and there are plenty of snug booths to sit in and enjoy their solid American menu.

MAP 2: 301 W. Jones St., 912/349-1000, www.crystalbeerparlor.com; daily 11am-10pm

★ MRS. WILKES' DINING ROOM ⑤⑤

The rise of Paula Deen and her Lady & Sons restaurant has only made local epicures even more exuberant in their praise for Mrs. Wilkes' Dining Room, Savannah's original comfort food mecca. The delightful Sema Wilkes herself has passed on, but nothing has changed—not the communal dining room, the cheerful service, the care taken with takeout customers, nor, most of all, the food, a succulent mélange of the South's greatest hits, including the best fried chicken in town, snap beans, black-eyed peas, and collard greens. While each day boasts a different set menu, almost all of the classics are on the table at each meal. Be prepared for a long wait, however; lines begin forming early in the morning.

MAP 2: 107 W. Jones St., 912/232-5997, www.mrswilkes.com; Mon.-Fri. 11am-2pm

FUSION
FORK & DAGGER ⑤

A unique, folksy, and affordable place within easy walking distance of Forsyth Park, Fork & Dagger has an eclectic breakfast and lunch menu combining Southern favorites, Caribbean dishes, and New York deli staples like the hot pastrami sandwich.

MAP 2: 609 Abercorn St., 912/712-5115, www.forkanddaggersav.com; Mon.-Sat. 8:30am-3pm

NEW SOUTHERN
★ ELIZABETH ON 37TH ⑤⑤⑤

Before there was Paula Deen, there was Elizabeth Terry, Savannah's first high-profile chef and founder of Elizabeth on 37th, Savannah's most elegant restaurant. Terry has since sold the place to two of her former waiters, Greg and Gary Butch, but this restaurant has continued to maintain her high standards. Executive chef Kelly Yambor uses eclectic, seasonally shifting ingredients that blend the South with the south of France. Along with generally attentive service, it makes for a wonderfully old-school fine-dining experience. Reservations are advised.

MAP 3: 105 E. 37th St., 912/236-5547; daily 6pm-10pm

COTTON & RYE ⑤⑤

One of the newer and more buzzworthy eat-and-drink spots in town is Cotton & Rye, which while off the usual tourist-beaten path is certainly well worth the trip if you want to go where the locals go. Set in a smallish, restored old bank building, the atmosphere is both upscale and invitingly cozy. The menu is strong on fresh artisanal meats in the Southern style; try the hanger steak or the fried chicken. In a neat twist, the entire wine and beer menu is all-American.

MAP 3: 1801 Habersham St., 912/777-6286, www.cottonandrye.com, Fri.-Sat. 5pm-10:30pm, Mon.-Thurs. 5pm-10pm

ATLANTIC ⑤

A new darling of Savannah foodies, Atlantic provides a curated seasonal menu in a boisterous, fun space located in a completely renovated historic gas station. Owner Jason Restivo focuses on upgrades of familiar comfort food items. A nice outdoor courtyard area is also a great option. Reservations aren't taken, so there might be a short wait at this popular place.

MAP 3: 102 E. Victory Dr., 912/417-8887, www.atlanticsavannah.com; Fri.-Sat. 5pm-10pm, Mon.-Thurs. 5pm-9pm

BURGERS
★ GREEN TRUCK NEIGHBORHOOD PUB ⑤

The cozy Green Truck Neighborhood Pub earns rave reviews with its delicious regionally sourced meat and produce offered at reasonable prices. (The large selection of craft beers on tap is a big draw too). The marquee item is the signature five-ounce grass-fed burger. A basic burger is $7, but several other increasingly more dressed-up versions are offered, none over $12.50. Burgers are also offered with chicken or veggie patties. It's a small room that often has a big line, and they don't take reservations. But the full menu is offered at the bar, which has a well-curated craft brew selection.

MAP 3: 2430 Habersham St., 912/234-5895, http://greentruckpub.com; Tues.-Sat. 11am-11pm

COFFEE, TEA, AND SWEETS

BACK IN THE DAY BAKERY $$

Primarily known for its sublime sweet treats, James Beard Award-nominated Back in the Day Bakery also offers a small but delightfully tasty (and tasteful) range of lunch soups, salads, and sandwiches (11am-2pm Tues.-Sat.). Lunch highlights include the baguette with camembert, roasted red peppers, and lettuce, as well as the caprese, the classic tomato, mozzarella, and basil trifecta on a perfect ciabatta. But whatever you do, save room for dessert, which runs the full sugar spectrum: red velvet cupcakes, lemon bars, macaroons, carrot cake, and many others.

MAP 3: 2403 Bull St., 912/495-9292, www.backinthedaybakery.com; Tues.-Fri. 9am-5pm, Sat. 8am-3pm

FOXY LOXY $

Foxy Loxy is a classic coffeehouse set within a cozy multistory Victorian on Bull Street. Bonuses include the authentic Tex-Mex menu, wine and beer offerings, and freshly baked sweet treats.

MAP 3: 1919 Bull St., 912/401-0543, www.foxyloxycafe.com; Mon.-Sat. 7am-11pm

THE SENTIENT BEAN $

The coffee at the Sentient Bean is all fair trade and organic, and the all-vegetarian fare is a major upgrade above the usual coffeehouse offerings. But "The Bean" is more than a coffeehouse—it's a community. Probably the best indie film venue in town, the Bean regularly hosts screenings of cutting-edge left-of-center documentary and kitsch films, as well as rotating art exhibits.

MAP 3: 13 E. Park Ave., 912/232-4447, www.sentientbean.com; daily 7:30am-10pm

Eastside

Map 4

CLASSIC SOUTHERN

DESPOSITO'S $$

Located just across the Wilmington River from the fishing village of Thunderbolt, Desposito's is a big hit with locals and visitors alike, although it's not in all the guidebooks. The focus here is on crab, shrimp, and oysters, and lots of them, all caught wild in local waters and served humbly on tables covered with newspapers.

MAP 4: 187 Old Tybee Rd., 912/897-9963, www.despositosseafood.com; Tues.-Fri. 5pm-10pm, Sat. noon-10pm

BARBECUE

★ SANDFLY BBQ ⑤

If you're out this way visiting Wormsloe or Skidaway Island State Park, or if you're just crazy about good barbecue, make a point to hit little Sandfly BBQ, unique in the area for its dedication to real Memphis-style barbecue. Anything is great—this is the best brisket in the area—but for the best overall experience try the Hog Wild platter. Service is friendly, the price is right, and everything on the menu is superb.

MAP 4: 8413 Ferguson Ave. 912/356-5463, www.sandflybbq.com; Mon.-Sat. 11am-8pm

Tybee Island   Map 5

BREAKFAST AND BRUNCH

THE BREAKFAST CLUB ⑤

Considered the best breakfast in the Savannah area for 30 years and counting, The Breakfast Club, with its brisk diner atmosphere and hearty Polish sausage-filled omelets, is like a little bit of Chicago in the South. Lines start early for a chance to enjoy such house specialties as Helen's Solidarity, the Athena Omelet, and the Chicago Bear Burger, but don't worry—you'll inevitably strike up a conversation with someone interesting while you wait.

MAP 5: 1500 Butler Ave., 912/786-5984, http://tybeeisland.com/breakfast-club; daily 6:30am-1pm

CASUAL DINING

THE CRAB SHACK ⑤⑤

Set in a large former fishing camp overlooking Chimney Creek, the Crab Shack is a favorite local seafood place and something of an attraction in itself. Don't expect gourmet fare or quiet seaside dining; the emphasis is on mounds of fresh, tasty seafood, heavy on the raw-bar action. Getting there is a little tricky: Take U.S. 80 to Tybee, cross the bridge over Lazaretto Creek, and begin looking for Estill Hammock Road to Chimney Creek on the right. Take Estill Hammock Road and veer right. After that, it's hard to miss.

MAP 5: 40 Estill Hammock Rd., 912/786-9857, www.thecrabshack.com; Mon.-Thurs. 11:30am-10pm, Fri.-Sun. 11:30am-11pm

HUC-A-POO'S BITES & BOOZE ⑤

Known far and wide for its sublime pizza is Huc-a-Poo's Bites & Booze. Individual slices run about $4, can easily feed two, and are quite delicious. Out of the tourist ruckus and tucked away within a small shopping center just as you arrive onto Tybee proper, Huc-a-Poo's also has a very lively bar scene.

MAP 5: 1213 E. U.S. 80, 912/786-5900, http://hucapoos.com; daily 11am-11pm

Top: interior of Elizabeth on 37th. **Bottom:** The Coffee Fox.

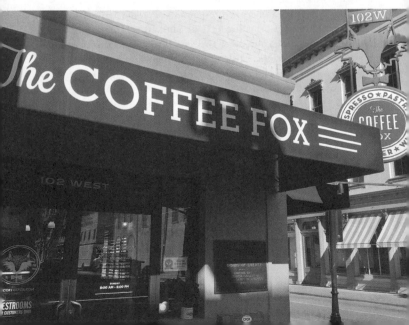

To Market, to Market

Savannah's first and still premier health-food market, **Brighter Day Natural Foods** (1102 Bull St., 912/236-4703, www.brighterdayfoods.com, Mon.-Sat. 9am-7pm, Sun. noon-5:30pm) has been the labor of love of Janie and Peter Brodhead for 30 years, all of them in the same location at the southern tip of Forsyth Park. Boasting organic groceries, regional produce, a sandwich and smoothie bar with a takeout window, and an extensive vitamin, supplement, and herb section, Brighter Day is an oasis in Savannah's sea of chain supermarkets.

Opened in 2013, **Whole Foods Market** (1815 E. Victory Dr., www.wholefoodsmarket.com, daily 8am-9pm) offers the chain's usual assortment of organic produce, with a very good fresh meat and seafood selection.

The thriving **Forsyth Park Farmers Market** (www.forsythfarmersmarket.org, Sat. 9am-1pm) happens in the south end of scenic and wooded Forsyth Park. You'll find very fresh fruit and produce from a variety of fun and friendly regional farmers. If you have access to a real kitchen while you're in town, you might be glad to know there's usually a very good selection of organic, sustainably grown meat and poultry products as well—not always a given at farmers markets.

If you need some good-quality groceries downtown—especially after hours—try **Parker's Market** (222 E. Drayton St., 912/231-1001, daily 24 hours). In addition to a pretty wide array of gourmet-style grab 'n' go victuals inside, there are gas pumps outside to fuel your vehicle.

There's one 24-hour full-service supermarket in downtown Savannah: **Kroger** (311 E. Gwinnett St., 912/231-2260, daily 24 hours).

NORTH BEACH GRILL ⑤⑤

One of Tybee's more cherished restaurants is on the north end in the shadow of the Tybee Light Station. Like a little slice of Jamaica near the dunes, the laid-back North Beach Grill deals in tasty Caribbean fare, such as its signature jerk chicken, fish sandwiches, and, of course, delicious fried plantains, all overseen by chef-owner "Big George" Spriggs. Frequent live music adds to the island vibe.

MAP 5: 33 Meddin Ave., 912/786-4442; daily 11:30am-10pm

TYBEE ISLAND SOCIAL CLUB ⑤⑤

For a leisurely and tasty dinner, try Tybee Island Social Club. Their menu is somewhat unusual for this seafood-heavy island: It's primarily an assortment of gourmet-ish tacos, including fish, duck, and lime- and tequila-marinated steak, all under $10 each. The beer and wine list is accomplished, and the live entertainment is usually very good—which is fortunate, since the service is on the slow side.

MAP 5: 1311 Butler Ave., 912/472-4044, http://tybeeislandsocialclub.com; Tues. 5pm-9:30pm, Wed.-Fri. noon-9:30pm, Sat.-Sun. 11:30am-10pm

The Pooler-West Chatham area is the fastest growing in the Savannah metro area. It is also dominated by new chain restaurants. Here are a couple of tasty departures from the mass-market trend for you to seek if you find yourself out that way.

POOLER-WEST CHATHAM

PIE SOCIETY ⑤

Get some incredibly tasty little pasties and meat pies, old English style, at this charming little family spot run by British expats. Everything is all homemade and usually fresh out of the oven. Note the early opening hours, all the better to get your piping hot, fresh breakfast baked items.

MAP 6: 115 Canal St., 912/856-4785, www.thebritishpiecompany.com; Mon.-Fri. 7am-6:30pm, Sat. 7am-5pm

MOLLY MACPHERSON'S SCOTTISH PUB AND GRILL ⑤⑤

A mirror image of the one on Congress Street in Savannah, this edition of Molly's delivers the same high-quality pub items like shepherd's pie and fish-and-chips, along with an outstanding selection of beers on tap and of course, scotch.

MAP 6: 110 Towne Center Dr., 912/348-3200, www.macphersonspub.com; Mon.-Sat. 11am-2am, Sun. 11am-11pm

INDIAN

NAAN APPETIT ⑤

This is unpretentious but tasty Indian food at a good price. Try the lamb masala curry or the chili paneer.

MAP 6: 1024 U.S. 80, 912/348-2446, www.naanappetit.com; Tues.-Fri. 11am-3pm, 5pm-9:30pm, Sat.-Sun. noon-3pm, 5pm-10:30pm

MIDWAY AND LIBERTY COUNTY

HOLTON'S SEAFOOD ⑤⑤

Many locals eat at least once a week at Holton's Seafood, an unpretentious and fairly typical family-run fried seafood place just off I-95 at the Midway exit.

MAP 6: 13711 E. Oglethorpe Hwy., Midway, 912/884-9151; daily lunch and dinner

SUNBURY CRAB COMPANY ⑤⑤

A restaurant of note in Midway is the Sunbury Crab Company, providing, you guessed it, great crab cakes in a casual atmosphere on the Midway River. Get here by taking Highway 38 east of Midway and then a left onto Fort Morris Road.

MAP 6: 541 Brigantine Dunmore Rd., Midway, 912/884-8640; Wed.-Fri. dinner, Sat.-Sun. lunch and dinner

RICHMOND HILL

STEAMERS RESTAURANT & RAW BAR ⑤⑤

A popular place on U.S. 17 is Steamers Restaurant & Raw Bar, home of some good Lowcountry boil in a relaxed, homey atmosphere.

MAP 6: 4040 U.S. 17, Richmond Hill, 912/756-3979; daily 5pm-10pm

THE UPPER CRUST PIZZERIA ⑤

There's no end to the chain food offerings in Richmond Hill, but one of the better restaurants in town is the Upper Crust, a casual American place with great pizza in addition to soups, salads, and hot sandwiches.

MAP 6: 1702 U.S. 17, Richmond Hill, 912/756-6990; Mon.-Sat. lunch and dinner, Sun. dinner

Nightlife and Events

Highlights

★ **Best Rooftop Bar:** The boutique **Rocks on the Roof** offers stunning wraparound alfresco views of the river and surrounding downtown area (page 114).

★ **Best Place to Get a Little Rowdy:** Sing karaoke with college students, have a Guinness with rugby players, do shots with roller derby girls, and more at **The Rail Pub** (page 115).

★ **Most Historical Tavern:** Abraham Lincoln never set foot in Savannah and Lincoln Street isn't named for him, but **Abe's on Lincoln** is the oldest surviving

bar in Savannah, with roots going back to colonial days (page 116).

★ **Most Authentic Irish Pub:** In a town with deep ties to Irish culture, tiny **O'Connell's** is without a doubt the closest thing here to an old school Emerald Isle pub (page 116).

★ **Diviest Bar:** Head to **The Original Pinkie Master's** for strong drinks, historic memorabilia, and the kitschy dive bar atmosphere (page 119).

★ **Biggest Party:** No other American city does **St. Patrick's Day** quite like Savannah (page 120).

Savannah's St. Patrick's Day Parade

Savannah is a hard-drinking town, and not just on St. Patrick's Day.

The ability to legally walk downtown streets with beer, wine, or a cocktail in hand definitely contributes to the overall *joie de vivre*. Bars close in Savannah at 3am. Savannah is known for its copious watering holes hosting a diverse range of local residents and adventurous visitors.

Bars close in Savannah at 3am. A citywide indoor smoking ban is in effect and you may not smoke cigarettes in any bar in Savannah. Recent legislation finally allows Savannah bars that don't serve food to open on Sundays, but not all have made the switch; call ahead.

Savannah's calendar fairly bursts with festivals, many outdoors. Dates shift from year to year, so it's best to consult the listed websites for details.

Previous: the Rail Pub; River Street at night.

Waterfront

Map 1

BARS AND PUBS

BAYOU CAFE

One of Savannah's favorite and most raucous historic taverns is possibly the River Street bar most visited by locals. The Bayou Cafe, overlooking River Street but situated on one of the cobblestone "ramps" going down from Bay Street to the waterfront, offers a convivial dive-bar type atmosphere and a solid Cajun-style pub food menu. The main floor is the traditional tavern, where the best local blues musicians play frequent gigs. The second floor is more of a game room and general younger folks' party area.

MAP 1: 4 N. Abercorn Ramp, 912/233-6411, daily 11am-3am

KEVIN BARRY'S IRISH PUB

The main landmark on the west end of River Street is the famous (or infamous, depending on which side of "The Troubles" you're on) Kevin Barry's Irish Pub, one of Savannah's most beloved establishments. KB's is open seven days a week, with evenings seeing performances by a number of Irish troubadours, all veterans of the East Coast trad circuit.

MAP 1: 117 W. River St., 912/233-9626, www.kevinbarrys.com; daily 11am-3am

★ ROCKS ON THE ROOF

One of the best hotel bars in the city is Rocks on the Roof, atop the Bohemian Hotel Savannah Riverfront on the waterfront. In good weather the exterior walls are opened up to reveal a large wraparound seating area with stunning views of downtown on one side and of the Savannah River on the other.

MAP 1: 102 W. Bay St., 912/721-3800; Fri.-Sat. 11am-1am, Sun.-Thurs. 11am-midnight

GAY AND LESBIAN

CHUCK'S BAR

A friendly, kitschy little tavern at the far west end of River Street near the Jefferson Street ramp, Chuck's Bar is a great place to relax and see some interesting local characters. Karaoke at Chuck's is especially a hoot, and they keep the Christmas lights up all year.

MAP 1: 301 W. River St., 912/232-1005; Mon.-Wed. 8pm-3am, Thurs.-Sat. 7pm-3am

CLUB ONE JEFFERSON

Any examination of gay and lesbian nightlife in Savannah must, of course, begin with Club One Jefferson of *Midnight in the Garden of Good and Evil* fame. Come for the famous drag shows upstairs in the cabaret, or the rockin' 1,000-square-foot dance floor downstairs. Cabaret showtimes are

Craft Breweries

Savannah is finally catching up to the craft brewery trend, and tasting events at **Southbound Brewing Company** (107 E. Lathrop Ave., 912/335-7716, http://southboundbrewingco.com, tours 5:30pm Wed.-Fri., 2pm Sat., $15) are getting rave reviews. Tours include 36 ounces of beer served on-site and your choice of a 22-ounce bomber, a 32-ounce growler fill, a six-pack, or a pint glass. The tastings attract a large crowd, so don't dillydally. Southbound's offerings include a rotating series of special-event beers and the occasional rock concert. As is the case with many up-and-coming breweries, the large restored warehouse space isn't in the most scenic neighborhood.

Savannah's other key craft brewery is **Service Brewing** (574 Indian St., http://servicebrewing.com, tours 5:30pm-7:30pm Thurs.-Fri., 2pm-4pm Sat., $12 pp), so named because its founders are former military; they donate a portion of all profits to veterans service organizations. Basic tastings include either a 36-ounce flight of 6 ounces per pour or three 12-ounce pours. Service is a wee bit closer to downtown than is Southbound, and within walking distance of the River Street-City Market area.

The state of Georgia has finally changed the law to allow retail package sales from craft breweries, so that is a great option as well.

Thursday-Saturday 10:30pm and 12:30am, Sunday 10:30pm, and Monday 11:30pm.

MAP 1: 1 Jefferson St., 912/232-0200, www.clubone-online.com; Mon.-Sat. 5pm-3am, Sun. 5pm-2am

City Market

Map 1

BARS AND PUBS
MOON RIVER BREWING COMPANY

Moon River Brewing Company offers half a dozen handcrafted beers in a rambling old space that housed Savannah's first hotel back in antebellum days. The particular highlight these days, however, is the dog-friendly enclosed beer garden, with frequent live music and a congenial alfresco atmosphere, as well as access to the full menu.

MAP 1: 21 W. Bay St., 912/447-0943, www.moonriverbrewing.com; Mon.-Thurs. 11am-11pm, Fri.-Sat. 11am-midnight, Sun. 11am-10pm

★ THE RAIL PUB

In the City Market area, your best bet is the Rail Pub, one of Savannah's oldest and most beloved taverns. This multifloor spot is a great place to get a pint or a shot or do karaoke in a quite boisterous but still cozy environment. You'll receive roasted peanuts with your drink; just let the shells fall on the floor like everyone else does.

MAP 1: 405 W. Congress St., 912/238-1311, www.therailpub.com; Mon.-Sat. 3pm-3am

In the modernist Andaz Savannah hotel overlooking bustling Ellis Square, 22 Square is a great place for an upscale cocktail and for meeting interesting people from all over. Try the refreshing Savannah Fizz or one of their mean Sazeracs.

MAP 1: 14 Barnard St., 912/233-2116, www.savannah.andaz.hyatt.com; Mon.-Thurs. 4pm-10pm, Fri.-Sat. 2pm-midnight, Sun. 4pm-10pm

LIVE MUSIC AND KARAOKE
THE JINX

Despite its high-volume offerings, The Jinx is a friendly watering hole and the closest thing Savannah has to a full-on music club, with a very active calendar of rock and metal shows. Shows start late here, never before 11pm and often later than that. If you're here for the music and have sensitive ears, bring earplugs. The beer offerings are okay, but this is the kind of place where many regular patrons opt for tallboy PBRs.

MAP 1: 127 W. Congress St., 912/236-2281, www.thejinx.net; Mon.-Sat. 4pm-3am

Historic District North
Map 1

BARS AND PUBS
★ ABE'S ON LINCOLN

No, Lincoln Street in Savannah isn't named for Abraham Lincoln. But dark, fun little Abe's is on Lincoln Street, and it's also the oldest bar in town, with a very eclectic clientele.

MAP 1: 17 Lincoln St., 912/349-0525, http://abesonlincoln.com; Mon.-Sat. 4pm-3am

CHIVE SEA BAR AND LOUNGE

For swank partying on Broughton Street, head to Chive Sea Bar and Lounge, which backs up its tasty menu with a high-end bar in a wonderful, modernist space.

MAP 1: 4 W. Broughton St., 912/233-1748, www.chivelounge.com; Mon.-Fri. 11am-10pm, Sat. noon-midnight, Sun. 5pm-10pm

CIRCA 1875

Circa 1875 is a hip hangout with an excellent menu—the burgers are as good as the martinis. The vintage vibe takes you back to the days of the Parisian salons.

MAP 1: 48 Whitaker St., 912/443-1875, www.circa1875.com; Mon.-Thurs. 6pm-10pm, Fri.-Sat. 6pm-11pm

★ O'CONNELL'S

Without question, the place in Savannah that comes closest to replicating an authentic Irish pub environment is tiny, cozy O'Connell's, where they

To-Go Cup Revelry

Arguably the single most civilized trait of Savannah, and certainly one of the things that most sets it apart, is the glorious old tradition of the "to-go cup." True to its history of hard partying and general open-mindedness, Savannah, like New Orleans, legally allows you to walk the streets downtown with an open container of your favorite adult beverage. Of course, you have to be 21 or over, and the cup must be Styrofoam or plastic, never glass or metal, and no more than 16 ounces. While there are boundaries to where to-go cups are legal, in practice this includes almost all areas of the historic district frequented by visitors. The quick and easy rule of thumb is to keep your to-go cups north of Jones Street.

Every downtown watering hole has stacks of cups at the bar for patrons to use. You can either ask the bartender for a to-go cup—a.k.a. a "go cup"—or just reach out and grab one yourself. Don't be shy; it's the Savannah way.

Have fun making up your own itinerary or sample **this to-go cup crawl:** Start with a beverage at legendary dive bar Pinkie Master's. Walk with your to-go cups north to 17Hundred90's classic historic bar. Then cut over to O'Connell's Pub for a taste of Ireland. Walk west to Congress Street for a stop at The Rail Pub, or perhaps to catch a late-night rock 'n' roll show at The Jinx, both near the City Market area.

know how to pour a Guinness, feature Magners cider on tap, and the house specialty is the "pickleback"—a shot of Jameson's followed by a shot of, yes, pickle brine. In classic Emerald Isle tradition, most seating is bench-style, to encourage conversation.

MAP 1: 42 Drayton St., 912/231-2298; daily 3pm-3am

Historic District South   Map 2

BARS AND PUBS
THE DISTILLERY

Yes, The Distillery is located in a former distillery. As such, the atmosphere isn't exactly dark and romantic—it's sort of one big open room—but the excellent location at the corner of MLK Jr. Boulevard and Liberty Street, the long vintage bar, and the great selection of beers on tap combine to make this a happening spot. The fish-and-chips are also great.

MAP 2: 416 W. Liberty St., 912/236-1772, www.distillerysavannah.com; Mon.-Sat. 11am-close, Sun. noon-close

THE CHROMATIC DRAGON

Gamers and geeks alike will enjoy video and board game action—as well as the food and drink—at this unique spot. While you can get a meal and a brew here, the focus is on the gaming, so much so that you are asked "analog

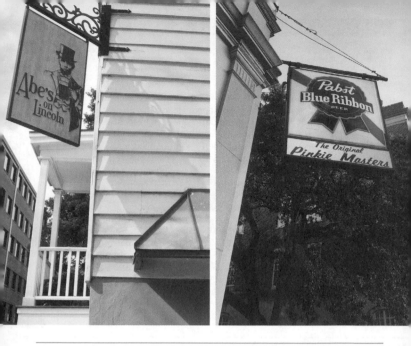

Clockwise from top left: Abe's on Lincoln; The Original Pinkie Master's; Chuck's Bar.

or digital?" (translation: board games or video consoles) as you walk in.
They offer a vast array of both, or you can bring your own.

MAP 3: 514 MLK Jr. Blvd., 912/289-0350, www.chromaticdragon.com; Thurs.-Sat. 11am-2am, Sun.-Wed. 11am-11pm

★ THE ORIGINAL PINKIE MASTER'S

For over 65 years, Savannah's most beloved dive bar has been the Original Pinkie Master's. For decades this has been a gathering place for local politicos; according to local lore, this is where President Jimmy Carter stopped during his visit for St. Patrick's Day (even though he's a teetotaler). A recent change of ownership has managed that rarest of accomplishments: They've lovingly retained the kitschy dive bar motif, complete with historic memorabilia, while expanding the drink menu and making things a bit more palatable for the general public.

MAP 2: 318 Drayton St., 912/999-7106, www.theoriginalsavannah.com; Mon.-Thurs. 3pm-3am, Fri.-Sat. noon-3am

LIVE MUSIC AND KARAOKE
MCDONOUGH'S

Savannah's undisputed karaoke champion is McDonough's, an advantage compounded by the fact that a lot more goes on here than karaoke. The kitchen at McDonough's is quite capable, and many locals swear you can get the best burger in town here. Despite the sports-bar atmosphere, the emphasis is on the karaoke, which ramps up every night at 9:30pm.

MAP 2: 21 E. McDonough St., 912/233-6136, www.mcdonoughsofsavannah.com; Mon.-Sat. 8pm-3am, Sun. 8pm-2am

SoFo District   Map 3

BARS AND PUBS
AMERICAN LEGION BAR

The real hipsters hang out in ironic fashion drinking PBRs at the American Legion Bar, located in, yes, an actual American Legion post. While the Legionnaires themselves are a straitlaced patriotic bunch, the patrons of "the Legion," as the bar is colloquially known, tend toward the counterculture. That said, in a clear nod to tradition, no profanity or public displays of affection are allowed. Here is where you'll find Savannah's movers and shakers in the grassroots arts and cultural community.

Fun historical fact: The building housing the Legion was the birthplace of the U.S. 8th Air Force during World War II.

MAP 3: 1108 Bull St., 912/233-9277, http://alpost135.com; Mon.-Sat. 4pm-2am

Festivals and Events

JANUARY

Floats and bands take part in the **Martin Luther King Jr. Day Parade** downtown to commemorate the civil rights leader and Georgia native. The bulk of the route is on historic MLK Jr. Boulevard, formerly West Broad Street.

Straddling January and February is the weeklong **PULSE Art + Technology Festival** (www.telfair.org), an adventurous event that brings video artists and offbeat electronic performance art into the modern Jepson Center for the Arts.

FEBRUARY

Definitely not to be confused with St. Patrick's Day, the **Savannah Irish Festival** (912/232-3448, www.savannahirish.org) focuses on Celtic music.

Hosted by the historically black Savannah State University at various venues around town, the monthlong **Black Heritage Festival** (912/691-6847) is tied into Black History Month and boasts name entertainers like the Alvin Ailey Dance Theatre (performing free!). This event also usually features plenty of historical lectures devoted to the very interesting and rich history of African Americans in Savannah.

Also in February is the quickly growing **Savannah Book Festival** (www.savannahbookfestival.org), modeled after a similar event in Washington DC and featuring many national and regional authors at various venues downtown.

MARCH
★ St. Patrick's Day

More than just a day, the citywide **St. Patrick's Day** (www.savannah-saintpatricksday.com) celebration generally lasts at least half a week and temporarily triples the population. The nearly three-hour parade—second biggest in the United States—always begins at 10am on St. Patrick's Day (unless that falls on a Sunday, in which case it's generally on the previous Saturday) and includes an interesting mix of marching bands, wacky floats, and sauntering local Irishmen in kelly-green jackets. The appeal comes not only from the festive atmosphere and generally beautiful spring weather, but also from Savannah's unique law allowing partiers to walk the streets with a cup filled with the adult beverage of their choice. While the parade itself is very family-friendly, afterward hard-core partiers generally head en masse to River Street—definitely not where you want to take small children. If you want to hear traditional Celtic music on St. Patrick's Day in Savannah, River Street also isn't the place to go, with the exception of Kevin

Other March Events

One of the most anticipated events for house-proud Savannahians, the **Tour of Homes and Gardens** (912/234-8054, www.savannahtourof-homes.org) offers guests the opportunity to visit six beautiful sites off the usual tourist-trod path. This is a great way to expand your understanding of local architecture and hospitality beyond the usual house museums.

One of Savannah's unique festivals is the multiday indie rock festival **Savannah Stopover** (www.savannahstopover.com) in early or mid-March. The idea is simple: Book bands that are already driving down to Austin, Texas, for the following week's South by Southwest so they can "stop over" and play at various venues in downtown Savannah. Get it? This is a great way to see up-and-coming bands before they blow up big; previous headliners have included St. Paul & The Broken Bones, Grimes, and Of Montreal. Admission is generally by ticketed wristband, and most venues are for ages 21 and over.

The three-week **Savannah Music Festival** (912/234-3378, www.savan-nahmusicfestival.org) is held at various historic venues around town and begins right after St. Patrick's Day. Past festivals have featured Wynton Marsalis, Dianne Reeves, and the Avett Brothers. The jazz portion is locked down tight, thanks to the efforts of festival director Rob Gibson, a Georgia native who cut his teeth as the founding director of Jazz at Lincoln Center. The classical side is helmed by one of the world's great young violinists, Daniel Hope, acting as associate director. Other genres are featured in abundance as well, including gospel, bluegrass, zydeco, world music, and the always-popular American Traditions vocal competition. The most economical way to enjoy the Savannah Music Festival is to purchase tickets online before December of the previous year at a 10 percent discount. However, if you just want to take in a few events, individual tickets are available at a tiered pricing system. You can buy tickets to individual events in town at the walk-up box office beside the Trustees Theater on Broughton Street.

APRIL

Short for "North of Gaston Street," the **NOGS Tour of Hidden Gardens** (912/961-4805, www.gcofsavnogstour.org, $30) is available two days in April and focuses on a selection of Savannah's amazing private gardens chosen for excellence of design, historical interest, and beauty.

Everyone loves the annual free **Sidewalk Arts Festival** (912/525-5865, www.scad.edu) presented by the Savannah College of Art and Design in Forsyth Park. Contestants claim a rectangular section of sidewalk on which to display their chalk art talent. There's a non-contest section with chalk provided.

A Southern St. Paddy's Day

Savannah's St. Patrick's Day Parade

Savannah hosts the second-largest St. Patrick's Day celebration in the world, second only to New York City's. With its fine spring weather and walkability—not to mention its liberal rules allowing you to carry an adult beverage on the street—Savannah is tailor-made for a boisterous outdoor celebration.

Ironically, given St. Patrick's Day's current close association with the Roman Catholic faith, the first parade in Savannah was organized by Irish Protestants. Thirteen members of the local Hibernian Society—the country's oldest Irish society—took part in a private procession to Independent Presbyterian Church in 1813. The first public procession was in 1824, when the Hibernians invited all local Irishmen to parade through the streets. The first recognizably modern parade, with bands and a "grand marshal," happened in 1870.

Organized by a "committee" of about 700 local Irish residents, today's three-hour procession includes marchers from all the local Irish organizations, in addition to marching bands and floats representing many local groups. The assembled clans wear kelly-green blazers, brandishing their walking canes and to-go cups, some pushing future committee members in strollers.

MAY

The SCAD-sponsored **Sand Arts Festival** (www.scad.edu) on Tybee Island's North Beach centers on a competition of sand castle design, sand sculpture, sand relief, and wind sculpture. You might be amazed at the level of artistry lavished on the sometimes-wondrous creations, only for them to wash away with the tide.

If you don't want to get wet, don't show up at the **Tybee Beach Bum Parade,** an uproarious event held the weekend prior to Memorial Day weekend. With a distinctly boozy overtone, this unique 20-year-old event features homemade floats filled with partiers who squirt the assembled crowds with various water pistols. The crowds, of course, pack their own heat and squirt back.

JULY

Two key events happen around **Fourth of July,** primarily the large fireworks show on River Street on July 4 but also an impressive fireworks display from the Tybee pier and pavilion on July 3. A nice bonus of the Tybee event is that sometimes you can look out over the Atlantic and see a similar fireworks display on nearby Hilton Head Island, South Carolina, a few minutes away by boat (but nearly an hour by car).

SEPTEMBER

Around the third week in September is when the free **Savannah Jazz Festival** (savannahjazzfest.com) happens, a week-long event at multiple venues, with highlighted evening gigs usually outside on the stage in Forsyth Park. The performers feature an interesting mix of touring national artists and well-established local and regional players.

Over Labor Day weekend you can check out the **Savannah Craft Brew Festival** (International Trade & Convention Center, 1 International Dr., www.savannahcraftbrewfest.com, $50). This daylong tasting event features a healthy range of breweries from around the nation as well as Georgia's own burgeoning craft brew industry.

OCTOBER

The Savannah Philharmonic Orchestra plays a free **Picnic in the Park** concert in Forsyth Park that draws thousands of noshers. Arrive early to check out the ostentatious, whimsical picnic displays, which compete for prizes. Then set out your blanket, open a bottle of wine, and enjoy the sweet sounds.

The combined aroma of beer, sauerkraut, and sausage that you smell coming from the waterfront is the annual **Oktoberfest on the River** (www.riverstreetsavannah.com), which has evolved to be Savannah's second-largest celebration (behind only St. Patrick's Day). Live entertainment of varying quality is featured, though the attraction, of course, is the aforementioned beer and German food. A highlight is Saturday morning's "Weiner Dog Races" involving, you guessed it, competing dachshunds.

It's a fairly new festival, but the **Tybee Island Pirate Festival** (http://tybeepiratefest.com) is a fun and typically rollicking Tybee event in October featuring, well, everybody dressing up like pirates, saying "Arr" a lot, eating, drinking, and listening to cover bands. It may not sound like much, and it's really not, but it's typically very well attended.

Sponsored by St. Paul's Greek Orthodox Church, the popular **Savannah Greek Festival** (www.stpaulsgreekorthodox.org) features food, music, and Greek souvenirs. The weekend event is held across the street from the church at the parish center—in the gym, to be exact, right on the basketball court. Despite the pedestrian location, the food is authentic and delicious, and the atmosphere convivial and friendly.

Hosted by the Savannah College of Art and Design, the weeklong **SCAD Savannah Film Festival** (www.scad.edu) beginning in late October is rapidly growing not only in size but in prestige as well. Lots of older, more established Hollywood names appear as honored guests for the evening events, while buzzworthy up-and-coming actors, directors, producers, writers, and animators give excellent workshops during the day. Many of these usually jaded showbiz types really let their hair down for this festival, because, as you'll see, Savannah is the real star. The best way to enjoy this excellent event is to buy a pass, which enables you to walk from event to event. Most importantly, the passes gain you admission to what many locals consider the best part of the festival: the after-parties, where you'll often find yourself face to face with some famous star or director.

One of Savannah's most unique events is late October's **"Shalom Y'all" Jewish Food Festival** (912/233-1547, www.mickveisrael.org), held in Forsyth Park and sponsored by the historic Temple Mickve Israel. Latkes, matzo, and other nibbles are all featured along with entertainment.

Arts and Shops

Highlights

★ **Classiest Night on the Town:**
The ornate gold-leafed interior of the historic
Lucas Theatre for the Arts is an echo
of the golden age of classic American movie
houses, now fully restored and offering a
packed schedule of screenings and live performances (page 129).

★ **Most Engaging Concertos:** In
a time where symphony orchestras are
often in financial straits, the **Savannah
Philharmonic** is going strong, offering
a vibrant and challenging season of opera,
classical music, and choral performances in
various venues all around town (page 129).

★ **Art Galleries:** Check out a number
of galleries featuring works by local artists,
many from the prestigious Savannah College
of Art & Design (page 130).

★ **Sweetest Shopping:** Now a growing regional boutique chain, **Savannah
Bee Company** offers an amazing and
delicious array of locally sourced honey,
honey-themed gifts, and cuisine comple-
ments (pages 128 and 131).

★ **Uniquely Euro Style:** A great mix
of hard-to-find genuine French vintage
home goods and regional boutique cosmet-
ics, bath items, and jewelry highlight **The
Paris Market & Brocante,** which also
sports a cool little coffee/tea café with a
great windowfront view of Broughton Street
(page 131).

★ **Most Old School Old Stuff:**
Savannah legend **Alex Raskin Antiques**
on Monterey Square is the most authentic
and delightful antiquing experience in town,
in a historic building festooned with world-
class wrought ironwork (page 133).

★ **Best Brush With Local Literati:**
Savannah takes its literary tradition seriously.
The Book Lady works overtime to highlight local and regional authors with frequent
signings and literary events (page 133).

There are more art galleries per capita in Savannah than in New York City—one gallery for every 2,191 residents, to be exact.

Savannah College of Art & Design (SCAD) galleries are in abundance all over town, displaying the handiwork of students, faculty, alumni, and important regional and national artists. Savannah's arts scene also shines a spotlight on theater, classical music, and cool movie houses.

Savannah has also perfected the fine art of shopping, with a focus on antiques and independent home goods stores, with some unique boutiques sprinkled throughout the city. Without question, downtown Savannah's main shopping district is **Broughton Street.** There are many vibrant local shops as well as a wide variety of the usual national chain stores on the avenue, such as Michael Kors, H&M, Victoria's Secret, and Banana Republic, to name just a few.

A bit south of downtown proper, but still a short drive away, is the **Starland District**. This up-and-coming mixed-use area is home to a growing variety of more hipster-oriented shops.

Focusing on upscale art and home goods, the small but chic and friendly **Downtown Design District** runs three blocks on Whitaker Street, a short walk from Forsyth Park.

SHOPS
Antiques
JERE'S ANTIQUES

One of the coolest antiques shops in town is Jere's Antiques. It's in a huge historic warehouse on Factor's Walk and has a concentration on fine European pieces.

MAP 1: 9 N. Jefferson St., 912/236-2815, www.jeresantiques.com; Mon.-Sat. 9:30am-5pm

Clothes
HARLEY-DAVIDSON

You won't be buying a Softail Deluxe at this retail merchandise store, but you can certainly clothe your inner biker here. This is more a place for accessories and lifestyle items.

MAP 1: 503 E. River St., 912/231-8000, www.savannahhd.com; Mon.-Sat. 10am-6pm, Sun. noon-6pm

THE MAD HATTER

Probably the closest thing to a unique shop on River Street proper is The Mad Hatter, which as the name suggests, offers a wide variety of headwear, from the whimsical to the practical.

MAP 1: 123 E. River St., 912/232-7566

Gourmet Treats
★ SAVANNAH BEE COMPANY

This popular locally based, regional chain offers a range of honey-based goods from lip balm to lotion to, yes, honey. This store is located on the ground floor of the Hyatt Regency hotel, and the flagship location is actually just a few blocks north on Broughton Street. All locations feature an educational component as well, about the value of bees and beehives to the ecosystem.

MAP 1: 1 W. River St., 912/234-7088, www.savannahbee.com; Mon.-Sat. 10am-7pm, Sun. 11am-8pm

RIVER STREET SWEETS

Cater to your sweet tooth—and buy some goodies to bring back with you—at River Street Sweets, where you can witness Southern delicacies like pralines being made as you shop. The bright, friendly shop never fails to attract visitors strolling up and down the street. And, of course, there are free samples.

MAP 1: 13 E. River St., 912/234-4608, www.riverstreetsweets.com; daily 9am-11pm

Pet Goods

BLACK DOG GENERAL STORE

The first Southern location of this national boutique chain offers upscale doggie treats and gear, as well as apparel and lifestyle and home items for their owners.

MAP 1: 211 W. River St., 912/335-7472, www.theblackdog.com; daily 10am-9pm

WOOF GANG BAKERY

On the opposite end of River Street from the Black Dog General store is Woof Gang Bakery, specializing in gourmet treats and food for your canine companion. Be forewarned: Some of the treats look tasty enough for you to want to sample yourself.

MAP 1: 425A E. River St., 912/999-6409, www.woofgangbakery.com; Fri.-Sat. 9am-9pm, Sun.-Thurs. 9am-8pm

Historic District North   Map 1

CINEMA

★ LUCAS THEATRE FOR THE ARTS

The ornate, beautifully restored Lucas Theatre for the Arts downtown is a classic Southern movie house. The Savannah Film Society and Savannah College of Art and Design host screenings there throughout the year. Check the website for schedules.

MAP 1: 32 Abercorn St., 912/525-5040, www.lucastheatre.com; most screenings under $10

MUSIC

★ SAVANNAH PHILHARMONIC

The Savannah Philharmonic is a professional symphony orchestra that performs concertos and sonatas at various venues around town, usually the Lucas Theatre, and is always worth checking out.

MAP 1: box office 216 E. Broughton St., 912/525-5050, www.savannahphilharmonic.org; Mon.-Fri. 10am-5pm

SHOPS

Art Supply

BLICK ART MATERIALS

A great art town needs a great art supply store, and in Savannah that would be Blick Art Materials, which has all the equipment and tools for the serious artist—priced to be affordable for students. But casual shoppers will enjoy it as well for its collection of offbeat gift items. The staff is very knowledgeable and helpful, and the space is cavernous but easily navigated.

MAP 1: 318 E. Broughton St., 912/234-0456, www.dickblick.com; Mon.-Fri. 8am-8pm, Sat. 10am-7pm, Sun. 11am-6pm

★ Art Galleries

Overlooking Ellis Square downtown is well-regarded **Kobo Gallery** (33 Barnard St., 912/201-0304, www.kobogallery.com), a local artist co-op featuring some of Savannah's best contemporary artists who frequently put on group shows.

Roots Up Gallery (412 Whitaker St., 912/677-2845) focuses on regional folk and outsider art with a strong emphasis on Southern roots and folkways.

Non-Fiction Gallery (1522 Bull St., 912/662-5152), south of Forsyth Park, exhibits work by many of Savannah's up-and-coming talents, often with exploratory themes.

Nearby is **Sulfur Studios** (2301 Bull St., sulfurstudios.org), which not only hosts rotating exhibits, but also coordinates many community forums and events of a cutting-edge nature.

Located inside the Mansion on Forsyth Park hotel, the **Grand Bohemian Gallery** (700 Drayton St., 912/721-5007) specializes in national and international artists working in a variety of media, from oils to jewelry.

Clothes and Fashion
GLOBE SHOE CO.

Broughton Street's oldest retailer still in operation, Globe Shoe Co. is a Savannah institution and a real throwback to a time of personalized retail service. They're all about simple one-to-one service, like in the old days, with a range of stylish shoes from the hip to the traditional.

MAP 1: 17 E. Broughton St., 912/232-8161; Mon.-Sat. 10am-6pm

CIVVIES NEW AND RECYCLED CLOTHING

Inhabiting a well-restored upstairs space, Civvie's is probably Savannah's best regarded vintage store, with a variety of retro clothes and shoes and a strong local following. They also have a nifty section of campy, kitschy gift items from various local vendors.

MAP 1: 14 E. Broughton St., 912/236-1551; Mon.-Sat. 11am-7pm, Sun. 11am-5pm

LEVY JEWELERS

At Bull and Broughton, Savannah's prime downtown corner, is century-old family-owned Levy Jewelers. They have a complete showcase of necklaces, watches, and rings from two dozen internationally recognized designers, in a large and attractive showroom.

MAP 1: 2 E. Broughton St., 912/233-1163; Mon.-Sat. 10am-9pm, Sun. noon-6pm

Gourmet Treats
CHOCOLAT BY ADAM TURONI

Chocolate lovers need to head straight to this tiny space with big taste. Adam's handcrafted, high-quality chocolates are miniature works of art—and delicious ones at that. The interior design elements of the store are incredible, incorporating the chocolatier's art.

MAP 1: 323 W. Broughton St., 912/335-2914, www.chocolatat.com; daily 11am-6pm

★ SAVANNAH BEE COMPANY

The closest thing to a can't-miss shopping experience locally, one of the most unique Savannah retail shops is the Savannah Bee Company, which carries an extensive line of honey and honey-based merchandise, from foot lotion to lip balm. All the honey comes from area hives owned by company founder and owner Ted Dennard. This flagship location provides plenty of sampling opportunities at the little café area and even boasts a small theater space for instructional films. The staff not only knows all about the products for sale, but how they are created and collected.

MAP 1: 104 W. Broughton St., 912/233-7873, www.savannahbee.com; Mon.-Sat. 10am-7pm, Sun. 11am-5pm

Home Goods
★ THE PARIS MARKET & BROCANTE

While Savannah is generally an Anglophile's dream, Francophiles will enjoy the Paris Market & Brocante, located on two floors on a beautifully restored corner of Broughton Street. Home and garden goods, bed and bath accoutrements, and a great selection of antique and vintage items combine for a rather opulent shopping experience. Plus there's an old-school Euro café inside, where you can enjoy a coffee, tea, or hot chocolate.

MAP 1: 36 W. Broughton St., 912/232-1500, www.theparismarket.com; Mon.-Sat. 10am-6pm, Sun. 11am-4pm

24E FURNISHINGS AT BROUGHTON

Those looking for great home decorating ideas with inspiration from both global and Southern aesthetics, traditional as well as sleekly modern, should check out 24e Furnishings at Broughton, located in an excellently restored 1921 storefront. You never know what you'll find here, from swanky style to repurposed aviation pieces. Be sure to check out the expansive second-floor showroom.

MAP 1: 24 E. Broughton St., 912/233-2274, www.twentyfoure.com; Mon.-Thurs. 10am-6pm, Fri.-Sat. 10am-7pm, Sun. noon-5pm

Outdoor Outfitters
HALF MOON OUTFITTERS

Outdoors lovers should make themselves acquainted with Half Moon Outfitters, a full-service camping, hiking, skiing, and kayaking store. Half Moon is part of a regional chain and the staff are particularly knowledgeable about local ecotourism.

MAP 1: 15 E. Broughton St., 912/201-9313, www.halfmoonoutfitters.com; Mon.-Sat. 10am-7pm, Sun. noon-6pm

Clockwise from top left: The Paris Market & Brocante; Savannah Bee Company; Chocolat by Adam Turoni.

PERFORMING ARTS
HISTORIC SAVANNAH THEATRE

The semipro troupe at the Historic Savannah Theatre performs a busy rotating schedule of oldies revues (a typical title: *Return to the '50s*), but they make up for their lack of originality with the tightness and energy of their talented young cast of regulars.

MAP 2: 222 Bull St., 912/233-7764, www.savannahtheatre.com

SHOPS
Antiques
★ ALEX RASKIN ANTIQUES

Possibly the most beloved antiques store in town is Alex Raskin Antiques in Monterey Square, catty-corner from the Mercer-Williams House Museum, set in the historic Hardee Mansion. A visit is worth it just to explore the home. But the goods Alex lovingly curates are among the best and most tasteful in the region.

MAP 2: 441 Bull St., 912/232-8205, www.alexraskinantiques.com; Mon.-Sat. 10am-5pm

THE CORNER DOOR

For a European take on antiques and collectibles, try the Corner Door, set in a unique building in the Downtown Design District and staffed by very friendly and knowledgeable antiques experts.

MAP 2: 417 Whitaker St., 912/238-5869; Tues.-Sat. 10am-5pm

SMALL PLEASURES

Small Pleasures is one of Savannah's hidden gems. They deal in a tasteful range of vintage and estate jewelry, in a suitably small but delightfully appointed space in the Downtown Design District.

MAP 2: 412 Whitaker St., 912/234-0277; Mon.-Sat. 10:30am-5pm

Books and Music
★ THE BOOK LADY

Specializing in "gently used" books in good condition, the Book Lady on Liberty Street features many rare first editions and lovably quirky items. Enjoy a gourmet coffee while you browse the stacks. They also host frequent author signings.

MAP 2: 6 E. Liberty St., 912/233-3628; Mon.-Sat. 10am-5:30pm

E. SHAVER BOOKSELLER

Locally owned independent E. Shaver Bookseller is one of the best bookstores in town. The friendly, well-read staff can help you around the

ARTS AND SHOPS
HISTORIC DISTRICT SOUTH

rambling old interior of their ground-level store and its generous stock of regionally themed books.

MAP 2: 326 Bull St., 912/234-7257; Mon.-Sat. 9am-6pm

V&J DUNCAN

The beautiful Monterey Square location and a mention in *Midnight in the Garden of Good and Evil* combine to make V&J Duncan a Savannah "must-shop." Owner John Duncan and his wife Virginia have collected an impressive array of prints, books, and maps over the past quarter century, and are themselves a treasure trove of information.

MAP 2: 12 E. Taylor St., 912/232-0338, www.vjduncan.com; Mon.-Sat. 10:30am-4:30pm

Clothes
CUSTARD BOUTIQUE

Custard Boutique in the Downtown Design District has a cute, cutting-edge selection of women's clothes in a range of styles, and is one of the more stylistically accessible boutiques in town.

MAP 2: 414 Whitaker St., 912/232-4733; Mon.-Sat. 10:30am-6pm, Sun. noon-5pm

Gifts and Souvenirs
FOLKLORICO

Set in a stunningly restored multilevel Victorian within a block of Forsyth Park, the globally conscious Folklorico brings in a fascinating and diverse collection of sustainably made jewelry, gifts, and home goods from around the world, focusing on Central and South America and Asia, at a variety of price points.

MAP 2: 440 Bull St., 912/232-9300; Mon.-Sat. 10am-5pm, Sun. 1pm-5pm

SAINTS AND SHAMROCKS

In this town so enamored of all things Irish, a great little locally owned shop is Saints and Shamrocks, across the intersection from the Book Lady. Pick up your St. Patrick's-themed gear and gifts to celebrate Savannah's highest holiday along with high-quality Irish imports.

MAP 2: 309 Bull St., 912/233-8858, www.saintsandshamrocks.org; Mon.-Sat. 9:30am-5:30pm, Sun. 11am-4pm

SHOPSCAD

Not only a valuable outlet for SCAD students and faculty to sell their artistic wares, shopSCAD is also one of Savannah's most unique boutiques. You never really know what you'll find, but whatever it is, it will be one-of-a-kind. The jewelry in particular is always cutting edge in design and high quality in craftsmanship. The designer T-shirts are a hoot too.

MAP 2: 340 Bull St., 912/525-5180, www.shopscadonline.com; Mon.-Wed. 9am-5:30pm, Thurs.-Fri. 9am-8pm, Sat. 10am-8pm, Sun. noon-5pm

MADAME CHRYSANTHEMUM

Madame Chrysanthemum, set in a charming, cozy corner spot in the Downtown Design District, deals in fun home items and gift ideas with a hip and enjoyable Savannah style.

MAP 2: 101 W. Taylor St., 912/238-3355; Mon.-Sat. 10am-5pm

ONE FISH TWO FISH

An eclectic European-style home goods store is One Fish Two Fish. Owner Jennifer Beaufait Grayson, a St. Simons Island native, came to town a decade ago to set up shop in this delightfully restored old dairy building in the Downtown Design District.

MAP 2: 401 Whitaker St., 912/484-4600; Mon.-Sat. 10am-5:30pm, Sun. noon-5pm

SoFo District

Map 3

SHOPS

Antiques

PICKER JOE'S ANTIQUE MALL & VINTAGE MARKET

Probably the best single antique/vintage store in town is Picker Joe's Antique Mall & Vintage Market, housed in an old mattress factory. There is a wide variety of consignment booths with great retro stuff. This store is more along the fun, serendipitous lines of the show "American Pickers" rather than the typical stuffy antiques shop. They make frequent picking trips all over the country, and you can sometimes catch them bringing in the new finds.

MAP 3: 217 E. 41st St., 912/239-4657, www.pickerjoes.com, Mon.-Sat. 10am-6pm, Sun. noon-5pm

Books and Music

GRAVEFACE RECORDS & CURIOSITIES

For the latest in vinyl, with new releases, vintage retro releases, locally released albums, and Record Store Day specials, check out Graveface in the Starland District. In addition to used and new vinyl, this is also a great place to get offbeat, kitschy gifts and unusual DVDs.

MAP 3: 5 W. 40th St., 912/335-8018; Mon.-Sat. 11am-7pm, Sun. noon-6pm

Clothes

GYPSY WORLD

Easily one of the best vintage stores in town, Gypsy World in the Starland District appeals to hipster and connoisseur alike and has a remarkable range of tasteful retro styles, including vintage furs, usually well within a reasonable budget.

MAP 3: 2405 Bull St., 912/704-2347; Tues.-Sat. 9:30am-5pm

SHOPS
Malls
KELLER'S FLEA MARKET
A local tradition for 20 years, Keller's Flea Market packs in about 10,000 shoppers over the course of a typical weekend. It offers a range of bargains in antiques, home goods, produce, and general kitsch, and there are concessions on-site.

MAP 6: 5901 Ogeechee Rd., I-95 exit 94, Southside, 912/927-4848, www.ilovefleas.com, Sat.-Sun. 8am-6pm

OGLETHORPE MALL
The mall closest to downtown—though not that close, at about 10 miles south—is Oglethorpe Mall in Southside. Its anchor stores are Sears, Belk, J. C. Penney, and Macy's.

MAP 6: 7804 Abercorn St., Southside, 912/354-7038, www.oglethorpemall.com; Mon.-Sat. 10am-9pm, Sun. noon-6pm

TANGER OUTLETS SAVANNAH
This outlet mall—actually in the adjacent city of Pooler, not Savannah—is marketed as a destination in itself, and it boasts a large number of stores even by the standards of outlet malls. Brands include American Eagle, Banana Republic, Chico's, Columbia, Gap, J. Crew, Cole Haan, Crocs, Oakley, Nike, and Under Armour.

MAP 6: 200 Tanger Outlet Blvd., Pooler, 912/348-3125, www.tangeroutlet.com; Mon.-Sat. 9am-9pm, Sun. 10am-7pm

Sports and Activities

Look for ★ to find
recommended activities

Highlights

★ **Best Birding:** Sitting smack dab on the coastal migratory flyway, **Skidaway Island State Park** offers a wealth of bird-watching in its expansive, wooded trail area, in addition to its marshfront (page 141).

★ **Closest Brush with The Babe:** Historic Grayson Stadium, home ballpark of the minor league baseball team **Savannah Bananas,** in its day hosted such greats as Babe Ruth, Mickey Mantle, Jackie Robinson, and Derek Jeter (page 143).

★ **Best Single Paddling Run:** The run across the Back River from Tybee to **Little Tybee Island** is a fun, marshy adventure (page 146).

★ **Best Historic Hiking:** For a brief period of time in the 1800s, the **Savannah-Ogeechee River Canal** did the job the railroad would later do, transporting goods inland to the Savannah River harbor. Today you can walk the old locks and enjoy scenic views of the Ogeechee River (page 148).

★ **Best Water that Looks Like Iced Tea:** Winding **Ebenezer Creek** outside of Savannah in Effingham County is a great place to take a scenic kayak or canoe run, its blackwater naturally stained dark from tree tannins (page 149).

★ **Most Expertly Repurposed Old Rice Plantation:** Now impounded for ecological purposes, old rice fields and paddies help form a thriving waterfowl and marsh habitat at the **Savannah National Wildlife Refuge,** a wonderful destination for kayakers (page 149).

a great blue heron at the Savannah National Wildlife Refuge

Savannah offers copious outdoor options that take full advantage of the city's temperate climate and the natural beauty of its marshy environment next to the Atlantic Ocean.

Savannah is a saltwater angler's paradise, rich in trout, flounder, and king and Spanish mackerel. Offshore there's a fair amount of deep-sea action, including large grouper, white and blue marlin, wahoo, snapper, sea bass, and big amberjack near some of the many offshore wrecks.

Diving is a challenge off the Georgia coast because of the silty nature of the water and its mercurial currents. Though not particularly friendly to the novice, plenty of great offshore opportunities abound around the many artificial reefs created by the Georgia Department of Natural Resources (www.coastalgadnr.org).

Other than some action around the pier, the surfing is poor on Tybee Island, with its broad shelf, tepid wave action, and lethal rip currents. But board surfers and kiteboarders have a lot of fun on the south end of Tybee beginning at about 17th Street. The craziest surf is past the rock jetty, but be advised that the rip currents are especially treacherous there.

Hiking in Savannah and the Lowcountry is largely a 2-D experience given the flatness of the terrain, but there are plenty of good nature trails from which to observe the area's rich flora and fauna up close, in beautiful settings.

Bicycling is fun all around the Savannah area. Plenty of folks ride their bikes downtown, and it is particularly enriching and fun to pedal around the squares. Legally, however, you're not allowed to ride through the squares; you're supposed to stay on the street around them. And always yield to traffic already within the square as you enter. Other good cycling opportunities are at Fort Pulaski and Tybee Island.

Savannah was the first city in Georgia to unveil a public **bike-share program** (http://catchacat.org, $2 per half hour, daily 5:30am-11pm), and you can now be the beneficiary. Head to Ellis Square adjacent to City Market; the rack is on the south side of the square.

Waterfront   Map 1

SPECTATOR SPORTS
SAVANNAH DERBY DEVILS
For sports action that's more hard-hitting and comes with a certain hip kitsch quotient, check out the bruising bouts of the women of the Savannah Derby Devils, who bring the roller derby thunder against other regional teams. They skate across the river at the Trade Center on Hutchinson Island, and the matches are usually quite well attended.

MAP 1: Savannah International Trade and Convention Center, 1 International Dr., 912/651-6556, www.savannahderby.com

SoFo District   Map 3

ECOTOURS
WILDERNESS SOUTHEAST
The nonprofit Wilderness Southeast offers guided trips (including paddles) to historic Mulberry Grove, birding trips, and beach explorations. Regularly scheduled "Walks on the Wild Side" run the gamut from "Alligators to Anhingas" to the "Urban Forest" to "Explore the Night Sky" to the "Blackwater River Float." Custom tours are also available.

MAP 3: 3025 Bull St., 912/897-5108, www.naturesavannah.org; $10-35

TENNIS
FORSYTH PARK

The closest public courts to the downtown area are at the south end of Forsyth Park, which features four free lighted courts. They are first-come, first-served and unstaffed, and as you might expect, they get serious use.

MAP 3: bordered by Drayton St., Gaston St., Whitaker St., and Park Ave., 912/351-3850; daily 8am-dusk; free

Southside   **Map 4**

BIRD-WATCHING
★ SKIDAWAY ISLAND STATE PARK

Skidaway Island State Park is part of the **Colonial Coast Birding Trail** (http://georgiawildlife.dnr.state.ga.us). Spring and fall bring a lot of the usual warbler action, while spring and summer feature nesting ospreys and painted buntings, always a delight.

MAP 4: 52 Diamond Causeway, 912/598-2300, www.gastateparks.org; daily 7am-10pm; parking $5 per vehicle per day

FISHING
MISS JUDY CHARTERS

Perhaps the best-known local angler is Captain Judy Helmey, a.k.a. "Miss Judy." In addition to her frequent and entertaining newspaper columns, she runs a variety of well-regarded charters; four-hour trips start at $500. To get here, go west on U.S. 80, take a right onto Bryan Woods Road, a left onto Johnny Mercer Boulevard, a right onto Wilmington Island Way, and a right down the dirt lane at her sign.

MAP 4: 124 Palmetto Dr., 912/897-2478, www.missjudycharters.com; from $500

TELECASTER CHARTERS

A great inshore charter service is offered by Telecaster Charters, with 4-, 6-, and 8-hour inshore trips priced from $300 for two anglers.

MAP 4: 2812 River Dr., Thunderbolt, 912/308-4622, www.telecastercharters.com; from $300

GOLF
WILMINGTON ISLAND CLUB

The Wilmington Island Club has arguably the quickest greens in town and is unarguably the most beautiful local course, set close by the Wilmington River amid lots of mature pines and live oaks.

MAP 4: 501 Wilmington Island Rd., 912/897-1612; greens fees about $70

HIKING

SKIDAWAY ISLAND STATE PARK

My favorite trails are at Skidaway Island State Park. The three-mile Big Ferry Trail is the best overall experience, taking you out to a wooden viewing tower from which you can see the vast expanse of the Skidaway Narrows. A detour takes you past a Native American shell midden, Confederate earthworks, and even a rusty old still—a nod to Skidaway Island's former notoriety as a bootlegger's sanctuary. The shorter but still fun Sandpiper Trail is wheelchair accessible.

MAP 4: 52 Diamond Causeway, 912/598-2300, www.gastateparks.org; daily 7am-10pm; parking $5 per vehicle per day

KAYAKING AND CANOEING

MOON RIVER KAYAK TOURS

Run by Captain Mike Neal, an experienced local boatman and conservationist, Moon River Kayak Tours focuses on 2.5-hour tours of the Skidaway Narrows and scenic Moon River, departing from the public boat ramp at the foot of the bridge to Skidaway Island. No kayaking experience is required.

MAP 4: 45 Diamond Causeway, 912/898-1800, www.moonriverkayak.com; $50

SKIDAWAY NARROWS

A pleasant kayaking route is the Skidaway Narrows. Begin this paddle at the public boat ramp, which you find by taking Waters Avenue all the way until it turns to Whitefield Avenue and then Diamond Causeway. Continue all the way over the Moon River to a drawbridge; park at the foot of the bridge. Once in the water, paddle northeast. Look for the osprey nests on top of the navigational markers in the narrows as you approach Skidaway Island State Park. Continuing on, you'll find scenic Isle of Hope high on a bluff to your left, with nearly guaranteed dolphin sightings around marker 62.

MAP 4: intersection of Moon River and Diamond Causeway

TENNIS

BACON PARK

On the south side, Bacon Park has 16 lighted hard courts. It's the city's best tennis facility, but it's the farthest from downtown. It's the most heavily trafficked of the city's courts, and a destination for local expert players.

MAP 4: 6262 Skidaway Rd., 912/351-3850; daily 8am-dusk; $3

FISHING
SAVANNAH FLY FISHING CHARTERS

Shallow-water fly-fishers might want to contact Savannah Fly Fishing Charters. Captain Scott Wagner takes half- and full-day charters both day and night from Savannah all the way down to St. Simons Island. Half-day rate starts at $300. Book early.

MAP 4: 56 Sassafras Trail, 912/308-3700, www.savannahfly.com; from $300

KAYAKING AND CANOEING
SAVANNAH CANOE & KAYAK

The most highly regarded local canoe and kayak tour operator and rental house is Savannah Canoe & Kayak, run by the husband-wife team of Nigel and Kristin Law. They offer several kayak trips, including a short jaunt to Little Tybee Island.

MAP 4: 414 Bonaventure Rd., 912/341-9502, www.savannahcanoeandkayak.com; half-day tour $55

TENNIS
DAFFIN PARK

South of Highway 80 is Daffin Park, where there are six clay courts and three lighted hard courts. This is mostly a locals-frequented spot, but the park is nice to visit.

MAP 4: 1001 E. Victory Dr., 912/351-3850; daily 8am-dusk; $3

SPECTATOR SPORTS
★ THE SAVANNAH BANANAS

A very popular local summer pastime is going to see the college summer league team the Savannah Bananas at historic Grayson Stadium in Daffin Park, where greats such as Babe Ruth and Jackie Robinson played back in the day. This isn't NCAA ball—these young players use real wooden bats and play for the love of the game while they're out of class for the summer. The off-field entertainment is a part of the experience, and is constant, very fun, and family-friendly. Most games sell out, so get tickets early.

MAP 4: 1401 E. Victory Dr., 912/712-2482, http://thesavannahbananas.com; $9

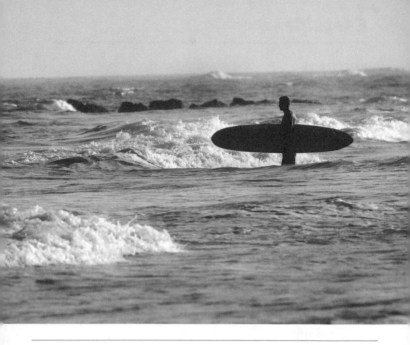

Top: a surfer on Tybee Island. Bottom: Savannah Fly Fishing Charters.

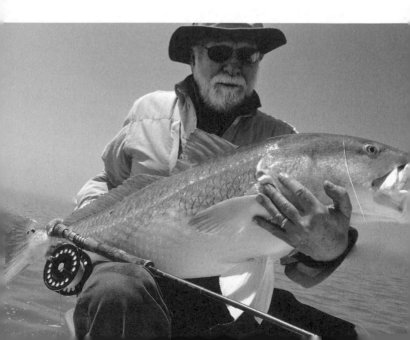

ECOTOURS

SUNDIAL NATURE TOURS

The best guided water tour in the area is Captain Rene Heidt's Sundial Nature Tours. Rene is an expert in local marine life and offers a variety of tours, including dolphin watches, fossil hunts, and trips to various barrier islands.

MAP 5: 1615 Chatham Ave., 912/786-9470, www.sundialcharters.com; from $160 for 2 people

BIKING

FORT PULASKI NATIONAL MONUMENT

Many locals like to load up their bikes and go to Fort Pulaski. From the grounds you can ride all over scenic and historic Cockspur Island.

MAP 5: 912/786-5787, www.nps.gov; daily 9am-5pm; $7, free under age 16

MCQUEEN'S ISLAND TRAIL

Outside town, much biking activity centers on Tybee Island, with the six-mile McQueen's Island Trail being a popular and simple ride. The trail started as a rail route for Central of Georgia Railway and was converted to a multiuse trail in the 1990s.

MAP 5: U.S. 80 near Fort Pulaski National Monument

BIRD-WATCHING

NORTH BEACH

An excellent birding spot on the **Colonial Coast Birding Trail** (http://georgiawildlife.dnr.state.ga.us) is Tybee Island's North Beach area. You'll see a wide variety of shorebirds and gulls, as well as piping plover, northern gannets, and in winter, purple sandpipers.

MAP 5: Savannah River to 1st St., Tybee Island; parking $5 per day, meters available

FISHING

AMICK'S DEEP SEA FISHING

A highly regarded local fishing charter is Tybee-based Amick's Deep Sea Fishing. Captain Steve Amick and crew run offshore charters daily. Go east on U.S. 80 and turn right just past the Lazaretto Creek Bridge.

MAP 5: 1 Old Hwy. 80, Tybee Island, 912/897-6759, www.amicksdeepseafishing.com; from $120 pp

KAYAKING AND CANOEING

LAZARETTO CREEK

Lazaretto Creek, on the western edge of Tybee island, is a great place to explore Tybee and environs. From here you can meander several miles through the marsh, or go the other way and head into a channel of the

Savannah River. If you're into ocean kayaking, you can even head into the Atlantic from here. Put in at the Lazaretto Creek landing, at the foot of the Lazaretto Creek bridge on the south side of U.S. 80 on the way to Tybee Island. This is a peaceful, pretty paddle for novice and experienced kayakers alike. You can also put in at the nearby **Tybee Marina** (4 Old Tybee Rd., 912/786-5554, www.tybeeislandmarina.com), also on Lazaretto Creek.

MAP 5: intersection of U.S. 80 and Tybee Island

★ LITTLE TYBEE ISLAND

Maybe the single best kayak or canoe adventure in Savannah is the run across the Back River from Tybee to Little Tybee Island, an undeveloped state heritage site that despite its name is actually twice as big as Tybee, albeit mostly marsh. Many kayakers opt to camp on the island. You can even follow the shoreline out into the Atlantic, but be aware that wave action can get intense offshore. Begin the paddle at the public boat ramp on the Back River. To get here, take Butler Avenue all the way to 18th Street and take a right, then another quick right onto Chatham Avenue. The parking lot for the landing is a short way up Chatham Avenue on your left. Warning: Do not attempt to swim to Little Tybee, no matter how strong a swimmer you think you are. Also, do not be tempted to walk far out onto the Back River beach at low tide. The tide comes in very quickly and often strands people on the sandbar.

MAP 5: south of Tybee Island

NORTH ISLAND SURF AND KAYAK

To rent an ocean-worthy kayak on Lazaretto Creek, stop by North Island Surf and Kayak, located at Tybee Marina. Reservations are recommended.

MAP 5: 1C Old Hwy. 80, 912/786-4000, www.northislandkayak.com; Mon.-Fri. 10am-5pm, Sat.-Sun. 9am-6pm; $45

SEA KAYAK GEORGIA

On U.S. 80 just as you get on Tybee is a quality tour service, Sea Kayak Georgia. Run by locals Marsha Henson and Ronnie Kemp, Sea Kayak offers many different types of kayak tours.

MAP 5: 1102 U.S. 80, 888/529-2542, www.seakayakgeorgia.com; half-day tour $55

SURFING AND BOARDING

HIGH TIDES SURF SHOP

The best—and pretty much only—surf shop in town is High Tides Surf Shop. You can get a good local surf report and forecasts at their website.

MAP 5: 405 U.S. 80, 912/786-6556, www.hightidesurfshop.com

TYBEE ISLAND MEMORIAL PARK

If you get the tennis jones on Tybee, there are two free hard courts at Tybee Island Memorial Park that are lighted.

MAP 5: Butler Ave. and 4th St., 912/786-4573, www.cityoftybee.org; daily 8am-dusk; free

Greater Savannah

BIRD-WATCHING

LAUREL HILL WILDLIFE DRIVE

Wading birds in particular are in wide abundance at the **Savannah National Wildlife Refuge.** The views are excellent all along the Laurel Hill Wildlife Drive, which takes you through the heart of the old paddy fields that once crisscrossed the entire area. To get here, take U.S. 17 north over the big Talmadge Bridge, over the Savannah River into South Carolina. Turn left on Highway 170 south and look for the entrance to Laurel Hill Wildlife Drive on the left.

MAP 6: 2 miles east of Port Wentworth, 843/784-2468, www.fws.gov/savannah; daily dawn-dusk; free

LECONTE-WOODMANSTON BOTANICAL GARDEN

LeConte-Woodmanston Botanical Garden is a bit hard to find. Part of William Bartram's historic nature trail, this was the home of Dr. Louis LeConte, renowned 19th-century botanist, and his sons John LeConte, first president of the University of California, Berkeley, and Joseph LeConte, who founded the Sierra Club with John Muir. The highlight here is the rare tidally influenced freshwater wetland, featuring the blackwater Bulltown Swamp. This visit is best done in a 4WD vehicle. The garden is about 40 minutes from Savannah. Take I-95 south to exit 76. Turn right on U.S. 84, then left on U.S. 17. Turn right on Barrington Ferry Road until the pavement ends at Sandy Run Road. Continue until you see the historical markers. Turn left onto the dirt road, then drive another mile.

MAP 6: 4918 Barrington Ferry Rd., Riceboro, 912/884-6500, www.leconte-woodmanston.org; daily 9am-5pm; $5

YOUMANS POND

Youmans Pond is a prime stop for migratory fowl. Its main claim to fame is that it was visited in 1773 by the great naturalist William Bartram on one of his treks across the Southeast. Youmans Pond has changed little since then, with its tree-studded pond and oodles of owls, ospreys, herons, egrets, wood storks, and many more. Youmans Pond is about 40 minutes from Savannah. To get here, take I-95 south to exit 76. Take a left onto Highway 38 (Islands Hwy.) and then a left onto Camp Viking Road. About one mile ahead, take a right onto Lake Pamona Drive. About 0.75 miles ahead, look for the pond on the right. It's unmarked, but there's a wooden boardwalk.

MAP 6: Lake Pamona Dr., Midway; daily; free

DIVING
GRAY'S REEF NATIONAL MARINE SANCTUARY

Certainly no underwater adventure in the area would be complete without a dive at Gray's Reef National Marine Sanctuary. Administered by the National Oceanic and Atmospheric Administration, this fully protected marine sanctuary 17 miles offshore is in deep enough water to provide divers good visibility of its live-bottom habitat. Not a classic living coral reef but rather one built by sedimentary deposits, Gray's Reef provides a look at a truly unique ecosystem. Some key dive charter operators that can take you to Gray's Reef are Captain Walter Rhame's **Mako Dive Charter** (600 Priest Landing Dr., 912/604-6256), which leaves from the Landings Harbor Marina; **Georgia Offshore** (1191 Lake Dr., Midway, 912/658-3884); and **Fantasia Scuba** (3 E. Montgomery Cross Rd., 912/921-8933).

The best all-around dive shop in town is **Diving Locker and Ski Chalet** (74 W. Montgomery Cross Rd., 912/927-6603, www.divinglockerskichalet.com, Mon.-Fri. 10am-6pm, Sat. 10am-5pm) on the south side.

MAP 6: 16 miles east of Sapelo Island, 912/598-2345, www.graysreef.noaa.gov

GOLF
CLUB AT SAVANNAH HARBOR

Across the Savannah River on Hutchinson Island and adjacent to the Westin Savannah Harbor Resort is the Club at Savannah Harbor, home to the Liberty Mutual Legends of Golf Tournament each spring. The club's tee times are 7:30am-3pm daily.

MAP 6: 2 Resort Dr., 912/201-2007, www.theclubatsavannahharbor.com; greens fees $135, twilight $70

HENDERSON GOLF CLUB

There are a couple of strong public courses in Savannah that are also very good bargains. Chief among these has to be the Henderson Golf Club, an excellent municipal course with very reasonable greens fees that include a half cart.

MAP 6: 1 Al Henderson Blvd., 912/920-4653, www.hendersongolfclub.com; greens fees Mon.-Fri. $28, Sat.-Sun. $33

HIKING
★ SAVANNAH-OGEECHEE RIVER CANAL

A relic of the pre-railroad days, the Savannah-Ogeechee River Canal is a 17-mile barge route joining the two rivers. Finished in 1830, it saw three decades of prosperous trade in cotton, rice, bricks, guano, naval stores, and food crops before the coming of the railroads finished it off. You can walk some of its length today near the Ogeechee River terminus, admiring the impressive engineering of its multiple locks used to stabilize the water level. Back in the day, the canal would continue through four lift locks as it traversed 16 miles before reaching the Savannah River. Naturalists will enjoy the built-in nature trail that walking along the canal provides. Be sure to check out the unique sand hills on a nearby trail, a vestige of a bygone geological era when this area was an offshore sandbar. Kids will enjoy the impromptu menagerie of gopher turtles near the site's entrance. Bring mosquito repellent, although often there's a community spray can at the front door of the little visitors center and museum where you pay your fee.

To get here, get on I-95 south, take exit 94, and go west on Fort Argyle Road (Hwy. 204). The canal is a little over two miles from the exit.

MAP 6: 681 Ft. Argyle Rd., 912/748-8068, www.savannahogeecheecanal.com; daily 9am-5pm; $2 adults, $1 students

KAYAKING AND CANOEING

★ EBENEZER CREEK

About 18 miles north of town, but worth the trip for any kayaker, is the beautiful blackwater Ebenezer Creek, near the tiny township of New Ebenezer in Effingham County. Cypress trees lining this nationally designated Wild and Scenic River hang overhead, and wildlife abounds on this peaceful paddle. Look for old wooden sluice gates, vestiges of the area's rice plantation past. To get here, take exit 109 off I-95. Go north on Highway 21 to Rincon, Georgia, then east on Highway 275 (Ebenezer Rd.). Put in at the private Ebenezer Landing.

MAP 6: intersection of Ebenezer Rd. and Savannah River, New Ebenezer; $5 put-in fee

★ SAVANNAH NATIONAL WILDLIFE REFUGE

One of the great overall natural experiences in the area is the massive Savannah National Wildlife Refuge. This 30,000-acre reserve—half in Georgia, half in South Carolina—is on the Atlantic flyway, so you'll be able to see birdlife in abundance, in addition to alligators and manatees. Earthen dikes crisscrossing the refuge are vestigial remnants of paddy fields from plantation days.

You can kayak on your own, but many opt to take guided tours offered by **Wilderness Southeast** (912/897-5108, www.wilderness-southeast. org, 2-hour trips from $38 for 2 people), **Sea Kayak Georgia** (888/529-2542, www.seakayakgeorgia.com, $55 pp), and **Swamp Girls Kayak Tours** (843/784-2249, www.swampgirls.com, $45). To get to the refuge, take U.S. 17 north over the big Talmadge Bridge, over the Savannah River into South Carolina. Turn left on Highway 170 south and look for the entrance to Laurel Hill Wildlife Drive on the left.

MAP 6: visitors center 694 Beech Hill Lane, Hardeeville, SC, 843/784-2468, www.fws.gov/ refuge/savannah; daily dawn-dusk; free

Hotels

The good news for visitors is that there are many comparatively new hotels of note directly in the downtown area within walking distance of most sites. Some of them are the more widely recognized chains, and others represent boutique companies

and provide a commensurately higher level of service. The less-good news, especially for locals, is that the ominously rising skyline that the newer, bigger hotels represent is a change from the friendly small-scale historical footprint Savannah is known for in the first place.

Savannah's many historic bed-and-breakfasts are competitive with the hotels on price, and often outperform them on service and ambience. If you don't need a swimming pool and don't mind climbing some stairs every now and then, a B&B is usually your best bet.

The best campground in town is at the well-managed and rarely crowded **Skidaway Island State Park** (52 Diamond Causeway, 912/598-2300, www.gastateparks.org; parking $5 per vehicle per day, tent and RV sites $26-40). There are 88 sites with 30-amp electric hookups. A two-night minimum stay is required on weekends, and there's a three-night minimum for Memorial Day, Labor Day, Independence Day, and Thanksgiving.

There's one campground on Tybee Island, the **River's End Campground and RV Park** (915 Polk St., 912/786-5518, www.cityofty-bee.org; water-and-electric sites $34, 50-amp full-hookup sites $45, cabins $150) on the north side. River's End offers 100 full-service sites plus some primitive tent sites. The highlight, however, are the incredibly cute little cabins; book well in advance. While During Tybee's sometimes-chilly

---

Previous: Mansion on Forsyth Park; the resort-style pool at the Westin Savannah Harbor Golf Resort & Spa.

Look for ★ to find
recommended hotels.

Highlights

★ **Best Scene:** The boutique **Bohemian Hotel Savannah Riverfront** has retro hip décor, a great waterfront location, and an amazing rooftop bar with wraparound views (page 153).

★ **Expertly Repurposed Coca-Cola Bottling Plant:** The historic building housing **The Brice** hasn't bottled soft drinks for decades, but it now hosts this tastefully modernist boutique hotel, complete with an upscale in-house Italian restaurant, Pacci. The Brice is in a comparatively quiet corner of downtown but still well within walking distance of most downtown attractions (page 153).

★ **Most Excellent View of Ellis Square:** A major part of the dramatic reclamation of Ellis Square was the building of the modernist **Andaz Savannah.** From its windows you get a great view of downtown, and the bar/restaurant combo is top-notch (page 154).

★ **Best Historic Hotel:** On bustling Broughton Street, **The Marshall House**

probably has the rooms with the most intact historic feel (page 154).

★ **Newest Old Name:** An extensive renovation and repurposing of a veteran name in local lodging puts **The DeSoto** at the top of any list of best hotels in town (page 156).

★ **Closest B&B to the Squares:** Probably the friendliest downtown B&B, **Foley House Inn** is also among the closest in walking distance to most of the downtown action (page 157).

★ **Classiest B&B near Forsyth Park:** It's not as close to the downtown squares as other places, but **The Gastonian** inn is a world-class stay just steps away from vast, green Forsyth Park and its iconic fountain (page 157).

★ **Best Stay on The Beach:** The lodging scene on Tybee Island is hit or miss. If you can get a room at the delightful and charming **Georgianne Inn,** circa 1910, you'll enjoy a peaceful stay that's still close to the entertainment on the south end of the island (page 158).

off-season (Nov.-Mar.), you can relax and get warm inside the common River Room. River's End also offers a swimming pool and laundry facilities.

Totally wilderness camping can be done on state-owned Little Tybee, accessible across the Back River by boat only; there are no facilities. The best camping and wilderness resource locally is **Half Moon Outfitters** (15 E. Broughton St., 912/201-9393, www.halfmoonoutfitters.com).

Waterfront

Map 1

★ BOHEMIAN HOTEL SAVANNAH RIVERFRONT ⑤⑤⑤

The Bohemian Hotel Savannah Riverfront has gained a reputation as one of Savannah's premier hotels, both for the casual visitor as well as visiting celebrities. Located between busy River Street and bustling City Market, this isn't the place for peace and quiet, but its combination of boutique-style retro-hip decor and happening rooftop bar scene makes it a great place to go for a fun stay that's as much Manhattan as Savannah. Valet parking is available, which you will come to appreciate.

MAP 1: 102 W. Bay St., 912/721-3800, www.bohemianhotelsavannah.com

★ THE BRICE ⑤⑤⑤

Housed in Savannah's first Coca-Cola bottling plant, The Brice brings a boutique-style upgrade to the historic building. With great service and 145 rooms, most complete with a modernized four-poster bed, The Brice also features **Pacci Italian Kitchen + Bar** (breakfast daily 7am-10:30am, brunch Sat.-Sun. 8am-3pm, dinner Sun.-Thurs. 5pm-10pm, Fri.-Sat. 5pm-10:30pm, $15-25), one of the better hotel restaurant/bar combos in town.

MAP 1: 601 E. Bay St., 912/238-1200, www.thebricehotel.com

HYATT REGENCY SAVANNAH ⑤⑤⑤

For years critics have called the modernist Hyatt Regency Savannah an insult to architecture and to history. Regardless, the Hyatt—a sort of exercise in cubism straddling an entire block of River Street—has avoided the neglect of many older chain properties downtown. Three sides of the hotel offer views of the bustling Savannah waterfront, with its massive ships coming in from all over the world.

MAP 1: 2 E. Bay St., 912/238-1234, www.savannah.hyatt.com

WESTIN SAVANNAH HARBOR GOLF RESORT AND SPA ⑤⑤

If you require a swank pool, look no farther than the Westin Savannah Harbor Golf Resort and Spa, which has a beautiful resort-style pool across the Savannah River from downtown and overlooking the old city. Accessing the hotel—located on a cross-channel island—is a bit of a process, but one made easier by charming river ferries that run regularly and free of charge. The attached golf course is a good one, and packages are available.

MAP 1: 1 Resort Dr., 912/201-2000, www.westinsavannah.com

City Market
Map 1

★ ANDAZ SAVANNAH $$$

Providing a suitably modernist decor to go with its somewhat atypical architecture for Savannah, the Andaz Savannah overlooks restored Ellis Square and abuts City Market with its shopping, restaurants, and nightlife. A boutique offering from Hyatt, the Andaz's guest rooms and suites feature top-of-the-line linens, extra-large and well-equipped baths, in-room snack bars, and technological features such as free Wi-Fi and, of course, the ubiquitous flat-screen TV. Customer service is a particular strong suit. Just off the lobby is a very hip lounge-wine bar that attracts locals as well as hotel guests. Keep in mind things can get a little noisy in this area at night on weekends.

MAP 1: 14 Barnard St., 912/233-2116, www.savannah.andaz.hyatt.com

Historic District North
Map 1

★ THE MARSHALL HOUSE $$$

Dominating most of a block of East Broughton Street is The Marshall House, Savannah's oldest hotel and a delightful throwback in a city increasingly populated with modernist boutique hotels. The craftsmanship devoted to preservation of this circa 1851 building is impressive. While that does mean the rooms aren't huge, you're paying for prime location in the heart of Savannah's commercial district and for distinctive retro style. If you're into ghosts, it is alleged to be a haunted property as well.

MAP 1: 123 E. Broughton St., 912/644-7896, www.marshallhouse.com

BALLASTONE INN $$$

Once a bordello, the 1838 mansion that is home to the 16-room Ballastone Inn is one of Savannah's favorite inns. Highlights include an afternoon tea service and one of the better full breakfasts in town. Note that some guest rooms are at what Savannah calls the "garden level," meaning sunken basement-level rooms with what amounts to a worm's-eye view.

MAP 1: 14 E. Oglethorpe Ave., 912/236-1484, www.ballastone.com

THE GREEN PALM INN $$

Easily the best bed-and-breakfast for the price in Savannah is The Green Palm Inn, a folksy and romantic little Victorian number with some neat gingerbread exterior stylings and four cute guest rooms, each named after a species of palm tree. It's situated on the very easternmost edge of the

Clockwise from top left: The DeSoto Savannah; The Kehoe House; The Marshall House.

Savannah Historic District—hence its reasonable rates. Delightful inn-keeper Diane McCray provides a very good and generous breakfast plus a pretty much constant dessert bar.

MAP 1: 546 E. President St., 912/447-8901, www.greenpalminn.com

17HUNDRED90 INN ⑤⑤

Famous for its host of resident ghosts—which many employees do swear aren't just tourist tales—17Hundred90 offers 14 cozy rooms within a historic building that dates from, yep, 1790. The addition of several nearby guest houses, booked through the inn, has expanded the footprint of this great old Savannah name. The great plus here—in addition to the ghost stories of course—is the excellent on-site restaurant and bar, popular with both locals and tourists alike.

MAP 1: 307 E. President St., 912/236-7122, www.17hundred90.com

THE KEHOE HOUSE ⑤⑤

One of Savannah's favorite bed-and-breakfasts, The Kehoe House is a great choice for its charm and attention to guests. Its historic location, on quiet little Columbia Square catty-corner to the Isaiah Davenport House, is within walking distance to all the downtown action, but far enough from the bustle to get some peace out on one of the rocking chairs on the veranda.

MAP 1: 123 Habersham St., 912/232-1020, www.kehoehouse.com

Historic District South   Map 2

ELIZA THOMPSON HOUSE ⑤⑤

One of Savannah's original historic B&Bs, the Eliza Thompson House is a bit out of the bustle on serene, beautiful Jones Street, but still close enough to get involved whenever you feel the urge. You can enjoy the various culinary offerings—breakfast, wine and cheese, nighttime munchies—either in the parlor or on the patio overlooking the house's classic Savannah garden.

MAP 2: 5 W. Jones St., 912/236-3620, www.elizathompsonhouse.com

★ THE DESOTO SAVANNAH ⑤⑤

One of Savannah's key downtown landmarks is the towering edifice of The DeSoto Savannah, usually just called The DeSoto in a nod to its long history here, which includes a now-demolished high Victorian resort by the same name. While the shell of the building dates from the 1960s in its incarnation as a Hilton property, the Sotheby brand recently acquired the hotel and has unveiled an extensive modernization and renovation. The rooms are sumptuous in the modern boutique hotel tradition, and the service at the hotel stands out. The location, at arguably Savannah's most important intersection, Bull and Liberty Streets, can't be beat. The independently run restaurant downstairs, the **1540 Room** (Tues.-Thurs. 5pm-10pm, Fri.-Sat.

5pm-11pm, Sun. 10:30am-3pm), boasts local culinary heavy-hitters. A few feet away is **Edgar's Proof & Provision,** an old-school hotel bar with a separate solid menu that's offered 6:30am-midnight daily. To top it off, Savannah's favorite dive bar, Pinkie Masters, is right across the street, though unaffiliated with the hotel.

MAP 2: 15 E. Liberty St., 912/232-9000, www.thedesotosavannah.com

★ FOLEY HOUSE INN $ $

The circa-1896 Foley House Inn is a four-diamond B&B with some rooms available at a three-diamond price. Its 19 individualized Victorian-decor guest rooms, in two town houses, range from the smaller Newport overlooking the "grotto courtyard" to the four-poster, bay-windowed Essex room, complete with a fireplace and a whirlpool bath. The location on Chippewa Square is pretty much perfect: well off the busy east-west thoroughfares but in the heart of Savannah's active theater district and within walking distance of anywhere.

MAP 2: 14 W. Hull St., 912/232-6622, www.foleyinn.com

Victorian District Map 3

DRESSER-PALMER HOUSE $ $

A short walk from Forsyth Park, the Dresser-Palmer House features 15 guest rooms in two wings but still manages to make things feel pretty cozy. Garden-level rooms go for under $200.

MAP 3: 211 E. Gaston St., 912/238-3294, www.dresserpalmerhouse.com

★ THE GASTONIAN $ $ $

The Gastonian inn, circa 1868, is a favorite choice for travelers to Savannah, mostly for its 17 sumptuously decorated guest rooms and suites, all with working fireplaces, and the always outstanding full breakfast. They pile on the epicurean delights with teatime, evening nightcaps, and complimentary wine.

MAP 3: 220 E. Gaston St., 912/232-2869, www.gastonian.com

MANSION ON FORSYTH PARK $ $ $

How ironic that a hotel built in a former mortuary would be one of the few Savannah hotels not to have a resident ghost story. But that's the case with Mansion on Forsyth Park, which dominates an entire block alongside Forsyth Park, including partially within the high-Victorian former Fox & Weeks Mortuary building. Its sumptuous guest rooms, equipped with big beds, big baths, and big-screen TVs, scream "boutique hotel," as does the swank little bar and the alfresco patio area.

MAP 3: 700 Drayton St., 912/238-5158, www.mansiononforsythpark.com

Most of the hotels on Tybee Island see a lot of wear and tear from eager vacationers. I encourage a B&B stay. Also be aware that places on Butler Avenue, even the substandard ones, charge a premium during the high season (Mar.-Oct.).

ATLANTIS INN $

For those looking for the offbeat, try the Atlantis Inn. Its reasonably priced, whimsically themed rooms are a hoot, and you're a short walk from the ocean and a very easy jaunt around the corner from busy Tybrisa Street. The downside, however, is no dedicated parking.

MAP 5: 20 Silver Ave., 912/786-8558, www.atlantisinntybee.com

★ THE GEORGIANNE INN $$

The best B&B-style experience on Tybee can be found at The Georgianne Inn, a short walk off the beach and close to most of the island's action, yet not so close that you can't get away when you want to. The complimentary bikes to use while you're there are a nice plus.

MAP 5: 1312 Butler Ave., 912/786-8710, www.georgianneinn.com

BEACHVIEW BED & BREAKFAST $$

For a classic B&B stay very close to the Tybrisa-south end action, Beachview is where to go. The food is great and the views from the extensive wraparound porches are wonderful, especially on a breezy Tybee night.

MAP 5: 1701 Butler Ave., 912/348-5202, www.beachviewbbtybee.com

LIGHTHOUSE INN $$

Tucked away on the north end near the Lighthouse, hence the name, the Lighthouse Inn offers a lot of privacy in a very cozy and lush corner lot. This is more the place for a quiet, secluded getaway.

MAP 5: 16 Meddin Dr., 912/786-0901, www.tybeebb.com

RIVER'S END CAMPGROUND $

RV campers and more adventurous trekkers have a great treat in store at River's End Campground, on Tybee's somewhat less-developed north end. There are plenty of full-hookup sites ($70-90), some limited service or tent sites ($60-70), and a set of adorable little cabins that sleep six (2-night minimum, $125-160).

MAP 5: 5 Fort Ave., 800/786-1016, www.riversendcampground.com

Stay the Week

For long-term stays on Tybee Island, weekly rentals are the name of the game. Though not cheap—expect to pay roughly $1,000 per week in the summer—they provide a higher level of accommodations than some hotels on the island. For weekly rentals, try **Oceanfront Cottage Rentals** (800/786-5889, www.oceanfrontcottage.com), **Tybee Island Rentals** (912/786-4034, www.tybeeislandrentals.com), or **Tybee Vacation Rentals** (866/359-0297, www.tybeevacationrentals.com).

Greater Savannah Map 6

MIDWAY AND LIBERTY COUNTY
DUNHAM FARMS ⑤⑤

While industry is coming quickly to Liberty County, it's still a small self-contained community with not much in the way of tourism amenities (many would say that is part of its charm). A great choice for a stay is Dunham Farms. The B&B ($165-205) is in the converted 1940s Palmyra Barn, and the self-catered circa-1840 Palmyra Cottage ($300) nearby is right on the river, with plenty of kayaking and hiking opportunities. Your hosts, Laura and Meredith Devendorf, couldn't be more charming or informed about the area, and the breakfasts are absurdly rich and filling in that hearty and deeply comforting Southern tradition.

MAP 6: 5836 Islands Hwy., Midway, 912/880-4500, www.dunhamfarms.com

HOTELS
GREATER SAVANNAH

Excursions

Just outside Savannah is a treasure trove of natural beauty, amazing recreation, and fascinating historic sights.

About an hour north of Savannah is Hilton Head Island in South Carolina, a scenic but entirely developed golf and tennis mecca. If you're not into golf, however, you're still in luck—there are also amazing opportunities to view wildlife and learn about the area's history.

To the south, the Georgia coast retains a timeless mystique evocative of an era before the coming of the Europeans, even before humankind itself. Often called the Golden Isles because of the play of the afternoon sun on the vistas of marsh grass, its other nickname, "the Debatable Land," is a nod to its centuries-long role as a constantly shifting battleground of European powers.

Highlights

★ **Pinckney Island National Wildlife Refuge:** This well-maintained sanctuary is a major birding location and a great getaway from nearby Hilton Head (page 166).

★ **Coastal Discovery Museum at Honey Horn:** This beautifully repurposed plantation house with spacious grounds is a great place to learn about Hilton Head history, both human and natural (page 166).

★ **Jekyll Island Historic District:** Relax and soak in the salty breeze at this onetime playground of the country's richest people (page 190).

★ **The Village:** The center of social life on St. Simons Island has shops, restaurants, a pier, and a beachside playground (page 198).

★ **Fort Frederica National Monument:** An excellently preserved tabby fortress dates from the first days of English settlement in Georgia (page 198).

★ **Harris Neck National Wildlife Refuge:** This former wartime airfield is now one of the East Coast's best birding locations (page 207).

★ **Cumberland Island National Seashore:** This undeveloped island paradise has wild horses, evocative abandoned ruins, and over 16 miles of gorgeous beach (page 212).

★ **Okefenokee National Wildlife Refuge:** More than just a swamp, the Okefenokee is a natural wonderland that takes you back into the mists of prehistory (page 218).

maritime forest on Cumberland Island National Seashore

Hilton Head Island

While the New York accents fly fast and furious on Hilton Head Island, that's no reason for you to rush. Plan on at least half a day just to enjoy the fine broad beaches alone. I recommend another half day to tour the island itself, maybe including a stop in Sea Pines for a late lunch or dinner.

The Golden Isles

Many travelers take I-95 south from Savannah to the Golden Isles, but **U.S. 17** roughly parallels the interstate—in some cases so closely that drivers on the two roads can see each other—and is a far more scenic and enriching drive for those with a little extra time to spend. Indeed, U.S. 17 is an intrinsic part of the life and lore of the region, and you are likely to spend a fair amount of time on it regardless.

Geographically, Brunswick is similar to Charleston in that it lies on a peninsula laid out roughly north-south. And like Charleston, it's separated from the Atlantic by barrier islands, in Brunswick's case St. Simons Island and Jekyll Island. Once you get within city limits, however, Brunswick has more in common with Savannah due to its Oglethorpe-designed grid layout. **Brunswick** itself can easily be fully experienced in a **single afternoon.** But really—as its nickname "Gateway to the Golden Isles" indicates—Brunswick is an economic and governmental center for Glynn County, to which Jekyll Island and St. Simons Island, the real attractions in this area, belong.

Both Jekyll Island and St. Simons Island are well worth visiting, and have their own separate pleasures—Jekyll more contemplative, St. Simons more upscale. Give an **entire day to Jekyll** so you can take full advantage of its relaxing, open feel. A **half day** can suffice for **St. Simons** because most of its attractions are clustered in the Village area near the pier, and there's little beach recreation to speak of.

Getting to the undeveloped barrier islands, Sapelo and Cumberland, takes planning because there is no bridge to either. Both require a ferry booking and hence a more substantial commitment of time. There are no real stores and few facilities on these islands, so pack along whatever you think you'll need, including food, water, medicine, suntan lotion, insect repellent, and so on. **Sapelo Island** is limited to **day use** unless you have prior reservations, with the town of Darien in McIntosh County as the gateway. The same is true for Cumberland Island National Seashore, with the town of St. Marys in Camden County as the gateway.

Hilton Head Island

Literally the prototype of the modern planned resort community, Hilton Head Island is also a case study in how a landscape can change when money is introduced. From Reconstruction until the post-World War II era, the island consisted almost entirely of African Americans with deep roots in the area. In the mid-1950s Hilton Head began its transformation into an almost all-white, upscale golf, tennis, and shopping mecca populated largely by Northern and Midwestern transplants and retirees. As you can imagine, the flavor here is now quite different from surrounding areas of the Lowcountry, to say the least, with an emphasis on material excellence, top prices, get-it-done-yesterday punctuality, and the attendant aggressive traffic.

These days, Hilton Head gets the most national media attention for the RBC Heritage golf tournament each April, when the entire island is packed with golf fans for this extremely popular PGA event.

HISTORY

The second-largest barrier island on the East Coast was named in 1663 by adventurer Sir William Hilton, who thoughtfully named the island—with its notable headland or "Head"—after himself. Later it gained fame as the first growing location of the legendary Sea Island cotton, a long-grain variety that, following its introduction in 1790 by William Elliott II of the Myrtle Bank Plantation, would soon be the dominant version of the cash crop.

Though it seems unlikely given the island's modern demographics, Hilton Head was almost entirely African American through much of the 20th century. When Union troops occupied the island at the outbreak of the Civil War, freed and escaped enslaved people flocked to the island, and many of the dwindling number of African Americans on the island today are descendants of this original Gullah population.

In the 1950s the Fraser family bought 19,000 of the island's 25,000 acres with the intent to continue forestry on them. But in 1956—not at all coincidentally the same year the first bridge to the island was built—Charles Fraser convinced his father to sell him the southern tip. Fraser's brainchild and decades-long labor of love—some said his obsession—Sea Pines Plantation became the prototype for the golf-oriented resort communities so common today on both U.S. coasts. Fraser himself was killed in a boating accident in 2002 and is buried under the famous Liberty Oak in Harbour Town.

SIGHTS

Contrary to what many think, there are things to do on Hilton Head that don't involve swinging a club at a little ball or shopping for designer labels, but instead celebrate the area's history and natural setting. The following

165

Hilton Head Island

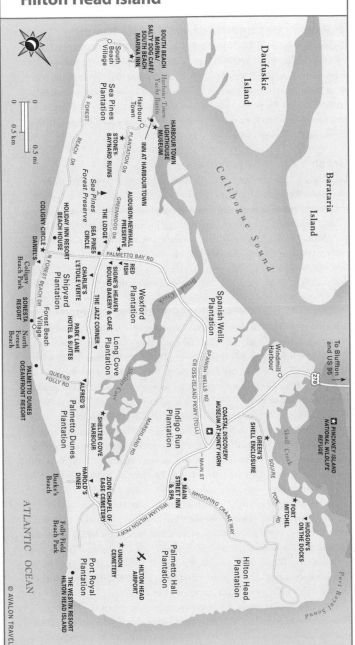

© AVALON TRAVEL

are some of those attractions, arranged in geographical order from where you first access the island.

★ Pinckney Island National Wildlife Refuge

Consisting of many islands and hammocks, **Pinckney Island National Wildlife Refuge** (912/652-4415, daily dawn-dusk, free) is the only part of this small but very well-managed 4,000-acre refuge that's open to the public. Almost 70 percent of the former rice plantation is salt marsh and tidal creeks, making it a perfect microcosm for the Lowcountry as a whole, as well as a great place to kayak or canoe. Some of the state's richest birding opportunities abound here.

Green's Shell Enclosure

Less known than the larger Native American shell ring farther south at Sea Pines, **Green's Shell Enclosure** (803/734-3886, daily dawn-dusk) is certainly easier to find, and you don't have to pay $6 to enter the area, as with Sea Pines. This three-acre heritage preserve dates back to at least the 1300s. The heart of the site is a low embankment, part of the original fortified village. To get here, take a left at the intersection of U.S. 278 and Squire Pope Road. Turn left into Green's Park, pass the office on the left, and park. The entrance to the shell enclosure is on the left behind a fence.

★ Coastal Discovery Museum at Honey Horn

With the acquisition of Honey Horn's 70-acre spread of historic plantation land, Hilton Head finally has a full-fledged museum worthy of the name, and the magnificent **Coastal Discovery Museum** (70 Honey Horn Dr., 843/689-6767, www.coastaldiscovery.org, Mon.-Sat. 9am-4:30pm, Sun. 11am-3pm, free) is a must-see, even for those who came to the island mostly to golf and soak up sun.

The facility centers on the expertly restored Discovery House, the only antebellum house still existing on Hilton Head, with exhibits and displays devoted to the history of the island. The museum is also a great one-stop place to sign up for a variety of specialty on-site and off-site guided tours, such as birding and Gullah history tours. The cost for most on-site tours is a reasonable $10 adults, $5 children.

But the real draw is the 0.5-mile trail through the Honey Horn grounds, including several boardwalk viewpoints over the marsh, a neat little butterfly habitat, a replica Native American shell ring, a wonderful heirloom camellia garden, and a stable and pasture that host Darling and Comet, the museum's two Marsh Tackies—short, tough little ponies descended from Spanish horses and used to great effect by Francis "Swamp Fox" Marion and his freedom fighters in the American Revolution.

While a glance at a map and area signage might convince you that you must pay the $1.25 toll on the Cross Island Parkway to get to Honey Horn, that isn't so. The exit to Honey Horn on the parkway is actually before you

Union Cemetery

A modest but key aspect of African American history on Hilton Head is at **Union Cemetery** (Union Cemetery Rd.), a small burial ground featuring several graves of black Union Army troops (you can tell by the designation "USCI" on the tombstone, for "United States Colored Infantry"). Also of interest are the charming hand-carved cement tombstones of nonveterans. To get here, turn north off William Hilton Parkway onto Union Cemetery Road. The cemetery is a short way ahead on the left. There is no signage or site interpretation.

Zion Chapel of Ease Cemetery

More like one of the gloriously desolate scenes common to the rest of the Lowcountry, this little cemetery in full view of the William Hilton Parkway at Folly Field Road is all that remains of one of the "Chapels of Ease," a string of chapels set up in the 1700s. The **Zion Chapel of Ease Cemetery** (daily dawn-dusk, free) is said to be haunted by the ghost of William Baynard, whose final resting place is in a mausoleum on the site (the remains of his ancestral home are farther south at Sea Pines Plantation).

Audubon-Newhall Preserve

Plant lovers shouldn't miss this small but very well-maintained 50-acre wooded tract in the south-central part of the island on Palmetto Bay Road between the Cross Island Parkway and the Sea Pines Circle. Almost all plantlife, even that in the water, is helpfully marked and identified. The **Audubon-Newhall Preserve** (year-round dawn-dusk, free) is open to the public, but you can't camp here. For more information, call the **Hilton Head Audubon Society** (843/842-9246).

Sea Pines Plantation

This private residential resort development at the extreme west end of the island—the first on Hilton Head and the prototype for every other such development in the country—hosts several attractions that collectively are worth the $6 per vehicle "road use" fee, which you pay at the main entrance gate.

HARBOUR TOWN

It's not particularly historic and not all that natural, but **Harbour Town** is still pretty cool. The dominant element is the squat, colorful **Harbour Town Lighthouse Museum** (149 Lighthouse Rd., 843/671-2810, www.harbourtownlighthouse.com, daily 10am-dusk, $4.25, free under age 5), which has never really helped a ship navigate. The 90-foot structure was built in 1970 purely to give visitors a little atmosphere, and that it does, as

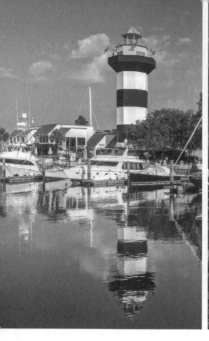

Clockwise from top left: the lighthouse on Hilton Head Island; a heron in the trees of Pinckney Island; shops in Harbour Town.

kids especially love climbing the stairs to the top and looking out over the island's expanse.

STONEY-BAYNARD RUINS

The **Stoney-Baynard ruins** (Plantation Dr., dawn-dusk, free), tabby ruins in a residential neighborhood, are what remains of the circa-1790 central building of the old Braddock's Point Plantation, first owned by patriot and raconteur Captain "Saucy Jack" Stoney and later by the Baynard family. Active during the island's heyday as a cotton center, the plantation was destroyed after the Civil War.

SEA PINES FOREST PRESERVE

The **Sea Pines Forest Preserve** (175 Greenwood Dr., 843/363-4530, free) is set amid the Sea Pines Plantation golf resort development, but you don't need a bag of clubs to enjoy this 600-acre preserve, which is built on the site of an old rice plantation (dikes and logging trails are still visible). Here you can ride a horse, fish, or just take a walk on the eight miles of trails (dawn-dusk) and enjoy the natural beauty around you. No bike riding is allowed on the trails, however.

In addition to the Native American shell ring farther north off Squire Pope Road, the Sea Pines Forest Preserve also boasts a shell ring set within a canopy of tall pines.

Tours and Cruises

Most guided tours on Hilton Head focus on the water. **Harbour Town Cruises** (843/363-9023, www.vagabondcruise.com, $30-60) offers several sightseeing tours as well as excursions to Daufuskie and Savannah. They also offer a tour on a former America's Cup racing yacht.

Dolphin tours are extremely popular on Hilton Head, and there is no shortage of operators. **Dolphin Watch Nature Cruises** (843/785-4558, $25 adults, $10 children) departs from Shelter Cove, as does **Lowcountry Nature Tours** (843/683-0187, www.lowcountrynaturetours.com, $40 adults, $35 children, free under age 3). **Outside Hilton Head** (843/686-6996, www.outsidehiltonhead.com) runs a variety of water ecotours and dolphin tours as well as a guided day-trip excursion to Daufuskie, complete with golf cart rental.

There is a notable land-based tour by **Gullah Heritage Trail Tours** (leaves from Coastal Discovery Museum at Honey Horn, 843/681-7066, www.gullahheritage.com, $32 adults, $15 children) delving into the island's rich, if poorly preserved, African American history from slavery through the time of the freedmen.

NIGHTLIFE

The highest-quality live entertainment on the island is at **The Jazz Corner** (1000 William Hilton Pkwy., 843/842-8620, www.thejazzcorner.com, dinner daily 6pm-9pm, late-night menu after 9pm, dinner $15-20, cover varies), which brings in big names in the genre to perform in this space in the unlikely setting of a boutique mall, the Village at Wexford. The dinners are actually quite good, but the attraction is definitely the music. Reservations are recommended. Live music starts around 7pm.

For years islanders jokingly referred to the "Barmuda Triangle," an area named for the preponderance of bars within vague walking distance of Sea Pines Circle. While some of the names have changed over the years, the longtime anchor of the Barmuda Triangle is the **Tiki Hut** (1 S. Forest Beach Dr., 843/785-5126, Sun.-Thurs. 11am-8pm, Fri.-Sat. 11am-10pm, bar until 2am), actually part of The Beach House hotel at the entrance to Sea Pines. This popular watering hole is the only beachfront bar on the island, which technically makes it the only place you can legally drink alcohol on a Hilton Head beach. Another Triangle fave is **The Lodge** (7 Greenwood Dr., 843/842-8966, www.hiltonheadlodge.com, daily 11:30am-midnight). After the martini-and-cigar craze waned, this popular spot successfully remade itself into a beer-centric place with 36 rotating taps.

Despite its location in the upscale strip mall of the Village at Wexford, the **British Open Pub** (1000 William Hilton Pkwy./U.S. 278, 843/686-6736, daily 11am-10pm) offers a fairly convincing English vibe with, as the name suggests, a heavy golf theme. The fish-and-chips and shepherd's pie are both magnificent.

Inside Sea Pines is the **Quarterdeck Lounge and Patio** (843/842-1999, www.seapines.com, Sun.-Thurs. 5:30pm-10pm, Fri.-Sat. 5:30pm-midnight) at the base of the Harbour Town Lighthouse. This is where the party's at after a long day on the fairways during the Heritage golf tournament. Within Sea Pines at the South Beach Marina is also where you'll find **The Salty Dog Cafe** (232 S. Sea Pines Dr., 843/671-2233, www.saltydog.com, lunch daily 11am-3pm, dinner daily 5pm-10pm, bar daily until 2am), one of the area's most popular institutions (some might even call it a tourist trap) and something akin to an island empire, with popular T-shirts, a gift shop, books, and an ice cream shop, all overlooking the marina. My suggestion, however, is to make the short walk to the affiliated **Wreck of the Salty Dog** (843/671-7327, daily until 2am), where the marsh views are better and the atmosphere not quite so tacky.

A gay-friendly bar on Hilton Head is **Cool Cats Lounge** (32 Palmetto Bay Rd., Mon.-Fri. 8pm-3am, Sat. 8pm-2am), with a welcoming dive-bar atmosphere and a small but lively dance floor.

ARTS AND CULTURE
Art Galleries

Despite the abundant wealth apparent in some quarters here, there's no freestanding art museum in the area, that role being filled by independent galleries. A good representative example is **Morris & Whiteside Galleries** (220 Cordillo Pkwy., 843/842-4433, www.morris-whiteside.com, Mon.-Fri. 9am-5pm, Sat. 10am-4pm), located in the historic Red Piano Too Art Gallery building, which features a variety of paintings and sculpture, heavy on landscapes but also showing some fine figurative work. The nonprofit **Art League of Hilton Head** (14 Shelter Cove Lane, 843/681-5060, Mon.-Sat. 10am-6pm) is located in the Walter Greer Art Gallery within the Arts Center of Coastal Carolina and displays work by member artists in all media. The **Nash Gallery** (13 Harbourside Lane, 843/785-6424, Mon.-Fri. 10am-9pm, Sat. 10am-8pm, Sun. 11am-5pm) in Shelter Cove Harbour deals more in North American craft styles. Hilton Head art isn't exactly known for its avant-garde nature, but you can find some whimsical stuff at **Picture This** (78D Arrow Rd., 843/842-5299, Mon.-Fri. 9:30am-5:30pm, Sat. 9:30am-12:30pm), including a selection of Gullah craft items.

Performing Arts

The range of offerings won't rival New York City, but because so many residents migrated here from art-savvy metropolitan areas in the Northeast, Hilton Head maintains a high standard of entertainment. Much of the activity centers on the multimillion-dollar **Arts Center of Coastal Carolina** (14 Shelter Cove Lane, 843/842-2787, www.artshhi.com), which hosts touring shows, resident companies, musical concerts, dance performances, and visual arts exhibits.

Under the direction of maestro John Morris Russell, the acclaimed **Hilton Head Symphony Orchestra** (843/842-2055, www.hhso.org) performs a year-round season of masterworks and pops programs at the First Presbyterian Church (540 William Hilton Pkwy./U.S. 278).

Cinema

There's an art house on Hilton Head, the charming **Coligny Theatre** (843/686-3500, www.colignytheatre.com) tucked away in the Coligny Plaza shopping center before you get to Sea Pines. For years this was the only movie theater for miles around, opening in 1972 and shuttering briefly in 1997. But since reopening in 2002 it has reincarnated as a primarily indie film venue. Look for the entertaining murals on the outside walls by local artist Ralph Sutton.

Festivals and Events

Late February-early March brings the **Hilton Head Wine and Food Festival** (www.hiltonheadhospitality.org), culminating in what they call "the East Coast's Largest Outdoor Public Tasting and Auction," which is generally held at the Coastal Discovery Museum at Honey Horn. Some events charge admission.

Without question, Hilton Head's premier event is the **RBC Heritage Golf Tournament** (843/671-2248, http://theheritagegolfsc.com), held each April, usually the week after the Masters, at the Harbour Town Golf Links on Sea Pines Plantation. Formerly known as the Verizon Heritage Classic, the event is South Carolina's only PGA Tour event and brings thousands of visitors to town. The entire island gets quite crowded during this time, so be aware.

A fun and fondly anticipated yearly event is the **Kiwanis Club Chili Cookoff** (www.hiltonheadkiwanis.org), held each October at Honey Horn on the south end. A low admission price gets you all the chili you can eat plus free antacids. All funds go to charity, and all excess chili goes to a local food bank.

Every November brings Hilton Head's second-largest event, the **Hilton Head Concours d'Elegance & Motoring Festival** (www.hhiconcours. com), a multiday affair bringing together vintage car clubs from throughout the nation and culminating in a prestigious "Best of Show" competition. It started as a fund-raiser for the Hilton Head Symphony, but now people come from all over the country to see these fine vintage cars in a beautiful setting.

SHOPS

As you'd expect, Hilton Head is a shopper's delight, with an emphasis on upscale stores and prices to match. Keep in mind that hours may be shortened in the off-season (Nov.-Mar.). Here's a rundown of the main island shopping areas in the order you'll encounter them as you enter the island.

Shelter Cove

Shelter Cove Towne Centre (40 Shelter Cove Lane, www.sheltercovetownecentre.com), a wonderfully repurposed former mall space, centers on a Belk anchor store and a Kroger but also offers a growing array of shops and new restaurants and watering holes in this brand new, attractive construction. Shelter Cove Community Park is adjacent, and features a safe playground space for young children and multiuse greenway. Retail highlights include **ArtWare** (23 Shelter Cove Lane, 843/682-3400, www. artwaredesigns.com), a whimsical boutique featuring clothing, home and garden goods, and pet goods, and **Spartina 449** (28 Shelter Cove Lane, 843/342-7722, www.spartina449.com), a women's clothing and accessory store with a distinctive Lowcountry flavor and color palette.

The nearby **Plaza at Shelter Cove** (50 Shelter Cove Lane, www.theplazaatsheltercove.com) features many shops, including a Whole Foods and the flagship location of **Outside Hilton Head** (843/686-6996, www. outsidehiltonhead.com, Mon.-Sat. 10am-5:30pm, Sun. 11am-5:30pm), a complete outdoor outfitter with a knowledgeable staff.

Village at Wexford

This well-shaded shopping center on William Hilton Parkway (U.S. 278), one of the older on the island, hosts plenty of well-tended shops, including the foodie equipment store **Le Cookery** (843/785-7171, Mon.-Sat. 10am-6pm), the Lily Pulitzer signature women's store **S. M. Bradford Co.** (843/686-6161, Mon.-Sat. 10am-6pm), and the aromatic **Scents of Hilton Head** (843/842-7866, Mon.-Fri. 10am-6pm, Sat. 10am-5pm).

My favorite shop at Wexford is **The Oilerie** (843/681-2722, www.oilerie. com, Mon.-Sat. 10am-7pm, Sun. noon-5pm). This franchise provides free samples of all its high-quality Italian olive oils and vinegars. After you taste around awhile, you pick what you want and the friendly staff bottles it for you in souvenir-quality glassware. They also have a selection of spices, soaps, and other goodies.

Coligny Circle

Often called "Hilton Head's downtown" because it was the first shopping area of note on the island, dating back to the 1950s, Coligny is the closest Hilton Head comes to funkier beach towns like Tybee Island or Folly Beach, although it doesn't really come that close. You'll find plenty somewhat quirky stores here, many keeping long hours in the summer, like the self-explanatory **Coligny Kite & Flag Co.** (843/785-5483, Mon.-Sat. 10am-9pm, Sun. 11am-6pm), the comprehensive and stylish **Quiet Storm Surf Shop** (843/671-2551, daily 10am-9pm), and **Fresh Produce** (843/842-3410, www.freshproduceclothes.com, Mon.-Sat. 10am-10pm, Sun. 10am-9pm), actually a very cute women's clothing store. Kids will love both **The Shell Shop** (843/785-4900, Mon.-Sat. 10am-9pm, Sun. noon-9pm) and **Black Market Minerals** (843/785-7090, Mon.-Sat. 10am-10pm, Sun. 11am-8pm). **The Bird's Nest** (843/785-3737) has a great selection of jewelry and fashionable handbags.

Harbour Town

The **Shoppes at Harbour Town** (www.seapines.com) are a collection of about 20 mostly boutique stores along Lighthouse Road in Sea Pines Plantation. At **Planet Hilton Head** (843/363-5177, www.planethiltonhead.com, daily 10am-9pm) you'll find some cute eclectic gifts and home goods. Other clothing highlights include **Knickers Men's Store** (843/671-2291, daily 10am-9pm) and **Radiance** (843/363-5176, Mon.-Tues. 10am-5pm, Wed.-Sat. 10am-9pm, Sun. 11am-9pm), a very cute and fashion-forward women's store.

The **Top of the Lighthouse Shoppe** (843/671-2810, www.harbourtownlighthouse.com, daily 10am-9pm) is where many a climbing visitor has been coaxed to part with some of their disposable income. And, of course, as you'd expect being near the legendary Harbour Town links, there's the **Harbour Town Pro Shop** (843/671-4485, daily 7am-5pm), routinely voted one of the best pro shops in the nation.

South Beach Marina

On South Sea Pines Drive at the marina you'll find several worthwhile shops, including a good marine store and all-around grocery dealer **South Beach General Store** (843/671-6784, daily 8am-10pm). I like to stop in **Blue Water Bait and Tackle** (843/671-3060, daily 7am-8pm) and check out the cool nautical stuff. They can also hook you up with a variety of kayak trips and fishing charters. And, of course, right on the water there's the ever-popular **Salty Dog Cafe** (843/671-2233, www.saltydog.com, lunch daily 11am-3pm, dinner daily 5pm-10pm), whose ubiquitous T-shirts seem to adorn every other person on the island.

SPORTS AND ACTIVITIES
Beaches

First, the good news: Hilton Head Island has 12 miles of some of the most beautiful, safe beaches you'll find anywhere. The bad news is that there are only a few ways to gain access, generally at locations referred to as "beach parks." Don't just drive into a residential neighborhood and think you'll be able to park and find your way to the beach; the vast majority of beach access on the island is in private hands, where trespassing and illegal parking is frowned upon.

Driessen Beach Park has 207 long-term parking spaces, costing $0.25 for 30 minutes. There's free parking but fewer spaces at the Coligny Beach Park entrance and at Fish Haul Creek Park. Also, there are 22 metered spaces at Alder Lane Beach Access, 51 at Folly Field Beach Park, and 13 at Burkes Beach Road. Most other beach parks have permit parking only. Clean, well-maintained public restrooms are available at all the beach parks. You can find **beach information** at 843/342-4580 and www.hiltonheadislandsc. gov. Beach park hours vary: Coligny Beach Park is open daily 24 hours; all other beach parks are open March-September daily 6am-8pm and October-February daily 6am-5pm. Alcohol is strictly prohibited on Hilton Head's beaches.

Kayaking

Kayakers will enjoy Hilton Head Island, which offers several gorgeous routes, including Calibogue Sound to the south and west and Port Royal Sound to the north. For particularly good views of life on the salt marsh, try Broad Creek, which nearly bisects Hilton Head Island, and Skull Creek, which separates Hilton Head from the natural beauty of Pinckney Island. Broad Creek Marina is a good place to put in.

If you want a guided tour, there are plenty of great kayak tour outfits to choose from in the area. Chief among them is **Outside Hilton Head** (32 Shelter Cove Lane, 800/686-6996, www.outsidehiltonhead.com).

Biking

Although the very flat terrain is not challenging, Hilton Head provides some scenic and relaxing cycling opportunities. Thanks to wise planning and foresight, the island has an extensive and award-winning 50-mile network of biking trails that does a great job of keeping cyclists out of traffic.

A big plus is the long bike path paralleling the William Hilton Parkway, enabling cyclists to use that key artery without braving its traffic. There is even an underground bike path beneath the parkway to facilitate crossing that busy road. In addition, there are also routes along Pope Avenue as well as North and South Forest Beach Drive. Go to www.hiltonheadisland.org/biking to download a map of the island's entire bike path network.

3006, www.palmettodunes.com) has a particularly nice 25-mile network
of bike paths that all link up to the island's larger framework.

Within the resort is **Palmetto Dunes Outfitters** (843/785-2449, www.
pdoutfitters.com, daily 9am-5pm), which will rent you any type of bike you
might need. Sea Pines Plantation also has an extensive 17-mile network of
bike trails; you can pick up a map at most information kiosks within the
plantation.

There's a plethora of bike rental facilities on Hilton Head with competitive rates. Be sure to ask if they offer free pickup and delivery. Try **Hilton
Head Bicycle Company** (112 Arrow Rd., 843/686-6888, daily 9am-5pm,
$16 per day).

Horseback Riding

Within the Sea Pines Forest Preserve is **Lawton Stables** (190 Greenwood
Dr., 843/671-2586, www.lawtonstableshhi.com), which features pony rides,
a small-animal farm, and guided horseback rides through the preserve. You
don't need any riding experience, but you do need reservations.

Bird-Watching

The premier birding locale in the area is the **Pinckney Island National
Wildlife Refuge** (U.S. 278 east, just before Hilton Head, 912/652-4415,
www.fws.gov, free). You can see bald eagles, ibis, wood storks, painted buntings, and many more species. Birding is best in spring and fall. The refuge
has several freshwater ponds that serve as wading bird rookeries. During
migration season, so many beautiful birds make such a ruckus that you'll
think you've wandered onto an Animal Planet shoot.

Golf

Hilton Head is one of the world's great golf centers, with no fewer than 23
courses, and one could easily write a book about nothing but that. This,
however, is not that book. Perhaps contrary to what you might expect, most
courses on the island are public, and some are downright affordable. All
courses are 18 holes unless otherwise described; greens fees are averages
and vary with season and tee time.

The best-regarded course, with prices to match, is **Harbour Town
Golf Links** (Sea Pines Plantation, 843/363-4485, www.seapines.com,
$239). It's on the island's south end at Sea Pines and is the home of the
annual RBC Heritage Classic, far and away the island's number-one tourist draw.

There are two Arthur Hills-designed courses on the island, **Arthur
Hills at Palmetto Dunes Resort** (843/785-1140, www.palmettodunes.
com, $125) and **Arthur Hills at Palmetto Hall** (Palmetto Hall Plantation,
843/689-4100, www.palmettohallgolf.com, $130), both of which now offer
the use of Segway vehicles on the fairways. The reasonably priced **Barony
Course** at Port Royal Plantation (843/686-8801, www.portroyalgolfclub.

com, $98) also boasts some of the toughest greens on the island. Another challenging and affordable course is the **George Fazio at Palmetto Dunes** Resort (843/785-1130, www.palmettodunes.com, $105).

It's wise to book tee times through the **Golf Island Call Center** (888/465-3475, www.golfisland.com), which can also hook you up with good packages.

Tennis

One of the top tennis destinations in the country, Hilton Head has over 20 tennis clubs, some of which offer court time to the public (walk-on rates vary; call for information). They are: **Palmetto Dunes Tennis Center** (Palmetto Dunes Resort, 843/785-1152, www.palmettodunes.com, $30 per hour), **Port Royal Racquet Club** (Port Royal Plantation, 843/686-8803, www.portroyalgolfclub.com, $25 per hour), **Sea Pines Racquet Club** (Sea Pines Plantation, 843/363-4495, www.seapines.com, $25 per hour), **South Beach Racquet Club** (Sea Pines Plantation, 843/671-2215, www.seapines.com, $25 per hour), and **Shipyard Racquet Club** (Shipyard Plantation, 843/686-8804, $25 per hour).

Free, first-come, first-served play is available at the following public courts, maintained by the Island Recreation Association (www.islandrec-center.org): **Chaplin Community Park** (Singleton Beach Rd., 4 courts, lighted), **Cordillo Courts** (Cordillo Pkwy., 4 courts, lighted), **Fairfield Square** (Adrianna Lane, 2 courts), **Hilton Head High School** (School Rd., 6 courts), and **Hilton Head Middle School** (Wilborn Rd., 4 courts).

Zip Line

Billing itself as the only zip line experience within 250 miles, the **Zip Line Hilton Head** (33 Broad Creek Marina Way, 843/682-6000, www.ziplinehiltonhead.com) offers an extensive canopy tour making great use of the area's natural scenery and features. You generally "fly" in groups of about eight. Reservations are strongly advised. The latest offering is "Aerial Adventure" ($50), a challenging two-hour trip with about 50 obstacles.

RESTAURANTS

Because of the cosmopolitan nature of the population, with so many transplants from the northeastern United States and Europe, there is uniformly high quality in Hilton Head restaurants. Hilton Head has shed its reputation as a somewhat stodgy food town and does offer some fun, cutting-edge, big city-style spots to enjoy.

Bistro

Combining rib-sticking comfort food with hearty European-style cuisine is ★ **Lucky Rooster** (841 William Hilton Pkwy., 843/681-3474, www.luckyroosterhhi.com, daily 5pm-10pm, $15). This really is one of the most vibrant and satisfying menus on the island, from the fried green tomatoes to the pan-fried sweetbread starters, to the short rib and shrimp and grits and mushroom lasagna entrées. A lively full bar complements the bistro-style scene.

An upgrade of a longtime island favorite called simply Daniel's, **Crave by Daniel's** (2 N. Forest Beach Dr., 843/341-9379, http://danielshhi.com, daily 4pm-2am, $25) is now an upscale steak house with a twist. In addition to offering gorgeous cuts of meat like a center-cut filet mignon, they specialize in what they call "big small plates." Try a sizzling cinnamon steak kebab or a gyro pizzetta.

Breakfast and Brunch

There are a couple of great diner-style places on the island. Though known more for its hamburgers and Philly cheesesteaks, **Harold's Diner** (641 William Hilton Pkwy., 843/842-9292, Mon.-Sat. 7am-3pm, $4-6) has great pancakes as well as its trademark brand of sarcastic service. The place is small, popular, and does not take reservations.

The French Bakery (28 Shelter Cove Lane, 843/342-5420, Mon.-Sat. 7am-4pm, Sun. 8am-3pm, frenchbakeryhiltonhead.com, $12) in the attractive new Shelter Cove Towne Centre is a great breakfast-brunch type spot, with an emphasis on rustic and hearty Euro-inspired breakfast sandwiches (breakfast is served through 11:30am) and various sweet and savory crepes. The lunch salads are outstanding.

If you need a bite in the Coligny Plaza area, go to **Skillets** (1 N. Forest Beach Dr., 843/785-3131, www.skilletscafe.com, breakfast daily 7am-5pm, dinner daily 5pm-9pm, $5-23) in Coligny Plaza. Their eponymous stock-in-trade is a layered breakfast dish of sautéed ingredients served in a porcelain skillet, like the "Kitchen Sink": pancakes ringed with potatoes, sausage, and bacon, topped with two poached eggs.

A great all-day breakfast place with a twist is ★ **Signe's Heaven Bound Bakery & Café** (93 Arrow Rd., 843/785-9118, www.signesbakery.com, Mon.-Fri. 8am-4pm, Sat. 9am-2pm, $5-10). Breakfast is tasty dishes like frittatas and breakfast polenta, while the twist is the extensive artisanal bakery, with delicious specialties like the signature key lime pound cake. Expect a wait during peak periods.

German

I'm pretty sure you didn't come all the way to South Carolina to eat traditional German food, but while you're here, check out ★ **Alfred's** (807 William Hilton Pkwy./U.S. 278, 843/341-3117, wwww.alfredshiltonhead.com, Mon.-Sat. 5pm-11pm, $20-30), one of the more unique spots on Hilton Head and a big favorite with the locals. Expect a wait. Bratwurst, veal cordon bleu, and of course Wiener schnitzel are all standouts. I recommend the German Mix Platter ($25), which features a brat, some sauerbraten, and a schnitzel.

Seafood and Southern

Honest-to-goodness Southern cookin' isn't always that easy to come by on this island full of transplants from outside the South. But a great place to find it is **A Lowcountry Backyard** (32 Palmetto Bay Rd., Suite 4A, www. hhbackyard.com, Mon.-Sat. 11am-3pm and 4:30pm-9pm, Sat. brunch 9am-noon, Sun. brunch 9am-3pm, $15). As the name implies, this is regional cuisine served in a relaxed and casual atmosphere fitting for island life. As with many Hilton Head establishments, it's located within a strip mall setting, the Village Exchange.

Not to be confused with Charley's Crab House next door to Hudson's, seafood lovers will enjoy the experience down near Sea Pines at ★ **Charlie's L'Etoile Verte** (8 New Orleans Rd., 843/785-9277, http:// charliesgreenstar.com, lunch Tues.-Sat. 11:30am-2pm, dinner Mon.-Sat. 5:30pm-10pm, $25-40), which is considered by many connoisseurs to be Hilton Head's single best restaurant. The emphasis here is on "French country kitchen" cuisine—think Provence, not Paris. In keeping with that theme, each day's menu is concocted from scratch and handwritten. Reservations are essential.

A longtime Hilton Head favorite is **Red Fish** (8 Archer Rd., 843/686-3388, www.redfishofhiltonhead.com, lunch Mon.-Sat. 11:30am-2pm, dinner daily beginning with early-bird specials at 5pm, $20-37). Strongly Caribbean in decor as well as menu, with romanticism and panache to match, this is a great place for couples. Reservations are essential.

Fresh seafood lovers will enjoy one of Hilton Head's staples, the huge **Hudson's on the Docks** (1 Hudson Rd., 843/681-2772, www.hudson-sonthedocks.com, lunch daily 11am-4pm, dinner daily from 5pm, $14-23) on Skull Creek just off Squire Pope Road on the less-developed north side. Much of the catch—though not all of it, by any means—comes directly off the boats you'll see dockside. Try the stuffed shrimp filled with crabmeat. Leave room for one of the homemade desserts crafted by Ms. Bessie, a 30-year veteran employee of Hudson's.

HOTELS

Generally speaking, accommodations on Hilton Head are often surprisingly affordable given their overall high quality and the breadth of their amenities.

Under $150

You can't beat the rates at **Park Lane Hotel and Suites** (12 Park Lane, 843/686-5700, www.hiltonheadparklanehotel.com, $130). This is your basic suite-type hotel (formerly a Residence Inn) with kitchens, laundry, a pool, and a tennis court. The allure here is the rates, hard to find anywhere these days at a resort location. For a nonrefundable fee, you can bring your pet. The one drawback is that the beach is a good distance away. The hotel does offer a free shuttle, however, so it would be wise to take advantage of that and avoid the usual beach-parking hassles. As you'd expect given the rates, rooms here tend to go quickly; reserve early.

A great place for the price is the **South Beach Inn** (232 S. Sea Pines Dr., 843/671-6498, www.sbinn.com, $186) in Sea Pines. Located near the famous Salty Dog Cafe and outfitted in a similar nautical theme, the inn not only has some pretty large guest rooms for the rates, it offers a lovely view of the marina and has a very friendly feel. As with all Sea Pines accommodations, staying on the plantation means you don't have to wait in line with other visitors to pay the $5-per-day "road fee." Sea Pines also offers a free trolley to get around the plantation.

One of Hilton Head's favorite hotels for beach lovers is **The Beach House** (1 S. Forest Beach Dr., 855/474-2882, www.beachhousehhi.com, $200), formerly the Holiday Inn Oceanfront and home of the famed Tiki Hut bar on the beach. Staff turnover is less frequent here than at other local accommodations, and while it's no Ritz-Carlton and occasionally shows signs of wear, it's a good value in a bustling area of the island.

One of the better resort-type places for those who prefer the putter and the racquet to the Frisbee and the surfboard is the **Inn and Club at Harbour Town** (7 Lighthouse Lane, 843/363-8100, www.seapines.com, $199) in Sea Pines. The big draw here is the impeccable service, delivered by a staff of "butlers" in kilts, mostly Europeans who take the venerable trade quite seriously. While it's not on the beach, you can take advantage of the free Sea Pines Trolley every 20 minutes.

Recently rated the number one family resort in the United States by *Travel + Leisure* magazine, the well-run ★ **Palmetto Dunes Oceanfront Resort** (4 Queens Folly Rd., 800/827-3006, www.palmettodunes.com, $150-300) offers something for everybody in terms of lodging. There are small, cozy condos by the beach or larger villas overlooking the golf course, and pretty much everything in between. The prices are perhaps disarmingly affordable considering the relative luxury and copious recreational amenities, which include 25 miles of very well-done bike trails, 11 miles of kayak and canoe trails, and, of course, three signature links. As with most developments of this type on Hilton Head, the majority of the condos are privately owned, and therefore each has its own particular set of guidelines and cleaning schedules.

A little farther down the island you'll find the **Sonesta Resort** (130 Shipyard Dr., 843/842-2400, www.sonesta.com/hiltonheadisland, $160-200), which styles itself as Hilton Head's only green-certified accommodations. The guest rooms are indeed state-of-the-art, and the expansive, shaded grounds near the beach are great for relaxation. No on-site golf here, but immediately adjacent is a well-regarded tennis facility with 20 courts.

Another good resort-style experience heavy on the golf is on the grounds of the Port Royal Plantation on the island's north side, **The Westin Resort Hilton Head Island** (2 Grasslawn Ave., 843/681-4000, www.westin.com/hiltonhead, from $200), which hosts three PGA-caliber links. The beach is also but a short walk away. This AAA four diamond-winning Westin offers a mix of suites and larger villas.

Vacation Rentals

Many visitors to Hilton Head choose to rent a home or villa for an extended stay, and there is no scarcity of availability. Try **Resort Rentals of Hilton Head** (www.hhivacations.com) or **Destination Vacation** (www.destinationvacationhhi.com).

TRANSPORTATION AND SERVICES

The best place to get information on Hilton Head, book a room, or secure a tee time is just as you come onto the island at the **Hilton Head Island Chamber of Commerce Welcome Center** (100 William Hilton Pkwy., 843/785-3673, www.hiltonheadisland.org, daily 9am-6pm).

Air

A few years back, the **Savannah/Hilton Head International Airport** (SAV, 400 Airways Ave., Savannah, 912/964-0514, www.savannahairport.com) added Hilton Head to its name specifically to identify itself with that lucrative market. Keep in mind that when your plane touches down in Savannah, you're still about a 45-minute drive to Hilton Head. From the airport, go north on I-95 into South Carolina, and take exit 8 onto U.S. 278 east.

There is a local regional airport as well, the **Hilton Head Island Airport** (HXD, 120 Beach City Rd., 843/689-5400, www.bcgov.net). While attractive and convenient, keep in mind that it only hosts propeller-driven commuter planes because of the runway length and concerns about noise.

Getting Around

Hilton Head Islanders have long referred to their island as the "shoe" and speak of driving to the toe or going to the heel. If you take a look at a map, you'll see why: Hilton Head bears an uncanny resemblance to a running shoe pointed toward the southwest, with the aptly named Broad Creek forming a near facsimile of the Nike "swoosh" symbol.

Running the length and circumference of the shoe is the main drag, U.S. 278 Business (William Hilton Parkway), which crosses onto Hilton Head right at the "tongue" of the shoe, a relatively undeveloped area. The Cross Island Parkway toll route (U.S. 278), beginning up toward the ankle as you first get on the island, is a quicker route straight to the toe near Sea Pines.

While making your way around the island, always keep in mind that the bulk of it consists of private developments, and local law enforcement frowns on people who aimlessly wander among the condos and villas.

Other than taxi services, there is no public transportation in Hilton Head, unless you want to count the free shuttle around Sea Pines Plantation. Taxi services include **Yellow Cab** (843/686-6666), **Island Taxi** (843/683-6363), and **Ferguson Transportation** (843/842-8088).

The Golden Isles

On a map it looks relatively short, but Georgia's coastline is the longest contiguous salt marsh environment in the world—a third of the country's remaining salt marsh. Abundant with wildlife, vibrant with exotic, earthy aromas, constantly refreshed by a steady, salty sea breeze, it's a place with no real match anywhere else.

Ancient Native Americans held the area in special regard. Avaricious for gold as they were, the Spanish also admired the almost monastic enchantment of Georgia's coast, choosing it as the site of their first colony in North America. They built a subsequent chain of Roman Catholic missions, now long gone.

While the American tycoons who used these barrier islands as personal playgrounds had avarice of their own, we must give credit where it's due: Their self-interest kept these places largely untouched by the kind of development that has plagued many of South Carolina's barrier islands to the north.

HISTORY

For over 5,000 years, the Golden Isles of what would become Georgia were an abundant food and game source for Native Americans. In those days, long before erosion and channel dredging had taken their toll, each barrier island was an easy canoe ride away from the next one—a sort of early Intracoastal Waterway—and there was bounty for everyone. But all that changed in 1526 when the Golden Isles became the site of the first European settlement in what is now the continental United States, the fabled San Miguel de Gualdape, founded nearly a century before the first English settlements in Virginia. Historians remain unsure where expedition leader Lucas de Ayllón actually set up camp with his 600 colonists and enslaved people, but recent research breakthroughs have put it somewhere around St. Catherine's Sound. San Miguel disintegrated within a couple of months, but it set the stage for a lengthy Spanish presence on the Georgia coast that culminated in the mission period (1580-1684). With cooperation from the coastal chiefdoms of Guale and Mocama, almost all of Georgia's barrier islands and many interior spots hosted Catholic missions, each with an accompanying contingent of Spanish regulars. The missions began retreating with the English incursion into the American Southeast in the 1600s, and the coast was largely free of European presence until an early English outpost, Fort King George near modern-day Darien, Georgia, was established decades later in 1721. Isolated and hard to provision, the small fort was abandoned seven years later.

The next English project was Fort Frederica on St. Simons Island, commissioned by General James Edward Oglethorpe following his establishment of Savannah to the north. Oglethorpe's settlement of Brunswick and Jekyll Island came soon afterward. With the final vanquishing of the Spanish at the Battle of Bloody Marsh near Fort Frederica, the Georgia

The Golden Isles

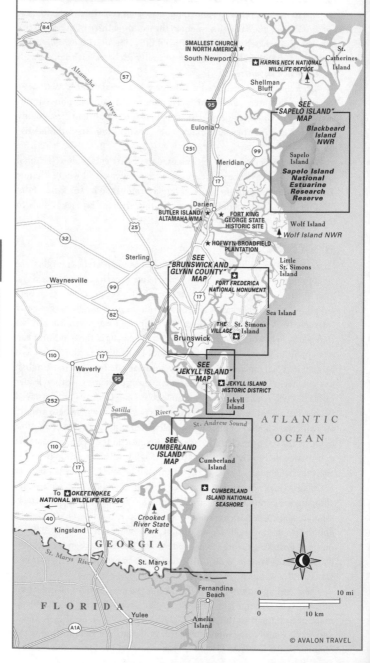

coast quickly emulated the profitable rice-based plantation culture of the South Carolina Lowcountry, and indeed many notable Carolina planters expanded their holdings with marshland on the Georgia coast.

During the Civil War the southern reaches of Sherman's March to the Sea came down as far as Darien, a once vital trading port that was burned to the ground by Union troops. With slavery gone and the plantation system in disarray, the coast's African American population was largely left to its own devices. Although the famous "40 acres and a mule" land and wealth redistribution plan for freed enslaved people would not come to fruition, the black population of Georgia's Sea Islands, like that of South Carolina's, developed an inward-looking culture that persists to this day. The generic term for this culture is Gullah, but in Georgia you'll also hear it referred to as Geechee, local dialect for the nearby Ogeechee River.

As with much of the South after the Civil War, business carried on, with the area becoming a center for lumber, the turpentine trade, and an increasing emphasis on fishing and shrimping. But by the start of the 20th century, the Golden Isles had become firmly established as a playground for the rich, who hunted and dined on the sumptuous grounds of exclusive retreats such as the Jekyll Island Club.

As it did elsewhere, World War II brought new economic growth in the form of military bases, even as German U-boats ranged off the coast. Today the federal presence is most obvious in the massive Trident submarine base at Kings Bay toward the Florida border.

BRUNSWICK AND GLYNN COUNTY

Consider Brunswick sort of a junior Savannah, sharing with that larger city to the north a heavily English flavor, great manners, a city plan with squares courtesy of General James Oglethorpe, a thriving but environmentally intrusive seaport, and a busy shrimping fleet. Despite an admirable effort at downtown revitalization, most visitors to the area seem content to employ Brunswick, as its nickname implies, as a "Gateway to the Golden Isles" rather than as a destination in itself.

Sights
BRUNSWICK HISTORIC DISTRICT
Most of the visitor-friendly activity centers on **Newcastle Street,** where you'll find the bulk of the galleries, shops, and restored buildings. Adjacent in the historic areas are some nice residential homes.

The new pride of downtown is **Old City Hall** (1212 Newcastle St., 912/265-4032, www.brunswickgeorgia.net), an amazing circa-1889 Richardsonian Romanesque edifice designed by noted regional architect Alfred Eichberg, who also planned many similarly imposing buildings in Savannah. Today it doubles as a rental event facility as well as a part-time courthouse; call ahead to look inside.

Another active restored building is the charming **Ritz Theatre** (1530 Newcastle St., 912/262-6934, www.goldenislearts.org), built in 1898

Brunswick and Glynn County

Brunswick River

To Jekyll Island

Mary Ross Waterfront Park

BAY ST

GLOUCESTER ST

4TH AVE

ALBEMARLE ST

GLYNN AVE

Overlook Park

Marshes of Glynn Park

MLK JR BLVD

NEWCASTLE ST

EGMONT ST

4TH ST

ALTAMA AVE

MLK ST

Brunswick

OCEAN HWY

SEE "BRUNSWICK" MAP

F.J. TORRAS CAUSEWAY

To Hofwyl-Broadfield Plantation and Darien

ST. SIMONS CAUSEWAY

Mackay River

Frederica River

Lanier Island

St. Simons Island

Dunbar Creek

SEA ISLAND RD

FREDERICA RD

DEMERE RD

KINGS WAY

FREDERICA RD

St. Simons Sound

Jekyll Island

THE VILLAGE
QUEENS COURT
RAFTERS/ PALMER'S
J. MAC'S
VISITORS CENTER
ST. SIMONS INN BY THE LIGHTHOUSE
ST. SIMONS LIGHTHOUSE
ST. SIMONS LIGHTHOUSE MUSEUM
KING AND PRINCE BEACH AND GOLF RESORT

EPWORTH BY THE SEA

VILLAGE INN AND PUB

MALCOLM MCKINNON AIRPORT

BLOODY MARSH BATTLEFIELD

DEMERE RD

OCEAN BLVD

FREDERICA RD

Massengale Park

East Beach

To FORT FREDERICA NATIONAL MONUMENT and Lodge on Little St. Simons Island

THE SEA ISLAND RESORT/ THE CLOISTER

SEA ISLAND DR

Sea Island

ATLANTIC OCEAN

0
0

1 km

1 mi

© AVALON TRAVEL

Brunswick

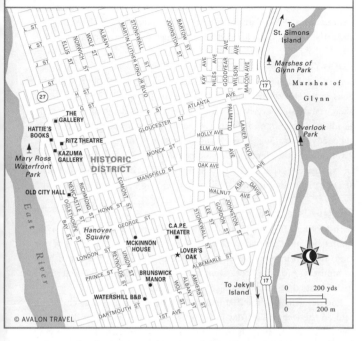

to house the Grand Opera House and the offices of the Brunswick and Birmingham Railroad. This ornate three-story Victorian transitioned with the times, becoming a vaudeville venue, then a movie house.

MARY ROSS WATERFRONT PARK

Mary Ross Waterfront Park, a downtown gathering place at Bay and Gloucester Streets, also has economic importance as a center of local industry—it's here where Brunswick's shrimp fleet is often moored and the town's large port facilities begin. In 1989 the park was dedicated to Mary Ross, member of a longtime Brunswick shrimping family and author of the popular Georgia history book *The Debatable Land.* At the entrance is a nice replica of a World War II Liberty Ship, a cargo vessel of the type which was manufactured in Brunswick for the war effort.

LOVER'S OAK

At the intersection of Prince and Albany Streets is the **Lover's Oak,** a nearly 1,000-year-old tree. Local lore says it has been a secret meeting place for young lovers for centuries, though one does wonder how much of a secret it actually could have been. It's about 13 feet in diameter and has 10 sprawling limbs.

Amid the light industrial sprawl of this area of the Golden Isles Parkway is the interesting little **Overlook Park,** just south of the visitors center on U.S. 17—a good, if loud, place for a picnic. From the park's picnic grounds or overlook you can see the fabled **Marshes of Glynn,** which inspired Georgia poet Sidney Lanier to write his famous poem of the same title under the **Lanier Oak,** located a little farther up the road in the median.

HOFWYL-BROADFIELD PLANTATION

South Carolina doesn't own the patent on well-preserved old rice plantations, as the **Hofwyl-Broadfield Plantation** (5556 U.S. 17, 912/264-7333, www.gastateparks.org, Wed.-Sun. 9am-5pm, last main house tour 4pm, $8 adults, $5 children), a short drive north of Brunswick, proves. With its old paddy fields along the gorgeous and relatively undeveloped Altamaha River estuary, the plantation's main home is an antebellum wonder, with an expansive porch and a nice house museum that includes silver, a model of a rice plantation, and a slide show. There's also a pleasant nature trail.

Festivals and Events

Each Mother's Day at noon, parishioners of the local St. Francis Xavier Church hold the **Our Lady of Fatima Processional and Blessing of the Fleet** (www.brunswick.net), begun in 1938 by the local Portuguese fishing community. After the procession, at about 3pm at Mary Ross Waterfront Park, comes the actual blessing of the shrimping fleet.

Foodies will enjoy the **Brunswick Stewbilee** ($9 adults, $4 children), held on the second Saturday in October 11:30am-3pm. Pro and amateur chefs showcase their skills in creating the local signature dish and vying for the title of "Brunswick Stewmaster." There are also car shows, contests, displays, and much live music.

Shops

Right in the heart of the bustle on Newcastle is a good indie bookstore, **Hattie's Books** (1531 Newcastle St., 912/554-8677, www.hattiesbooks.com, Mon.-Fri. 10am-5:30pm, Sat. 10am-4pm). Not only do they have a good selection of local and regional authors, you can also get a good cup of coffee.

Like Beaufort, South Carolina, Brunswick has made the art gallery a central component of its downtown revitalization, with nearly all of them on Newcastle Street. Near Hattie's you'll find the **Ritz Theatre** (1530 Newcastle St., 912/262-6934, Tues.-Fri. 9am-5pm, Sat. 10am-2pm), which has its own art gallery inside. Farther down is **The Gallery on Newcastle Street** (1626 Newcastle St., 912/554-0056, www.thegalleryonnewcastle. com, Thurs.-Sat. 11am-5pm), showcasing the original oils of owner Janet Powers.

Restaurants

Brunswick isn't known for its breadth of cuisine options, and, frankly, most discriminating diners make the short drive over the causeway to St. Simons Island. One exception in Brunswick that really stands out, however,

Brunswick Stew

Virginians insist that the distinctive Southern dish known as Brunswick stew was named for Brunswick County, Virginia, in 1828, where a political rally featured stew made from squirrel meat. But all real Southern foodies know the dish is named for Brunswick, Georgia. Hey, there's a plaque to prove it in downtown Brunswick—although it says the first pot was cooked on July 2, 1898, on St. Simons Island, not in Brunswick at all. However, I think we can all agree that "Brunswick stew" rolls off the tongue much more easily than "St. Simons stew." You can find the famous pot in which the first batch was cooked on F Street near Mary Ross Waterfront Park.

It seems likely that what we now know as Brunswick stew is based on an old colonial recipe, adapted from Native Americans, that relied on the meat of small game—originally squirrel or rabbit but nowadays mostly chicken or pork—along with vegetables like corn, onions, and okra simmered over an open fire. Today, this tangy, thick, tomato-based delight is a typical accompaniment to barbecue throughout the Lowcountry and the Georgia coast, as well as a freestanding entrée on its own. Here's a typical recipe from Glynn County, home of the famous Brunswick Stewbilee festival held the second Saturday of October:

Sauce
Melt ¼ cup butter over low heat, then add:
1¾ cups ketchup
¼ cup yellow mustard
¼ cup white vinegar
Blend until smooth, then add:
½ tablespoon chopped garlic
1 teaspoon ground black pepper
½ teaspoon crushed red pepper
½ ounce Liquid Smoke
1 ounce Worcestershire sauce
1 ounce hot sauce
½ tablespoon fresh lemon juice
Blend until smooth, then add:
¼ cup dark brown sugar
Stir constantly and simmer for 10 minutes, being careful not to boil. Set aside.

Stew
Melt ¼ pound butter in a two-gallon pot, then add:
3 cups diced small potatoes
1 cup diced small onion
2 14½-ounce cans chicken broth
1 pound baked chicken
8-10 ounces smoked pork
Bring to a boil, stirring until potatoes are nearly done, then add:
1 8½-ounce can early peas
2 14½-ounce cans stewed tomatoes
1 16-ounce can baby lima beans
¼ cup Liquid Smoke
1 14½-ounce can creamed corn
Stir in sauce. Simmer slowly for two hours. Makes one gallon of stew.

is **Indigo Coastal Shanty** (1402 Reynolds St., 912/265-2007, www.indigo-coastalshanty.com, Tues.-Thurs. 11am-3pm, Fri. 11am-3pm and 5pm-10pm, Sat. 5pm-10pm, $12). This friendly, smallish place specializes in creative coastal themes, with dishes like the Charleston Sauté (shrimp and ham with peppers), Fisherman's Bowl (shrimp and fish in a nice broth), and even that old Southern favorite, a pimento cheeseburger.

Hotels

In addition to the usual variety of chain hotels—most of which you should stay far away from—there are some nice places to stay in Brunswick at very reasonable prices if you want to make the city a base of operations. In the heart of Old Town in a gorgeous Victorian is the ★ **McKinnon House** (1001 Egmont St., 912/261-9100, www.mckinnonhousebandb.com, $125), which had a cameo role in the 1974 film *Conrack*. Today, this bed-and-breakfast is Jo Miller's labor of love, a three-suite affair with some plush interiors and an exterior that is one of Brunswick's most photographed spots. Surprisingly affordable for its elegance, the **WatersHill Bed & Breakfast** (728 Union St., 912/264-4262, www.watershill.com, $100) serves a full breakfast and offers a choice of five themed suites, such as the French country Elliot Wynell Room or the large Mariana Mahlaney Room way up in the restored attic. Another good B&B is the **Brunswick Manor** (825 Egmont St., 912/265-6889, www.brunswickmanor.com, $130), offering four suites in a classic Victorian and a tasty meal each day.

The most unique lodging in the area is the ★ **Hostel in the Forest** (Hwy. 82, 912/264-9738, www.foresthostel.com, $25, cash only). Formed more than 30 years ago as an International Youth Hostel, the place initially gives off a hippie vibe, with an evening communal meal (included in the rates) and a near-total ban on cell phones. But don't expect a wild time: No pets are allowed, the hostel discourages young children, and quiet time is strictly enforced beginning at 11pm. To reach the hostel, take I-95 exit 29 and go west for two miles. Make a U-turn at the intersection at mile marker 11. Continue east on Highway 82 for 0.5 miles. Look for a dirt road on the right with a gate and signage. This is now a "membership" organization, so you'll need to join before booking.

Transportation and Services

Brunswick is directly off I-95. Take exit 38 to the Golden Isles Parkway, and take a right on U.S. 17. The quickest way to the historic district is to make a right onto Gloucester Street. Plans and funding for a citywide public transit system are pending, but currently Brunswick has no public transportation.

A downtown **information station** (912/262-6934, Tues.-Fri. 9am-5pm, Sat. 10am-2pm) is in the Ritz Theatre (1530 Newcastle St.).

The newspaper of record in town is the *Brunswick News* (www.the-brunswicknews.com). The main **post office** (805 Gloucester St., 912/280-1250) is downtown.

Jekyll Island

Driftwood Beach

CLAM CREEK PICNIC AREA

Brunswick River

North Beach

JEKYLL ISLAND

HORTON HOUSE TABBY RUINS

MAJOR HORTON RD

N BEACHVIEW DR

N RIVERVIEW DR

Jekyll Creek

CAPTAIN WYLLY RD

To Brunswick

GEORGIA SEA TURTLE CENTER

JEKYLL ISLAND CLUB/ COURTYARD AT CRANE

STABLE RD

JEKYLL ISLAND GOLF RESORT

PIER RD

WELCOME CENTER

JEKYLL ISLAND CAUSEWAY

CAFÉ SOLTERRA

SHELL RD

JEKYLL ISLAND HISTORIC DISTRICT

TOLL STATION

TIDELANDS 4-H CENTER

SUMMER WAVES

Jekyll Sound

HAMPTON INN & SUITES JEKYLL ISLAND

St. Andrews Park

Intracoastal Waterway

S RIVERVIEW DR

S BEACHVIEW DR

South Dunes

ATLANTIC OCEAN

0   1 mi

0   1 km

© AVALON TRAVEL

Few places in the United States have as paradoxical a story as Jekyll Island (www.jekyllisland.com). Once the playground of the world's richest people—whose indulgence allowed the island to escape the overdevelopment that plagues nearby St. Simons—Jekyll then became a dedicated vacation area for Georgians of modest means, by order of the state legislature. Today, it's somewhere in the middle—a great place for a relaxing nature-oriented vacation that retains some of the perks of luxury of its Gilded Age pedigree.

After securing safe access to the island from the Creek people in 1733, Georgia's founder, General James Oglethorpe, gave the island its modern name, after his friend Sir Joseph Jekyll. In 1858, Jekyll Island was the final port of entry for the infamous voyage of *The Wanderer,* the last American slave ship. After intercepting the ship and its contraband manifest of 409 enslaved Africans—the importation of enslaved people having been banned in 1808—its owners and crew were put on trial and acquitted in Savannah.

As a home away from home for the country's richest industrialists—including J. P. Morgan, William Rockefeller, and William Vanderbilt—in the late 1800s and early 1900s, Jekyll Island was the unlikely seat of some of the most crucial events in modern American history. It was at the Jekyll Island Club in 1910 that the Federal Reserve banking system was set up, the result of a secret convocation of investors and tycoons. Five years later on the grounds of the club, AT&T president Theodore Vail would listen in on the first transcontinental phone call.

Orientation

You'll have to stop at the entrance gate and pay a $6 "parking fee" to gain daily access to this state-owned island; a weeklong pass is $28. (Bicyclists and pedestrians don't need to pay.) Debit and credit cards are accepted.

As the smallest of Georgia's barrier islands, Jekyll is very easy to get around on. North and South Beachview Roads essentially circle the perimeter of the island, with dedicated, separate bike paths more or less paralleling that route.

Sights

★ JEKYLL ISLAND HISTORIC DISTRICT

A living link to one of the most glamorous eras of American history, the **Jekyll Island Historic District** is also one of the largest ongoing restoration projects in the southeastern United States. A visit to this 240-acre riverfront area is like stepping back in time to the Gilded Age, with croquet grounds, manicured gardens, and even ferry boats with names like the *Rockefeller* and the *J. P. Morgan.* The historic district essentially comprises the buildings and grounds of the old **Jekyll Island Club,** not only a full-service resort complex—consisting of the main building and several amazing "cottages" that are mansions themselves—but a sort of living-history exhibit chronicling that time when Jekyll was a gathering place for the world's richest and most influential people.

The Queen Anne-style main clubhouse, with its iconic turret, dates from 1886. Within a couple of years the club had already outgrown it, and the millionaires began building the ornate cottages on the grounds surrounding it. In 2000 renovations were done on the most magnificent outbuilding, the 24-bedroom Crane Cottage, a Mediterranean villa that also hosts a fine restaurant. Other historic outbuildings are used as charming little shops.

GEORGIA SEA TURTLE CENTER

Within the historic district in a whimsically renovated 1903 building is the **Georgia Sea Turtle Center** (214 Stable Rd., 912/635-4444, www.georgia-seaturtlecenter.org, daily 9am-5pm, $8 adults, $6 children), which features interactive exhibits on these important marine creatures, for whom Jekyll Island is a major nesting ground. Don't miss the attached rehabilitation building, where you can see the center's turtles in various states of treatment and rehabilitation before they are released into the wild. Children and adults alike will enjoy this unique opportunity to see these creatures up close and learn about the latest efforts to protect them.

In an effort to raise awareness about the need to protect the nesting areas of the big loggerheads that lay eggs on Jekyll each summer, the Sea Turtle Center also guides **nighttime tours** (early June-Aug. daily 8:30pm

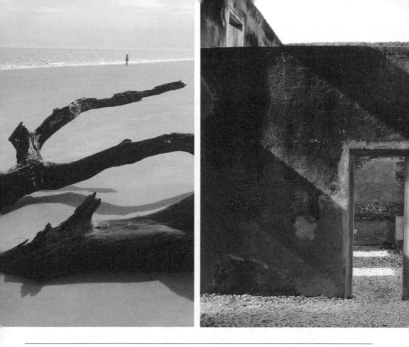

Clockwise from top left: Jekyll's Driftwood Beach; the tabby ruins of the Horton House; the legendary Jekyll Island Club.

and 9:30pm) on the beach in order to explain about the animals and their habitat and hopefully to see some loggerheads in action. These tours fill up fast, so make reservations in advance.

DRIFTWOOD BEACH

Barrier islands like Jekyll are in a constant state of southward flux as currents erode the north end and push sand down the beach to the south end. This phenomenon has created **Driftwood Beach,** as the soil has eroded from under the large trees, causing them to fall and settle into the sand. In addition to being a naturalist's wonderland, it's also a starkly beautiful and strangely romantic spot. Drive north on Beachview Drive until you see a pullover on your right immediately after the Villas by the Sea (there's no signage). Park and take the short trail through the maritime forest, and you'll find yourself right there among the fallen trees and sand. Dogs are allowed on Driftwood Beach, off-leash as long as they are under voice control.

HORTON HOUSE TABBY RUINS

Round the curve and go south on Riverview Drive, and you'll see the large frame of a two-story house on the left (east) side of the road. That is the magnificent tabby ruins of the old **Horton House,** built by Jekyll's original English-speaking settler, William Horton. The house has survived two wars, a couple of hurricanes, and a clumsy restoration in 1898. Its current state of preservation is thanks to the Jekyll Island Authority and various federal, state, and local partners.

Frenchman Christophe Poulain du Bignon would live in the Horton House for a while after purchasing the island in the 1790s. Across the street from the house is the poignant little **Du Bignon Cemetery,** around which winds a nicely done pedestrian and bike path overlooking one of the most beautiful areas of marsh you'll see in all the Golden Isles.

Nightlife

There's not much nightlife on Jekyll, it being intended for quiet, affordable daytime relaxation. The focus instead is on several annual events held at the **Jekyll Island Convention Center** (1 N. Beachview Dr., 912/635-3400), which has undergone a massive restoration to bring it in line with modern convention standards. The convention center itself is part of a dramatic new reinvestment called the Jekyll Island Beach Village, which comprises the convention center, a retail area, and the new Westin hotel.

Festivals and Events

At the beginning of the New Year comes one of the area's most beloved and well-attended events, the **Jekyll Island Bluegrass Festival** (www. adamsbluegrass.com). Many of the genre's biggest traditional names come to play at this casual multiday gathering. The focus here is on the music, not the trappings, so come prepared to enjoy wall-to-wall bluegrass played by the best in the business.

Jekyll Island's Millionaires' Club

After the Civil War, as the Industrial Revolution gathered momentum seemingly everywhere but Georgia's Golden Isles, a couple of men decided to do something to break the foggy miasma of Reconstruction that had settled into the area and make some money in the process. In the late 1870s, John Eugene DuBignon and his brother-in-law Newton Finney came up with a plan to combine DuBignon's long family ties to Jekyll with Finney's extensive Wall Street connections in order to turn Jekyll into an exclusive winter hunting club. Their targeted clientele was a no-brainer: the newly minted American mega-tycoons of the Industrial Age. Finney found 53 such elite millionaires willing to pony up to become charter members of the venture, dubbed the Jekyll Island Club. Among them were William Vanderbilt, J. P. Morgan, and Joseph Pulitzer. As part of the original business model, in 1886 Finney purchased the island from DuBignon for $125,000.

With the formal opening two years later began Jekyll Island's half century as a premier playground for the country's richest citizens, centered on the Victorian winter homes, called "cottages," built by each member and preserved today in the historic district.

In 1910, secret meetings of the so-called "First Name Club" led to the development of the Aldrich Plan, which laid the groundwork for the modern Federal Reserve System. A few years later, AT&T president Theodore Vail, nursing a broken leg at his Mound Cottage on Jekyll, participated in the first transcontinental telephone call on January 25, 1915, among New York City, San Francisco, and the special line strung down the coast from New York and across Jekyll Sound to the club grounds. Also on the line were the telephone's inventor, Alexander Graham Bell, his assistant Thomas Watson, the mayors of New York and San Francisco, and President Woodrow Wilson.

The millionaires continued to frolic on Jekyll through the Great Depression, but worsening international economic conditions reduced the club's numbers, even though the cost of membership was lowered in 1933. The outbreak of World War II and the resulting drain of labor into the armed forces put a further cramp in the club's workings, and it finally closed for good in 1942. The state would acquire the island after the war in 1947, turning the once-exclusive playground of millionaires into a playground for all the people.

In September as the harvest comes in off the boats, the **Wild Georgia Shrimp and Grits Festival** (www.jekyllisland.com, free admission) promotes the value of the Georgia shrimping industry by focusing on how good the little critters taste in various regional recipes.

Shops

The best bet for unique shopping opportunities on Jekyll is in the Historic District near the Jekyll Island Club, in the collection of venues called the **Pier Road Shops.** These are in various cute historic outbuildings. Highlights include the tiny but fun Goodyear Shop, featuring arts and crafts from Jekyll Island Art Association members, and Gypsea Glass, for individually handblown art glass items.

The new Beach Village shops, in the area of the Convention Center and the new Westin, include **Kennedy Outfitters** (31 Main St., 912/319-2079) for your outdoorsy needs, and **Whittle's Gift Shop** (31 Main St., 912/635-2552) for trinkets and fun stuff.

Sports and Activities
HIKING AND BIKING

Quite simply, Jekyll Island is a paradise for bicyclists and walkers, with a well-developed and very safe system of paths totaling about 20 miles and running the circumference of the island. The paths go by all major sights, including the Jekyll Island Club in the historic district. In addition, walkers and bicyclists can enjoy much of the seven miles of beachfront at low tide.

GOLF AND TENNIS

True to Jekyll Island's intended role as a playground for Georgians of low to medium income, its golf and tennis facilities—all centrally located at the middle of the island—are quite reasonably priced. The **Jekyll Island Golf Resort** (322 Captain Wylly Rd., 912/635-2368, www.jekyllisland.com, greens fees $40-60) is the largest public golf resort in Georgia. A total of 63 holes on four courses—Pine Lakes, Indian Mound, Oleander, and Ocean Dunes (nine holes)—await. Check the resort's website for "golf passport" packages that include local lodging.

The adjacent **Jekyll Island Tennis Center** (400 Captain Wylly Rd., 912/635-3154, $25 per hour) boasts 13 courts, 7 of them lighted, as well as a pro shop (daily 9am-6pm). Reservations are required for court time.

Great Dunes (100 Great Dune Lane, 912/635-2170, $15-25) offers both a 9-hole course and a cute and well-lit mini-golf course ($6.50 per round).

WATER PARKS

Summer Waves (210 S. Riverview Dr., 912/635-2074, www.jekyllisland.com, Memorial Day-Labor Day, $20 adults, $16 children under 48 inches tall) is just what the doctor ordered for kids with a surplus of energy. The 11-acre facility has a separate section for toddlers to splash around in, with the requisite more daring rides for hard-charging preteens. Hours vary, so call ahead.

HORSEBACK RIDING AND TOURS

Three Oaks Carriage and Trail (Clam Creek Rd., 912/635-9500, www.threeoaksfarm.org) offers numerous options. Horseback rides include guided beach rides (from $58 pp). These leave from the Clam Creek Picnic Area on the north end of the island, directly across the street from the Jekyll Island Campground. Horse-drawn carriage tours with a guide leave from the river side of the Jekyll Island Club and start at $15pp for daytime tours, with private evening tours at $40 for two people.

The **Tidelands 4-H Center** (912/635-5032) gives 1.5- to 2-hour Marsh Walks (Mon. 9am, $5 adults, $3 children) leaving from Clam Creek Picnic Area, and Beach Walks ($5 adults, $3 children) leaving at 9am Wednesday

Restaurants

Culinary offerings are few and far between on Jekyll. I'd suggest you patronize one of the dining facilities at the **Jekyll Island Club** (371 Riverview Dr.), which are all open to nonguests. They're not only delicious but pretty reasonable as well, considering the swank setting. My favorite is the ★ **Courtyard at Crane** (912/635-2400, lunch Sun.-Fri. 11am-4pm, Sat. 11am-2pm, dinner Sun.-Thurs. 5:30pm-9pm, $27-38). Located in the circa-1917 Crane Cottage, one of the beautifully restored tycoon villas, the Courtyard offers romantic evening dining (call for reservations) as well as tasty and stylish lunch dining in the alfresco courtyard area or inside.

For a real and figurative taste of history, make a reservation at the **Grand Dining Room** (912/635-2400, breakfast Mon.-Sat. 7am-11am, Sun. 7am-10am, lunch Mon.-Sat. 11:30am-2pm, brunch Sun. 10:45am-2pm, dinner daily 6pm-10pm, dinner $26-35), the club's full-service restaurant. Focusing on continental cuisine—ordered either à la carte or as a prix fixe "sunset dinner"—the Dining Room features a pianist each evening and for Sunday brunch. Jackets or collared shirts are required for men.

For a tasty breakfast, lunch, or dinner on the go or at odd hours, check out **Café Solterra** (912/635-2600, daily 7am-10pm, $8-12), great for deli-type food and equipped with Starbucks coffee.

There is a great riverfront dining place within a stone's throw of the Jekyll Island Club: **The Wharf** (371 Riverview Dr., 912/635-3612, www.jekyllwharf.com, Tues.-Sun. 11:30am-9:30pm, $12-25) is an upscale seafood-oriented spot with frequent live music. Go for the chilled seafood platter.

Hotels

UNDER $150

The **Days Inn** (60 S. Beachview Dr., 912/635-9800, www.daysinnjekyll.com, $100) has undergone remodeling lately and is the best choice if budget is a concern (and you don't want to camp, that is). It has a good location on the south side of the island with nice ocean views.

$150-300

Any discussion of lodging on Jekyll Island begins with the legendary ★ **Jekyll Island Club** (371 Riverview Dr., 800/535-9547, www.jekyllclub.com, $199-490), which is reasonably priced considering its history, postcard-perfect setting, and delightful guest rooms. Some of its 157 guest rooms in the club and annex areas are available for under $200. There are 60 guest rooms in the main club building, and several outlying cottages, chief among them the Crane, Cherokee, and Sans Souci Cottages, are also available. All rates include use of the big outdoor pool overlooking the river, and a neat amenity is a choice of meal plans for an extra daily fee.

The first hotel built on the island in 35 years, the ★ **Hampton Inn &**

Suites Jekyll Island (200 S. Beachview Dr., 912/635-3733, www.hampton inn.com, $180-210) was constructed according to an exacting set of conservation guidelines, conserving much of the original tree canopy and employing various low-impact design and building techniques. It's one of the best eco-friendly hotel designs I've experienced.

The **Westin Jekyll Island** (110 Ocean Way, 912/635-4545, www.westinjekyllisland.com, $200) is part of the larger Jekyll Island Beach Village development, essentially one of the first things you encounter when first coming on the island. These rooms are the newest on the island and range from large ocean-view suites to smaller "coastal studio suites."

CAMPING

One of the niftiest campgrounds in the area is the **Jekyll Island Campground** (197 Riverview Dr., 912/635-3021, tent sites $26, RV sites $41). It's a friendly place with an excellent location at the north end of the island. There are more than 150 sites, from tent to full-service pull-through RV sites. There's a two-night minimum on weekends and a three-night minimum on holiday and special-event weekends; reservations are recommended.

Transportation and Services

Jekyll Island is immediately south of Brunswick. You'll have to pay a $6 per vehicle fee to get onto the island. Once on the island, most sites are on the north end (a left as you reach the dead-end at Beachview Dr.). The main circuit route around the island is Beachview Drive, which suitably enough changes into Riverview Drive as it rounds the bend to landward at the north end.

Many visitors choose to bicycle around the island once they're here, which is certainly the best way to experience both the sights and the beach itself at low tide.

The **Jekyll Island Visitor Center** (901 Downing Musgrove Causeway, 912/635-3636, daily 9am-5pm) is on the long causeway along the marsh before you get to the island. Set in a charming little cottage it shares with the Georgia State Patrol, the center has a nice gift shop and loads of brochures on the entire Golden Isles region.

ST. SIMONS ISLAND

Despite a reputation for aloof affluence, the truth is that St. Simons Island is also very visitor-friendly, and there's more to do here than meets the eye.

Fort Frederica, now a National Monument, was a key base of operations for the British struggle to evict the Spanish from Georgia—which culminated in 1742 in the decisive Battle of Bloody Marsh. In the years after American independence, St. Simons woke up from its slumber as acre after acre of virgin live oak was felled to make the massive timbers of new warships for the U.S. Navy, including the USS *Constitution*. In their place was

And now from the Vast of the Lord will the waters of sleep
Roll in on the souls of men,
But who will reveal to our waking ken
The forms that swim and the shapes that creep
Under the waters of sleep?
And I would I could know what swimmeth below when the tide
comes in
On the length and the breadth of the marvelous marshes of Glynn.

Sidney Lanier

Many authors have been inspired by their time in the Golden Isles, whether to pen flights of poetic fancy, page-turning novels, or politically oriented chronicles. Here are a few of the most notable names:

- **Sidney Lanier:** Born in Macon, Georgia, Lanier was a renowned linguist, mathematician, and legal scholar. Fighting for the Confederacy during the Civil War, he was captured while commanding a blockade runner and taken to a POW camp in Maryland, where he came down with tuberculosis. After the war, he stayed at his brother-in-law's house in Brunswick to recuperate, and it was during that time that he took up poetry, writing the famous "Marshes of Glynn," quoted above.

- **Eugenia Price:** Although not originally from St. Simons, Price remains the best-known local cultural figure, setting her *St. Simons Trilogy* here. After relocating to the island in 1965, she stayed here until her death in 1996. She's buried in the Christ Church cemetery on Frederica Road.

- **Tina McElroy Ansa:** Probably the most notable literary figure currently living on St. Simons Island is award-winning African American author Tina McElroy Ansa. Few of her books are set in the Golden Isles region, but they all deal with life in the South, and Ansa is an ardent devotee of St. Simons and its relaxed, friendly ways.

- **Fanny Kemble:** In 1834, this renowned English actress married Georgia plantation heir Pierce Butler, who would become one of the largest slave owners in the United States. Horrified by the treatment of the enslaved people at Butler Island, just south of Darien, Georgia, Kemble penned one of the earliest antislavery chronicles, *Journal of a Residence on a Georgian Plantation in 1838-1839*. Kemble's disagreement with her husband over slavery hastened their divorce in 1849.

planted a new crop—cotton. The island's antebellum plantations boomed to world-class heights of profit and prestige when the superior strain of the crop known as Sea Island cotton came in the 1820s.

The next landmark development for St. Simons didn't come until the building of the first causeway in 1924, which led directly to the island's resort development by the megarich industrialist Howard Coffin of Hudson Motors fame, who also owned nearby Sapelo Island to the north.

Orientation

Because it's only a short drive from downtown Brunswick on the Torras Causeway, St. Simons has much less of a remote feel than most other Georgia barrier islands, and it's much more densely populated than any other Georgia island except Tybee. Most visitor-oriented activity on this 12-mile-long, heavily residential island is clustered at the south end, where St. Simons Sound meets the Atlantic.

Sights
★ THE VILLAGE

Think of **The Village** at the extreme south end of St. Simons as a mix of Tybee's downscale accessibility and Hilton Head's upscale exclusivity. This compact, bustling area only a few blocks long offers not only boutique shops and stylish cafés, but also vintage stores and busking musicians.

On the Village waterfront you'll find the **St. Simons Island Pier,** which, while not extremely long, does offer attractive views of the island. Adjacent to the pier is oak-lined **Neptune Park**, a family-friendly play area. Overlooking Neptune Park is the old **St. Simons Casino Building**, now the home of the theater troupe St. Simons Players, as well as the St. Simons Public Library.

ST. SIMONS LIGHTHOUSE MUSEUM

Unlike many East Coast lighthouses, which tend to be in hard-to-reach places, anyone can walk right up to the **St. Simons Lighthouse Museum** (101 12th St., 912/638-4666, www.coastalgeorgiahistory.org, Mon.-Sat. 10am-5pm, Sun. 1:30pm-5pm, $12 adults, $5 children). Once inside, you can enjoy the museum's exhibit and take the 129 steps up to the top of the 104-foot beacon—which is, unusually, still active—for a gorgeous view of the island and the ocean beyond.

★ FORT FREDERICA NATIONAL MONUMENT

The expansive and well-researched **Fort Frederica National Monument** (Frederica Rd., 912/638-3639, www.nps.gov/fofr, daily 9am-5pm, free) lies on the landward side of the island. Established by General James Oglethorpe in 1736 to protect Georgia's southern flank from the Spanish, the fort (as well as the village that sprang up around it, in which the Wesley brothers preached for a short time) was named for Frederick Louis, the Prince of Wales. The feminine suffix -*a* was added to distinguish it from the older Fort Frederick in South Carolina.

You don't just get to see a military fort here (actually the remains of the old powder magazine—most of the fort itself eroded into the river long ago); this is an entire colonial town site a mile in circumference, originally modeled after a typical English village. A self-guided walking tour through the beautiful grounds shows foundations of building sites that have been uncovered, including taverns, shops, and the private homes of influential citizens. Closer to the river is the large tabby structure of the garrison barracks.

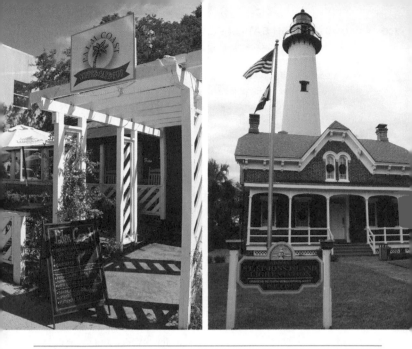

Clockwise from left top: Palm Coast Coffee, Cafe, and Pub; the historic lighthouse on St. Simons; Fort Frederica National Monument.

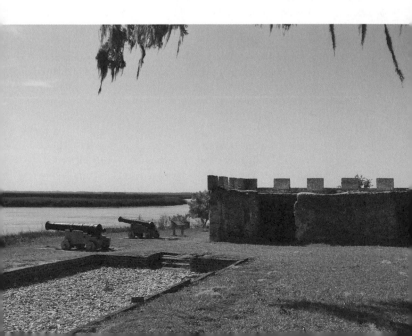

There's not a lot to see at the site of the **Battle of Bloody Marsh** (Frederica Rd., 912/638-3639, www.nps.gov/fofr, daily 8am-4pm, free). Essentially just a few interpretive signs overlooking a beautiful piece of salt marsh, the site is believed to be near the place where British soldiers from nearby Fort Frederica ambushed a force of Spanish regulars on their way to besiege the fort. The battle wasn't actually that bloody—some accounts say the Spanish lost only seven men—but the stout British presence convinced the Spanish to leave St. Simons a few days later, never again to project their once-potent military power that far north in the New World.

While the Battle of Bloody Marsh site is part of the National Park Service's Fort Frederica unit, it's not at the same location. Get to the battlefield from the fort by taking Frederica Road south, and then a left (east) on Demere Road. The site is on the left as Demere Road veers right, in the 1800 block.

CHRIST CHURCH

Just down the road from Fort Frederica is historic **Christ Church** (6329 Frederica Rd., 912/638-8683, www.christchurchfrederica.org, daily 2pm-5pm). The first sanctuary dates from 1820, but the original congregation at the now-defunct town of Frederica held services under the oaks at the site as early as 1736. The founder of Methodism, John Wesley, and his brother Charles both ministered to island residents during 1736-1737.

Christ Church's claim to fame in modern culture is as the setting of local novelist Eugenia Price's *The Beloved Invader,* the first work in her Georgia trilogy. The late Price, who died in 1996, is buried in the church cemetery.

TOURS

St. Simons Island Trolley Tours (912/638-8954, www.stsimonstours. com, Sept.-Mar. daily 11am, Apr.-Aug. daily 11am and 1pm, $20 adults, $10 ages 4-12, free under age 4) offers a ride around the island in comparative comfort, departing from the pier.

Nightlife

Unlike some areas this far south on the Georgia coast, there's usually a sizable contingent of young people on St. Simons out looking for a good time. The island's main club for the younger party set is **Rafters** (315½ Mallory St., 912/634-9755, www.raftersblues.com, Mon.-Sat. 4:30pm-2am). For more of a classic friendly dive bar feel, try out **Murphy's** (415 Mallory St., 912/638-8966).

My favorite spot on St. Simons for a drink or an espresso—or a panini, for that matter—is **Palm Coast Coffee, Cafe, and Pub** (316 Mallory St., 912/634-7517, www.palmcoastssi.com, daily 8am-10pm). This handy little spot, combining a hip, relaxing coffeehouse with a hearty menu of brunch items, is in the heart of the Village. The kicker, though, is the cute little bar the size of a large walk-in closet right off the side of the main room—a little bit of Key West on St. Simons.

Inside the Village Inn is the popular nightspot the **Village Pub** (500 Mallory St., 912/634-6056, www.villageinnandpub.com, Mon.-Sat. 5pm-midnight, Sun. 5pm-10pm). Slightly more upscale than most watering holes on the island, this is the best place for a quality martini or other premium cocktail.

Shops

Most visitor-oriented shopping on St. Simons is concentrated in the Village and is a typical beach town mix of hardware and tackle, casual clothing, and souvenir stores. A funky highlight is **Beachview Books** (215 Mallory St., 912/638-7282, Mon.-Sat. 10:30am-5:30pm, Sun. 11:30am-3pm), a rambling used bookstore with lots of regional and local goodies, including books by the late great local author Eugenia Price. Probably the best antiques shop in this part of town is **Village Mews** (504 Beachview Dr., 912/634-1235, Mon.-Sat. 10am-5pm).

The local edition of the **Savannah Bee Company** (315 Mallory St., 912/771-8972, www.savannahbee.com) might be the best in the regional franchise, with a very friendly staff and an immaculate, and very interesting, store with all the honey-based edible and cosmetic products the company offers.

The **Shops at Pier Village Market** is a collection of übercute shops in a cluster of mini-cottages, including Island Pearl Boutique, All Things Princess & Fairy, and the Island Gallery. This is a great place for families to wander and browse. The shops keep varying hours, both daily and seasonally.

Sports and Activities
BEACHES

Keep going from the pier past the lighthouse to find **Massengale Park** (daily dawn-dusk), with a playground, picnic tables, and restrooms right off the beach on the Atlantic side. The beach itself on St. Simons is underwhelming compared to some in these parts, but it's easily accessible from the pier area and good for a romantic stroll if it's not high tide. There's a great playground, Neptune Park, right next to the pier overlooking the waterfront.

KAYAKING AND BOATING

With its relatively sheltered landward side nestled in the marsh and an abundance of wildlife, St. Simons Island is an outstanding kayaking site, attracting connoisseurs from all over. A good spot to put in on the Frederica River is the **Golden Isles Marina** (206 Marina Dr., 912/634-1128, www.gimarina.com), which is actually on little Lanier Island on the Torras Causeway right before you enter St. Simons proper. For a real adventure, put in at the ramp at the end of South Harrington Street off Frederica Road, which will take you out Village Creek on the seaward side of the island.

Undoubtedly the best kayaking outfitter and tour operator in this part of the Golden Isles is **SouthEast Adventure Outfitters** (313 Mallory St., 912/638-6732, www.southeastadventure.com, daily 10am-6pm), which also has a location in nearby Brunswick.

BIKING

The best place to rent bikes is **Monkey Wrench Bicycles** (1700 Frederica Rd., 912/634-5551). You can rent another kind of pedal-power at **Wheel Fun Rentals** (532 Ocean Blvd., 912/634-0606), which deals in four-seat pedaled carts with steering wheels.

GOLF AND TENNIS

A popular place for both sports is the **Sea Palms Golf and Tennis Resort** (5445 Frederica Rd., 800/841-6268, www.seapalms.com, greens fees $70-80) in the middle of the island, with three 9-hole public courses and three clay courts. The **Sea Island Golf Club** (100 Retreat Rd., 800/732-4752, www.seaisland.com, greens fees $185-260) on the old Retreat Plantation as you first come onto the island has two award-winning 18-hole courses, the Seaside and the Plantation. Another public course is the 18-hole **Hampton Club** (100 Tabbystone Rd., 912/634-0255, www.hamptonclub.com, greens fees $95) on the north side of the island, part of the King and Prince Beach and Golf Resort.

Restaurants

While the ambience at St. Simons has an upscale feel, don't feel like you have to dress up to get a bite to eat—the emphasis is on relaxation and having a good time.

BREAKFAST AND BRUNCH

★ **Palmer's Village Cafe** (223 Mallory St., 912/634-5515, www.palmersvillagecafe.com, Tues.-Sun. 7:30am-2pm, $10-15), formerly called Dressner's, is right in the middle of the Village's bustle. It's one of the island's most popular places but still has enough seats that you usually don't have to wait. Sandwiches and burgers are great, but breakfast all day is the real attraction and includes lovingly crafted omelets, hearty pancakes, and a "build your own biscuit" menu.

SEAFOOD

A popular seafood place right in the action in the Village is **Barbara Jean's** (214 Mallory St., 912/634-6500, www.barbarajeans.com, Sun.-Thurs. 11am-9pm, Fri.-Sat. 11am-10pm, $7-20), which also has a variety of imaginative veggie dishes to go along with its formidable seafood menu, including some excellent she-crab soup and crab cakes. They also have plenty of good landlubber treats.

★ **Nancy** (26 Market St., 912/634-0885, www.nancyssi.com, lunch Tues.-Sat. 11:30am-2pm, dinner Thurs.-Sat. 6pm-10pm, $30) is an interesting concept: an upscale fine-dining spot with an affiliated women's clothing boutique. Nancy Herdlinger and chef Abney Harper run this enterprise in a newer area a short drive outside the Village. It's one of the premier fine-dining spots on the Georgia coast south of Savannah. Any seafood dish is great, but I suggest the short ribs if they're on the tightly curated menu.

Inside the King and Prince Resort, you'll find the old-school glory of the **Blue Dolphin** (201 Arnold Rd., 800/342-0212, lunch daily 11am-4pm, dinner daily 5pm-10pm, $15-30), redolent of the *Great Gatsby* era. The Blue Dolphin claims to be the only oceanfront dining on the island, and the views are certainly magnificent.

Hotels
UNDER $150
A charming and reasonable place a stone's throw from the Village is **Queens Court** (437 Kings Way, 912/638-8459, $85-135), a traditional roadside motel from the late 1940s, with modern upgrades that include a nice outdoor pool in the central courtyard area. Despite its convenient location, you'll feel fairly secluded.

You couldn't ask for a better location than that of the **St. Simons' Inn by the Lighthouse** (609 Beachview Dr., 912/638-1101, www.saintsimonsinn.com, $120-300), which is indeed in the shadow of the historic lighthouse and right next to the hopping Village area. A so-called "condo-hotel," each of the standard and deluxe suites at the inn are individually owned by off-site owners—however, each gets full maid service and complimentary breakfast.

$150-300
The best-known lodging on St. Simons Island is the ★ **King and Prince Beach and Golf Resort** (201 Arnold Rd., 800/342-0212, $249-320). Originally opened as a dance club in 1935, the King and Prince brings a swank old-school glamour similar to the Jekyll Island Club (though less imposing). And like the Jekyll Island Club, the King and Prince is also designated as one of the Historic Hotels of America. Its nearly 200 guest rooms are spread over a complex that includes several buildings, including the historic main building, beach villas, and freestanding guesthouses. Some standard rooms can go for under $200 even in the spring high season. Winter rates for all guest rooms are appreciably lower and represent a great bargain. For a dining spot overlooking the sea, try the **Blue Dolphin** (lunch daily 11am-4pm, dinner daily 5pm-10pm, $15-30). The resort's Hampton Club provides golf for guests and the public.

An interesting B&B on the island that's also within walking distance of most of the action on the south end is the 28-room **Village Inn & Pub** (500 Mallory St., 912/634-6056, www.villageinnandpub.com, $160-245), nestled among shady palm trees and live oaks. The pub, a popular local hangout in a renovated 1930 cottage, is a nice plus.

OVER $300

Affiliated with the Sea Island Resort, the **Lodge at Sea Island** (100 Retreat Ave., 912/638-3611, $650-2,500) is actually on the south end of St. Simons Island on the old Retreat Plantation. Its 40 grand guest rooms and suites all have great views of the Atlantic Ocean, the associated Plantation Course links, or both. Full butler service makes this an especially pampered and aristocratic stay.

Transportation and Services

Get to St. Simons through the gateway city of Brunswick. Take I-95 exit 38 for Golden Isles, which will take you to the Golden Isles Parkway. Take a right onto U.S. 17 and look for the intersection with the Torras Causeway, a toll-free road that takes you the short distance onto St. Simons.

The **St. Simons Visitors Center** (530-B Beachview Dr., 912/638-9014, www.bgivb.com, daily 9am-5pm) is across the street from the old Casino Building near Neptune Park and the Village. The main newspaper in St. Simons is the *Brunswick News* (www.thebrunswicknews.com). The **U.S. Postal Service** (800/275-8777) has an office at 620 Beachview Drive.

Little St. Simons Island

This 10,000-acre privately owned island, accessible only by water, is almost totally undeveloped—thanks to its salt-stressed trees, which discouraged timbering—and boasts seven miles of beautiful beaches. All activity centers on the circa-1917 ★ **Lodge on Little St. Simons Island** (1000 Hampton Point Dr., 888/733-5774, www.littlestsimonsisland.com, from $625), named one of the top five U.S. resorts by *Condé Nast Traveler* in 2016. Within it lies the famed Hunting Lodge, where meals and cocktails are served. With 15 ultra-plush guest rooms and suites in an assortment of historic buildings, all set amid gorgeous natural beauty—there are five full-time naturalists on staff—the lodge is a reminder of what St. Simons used to look like. The guest count is limited to 30 people.

TRANSPORTATION

Unless you enlist the aid of a local kayaking charter company, you have to be a guest of the lodge to have access to Little St. Simons. The ferry, a 15-minute ride, leaves from a landing at the northern end of St. Simons at the end of Lawrence Road. Guests have full use of bicycles once on the island and can also request shuttle transportation just about anywhere.

Sea Island

The only way to enjoy Sea Island—basically a tiny appendage of St. Simons facing the Atlantic Ocean—is to be a guest at ★ **The Sea Island Resort** (888/732-4752, www.seaisland.com, from $700). The legendary facility, which underwent extensive renovations in 2008, is routinely ranked as one of the best resorts in the United States. The rooms at the resort's premier lodging institution, **The Cloister,** nearly defy description—enveloped in Old World luxury, they also boast 21st-century technology.

TRANSPORTATION

Get to Sea Island by taking Torras Causeway onto the island and then making a left onto Sea Island Causeway, which takes you all the way to the gate marking the only land entrance to the island.

DARIEN AND MCINTOSH COUNTY

The small fishing and shrimping village of Darien in McIntosh County has an interesting and historic pedigree of its own. It is centrally located near some of the best treasures the Georgia coast has to offer, including the Harris Neck National Wildlife Refuge, the beautiful Altamaha River, and the sea island of Sapelo, and it also boasts what many believe to be the best traditional seafood restaurants in the state.

Unlike Anglophilic Savannah to the north, the Darien area has had a distinctly Scottish flavor from the beginning. In 1736, Scottish Highlanders established a settlement at the mouth of the Altamaha River at the bequest of General James Oglethorpe, who wanted the tough Scots protecting his southern border from the Spanish.

Darien's heyday was in that antebellum period, when for a brief time the town was the world's largest exporter of cotton, floated down the Altamaha on barges and shipped out through the town's port. The Bank of Darien was the largest bank south of Philadelphia in the early 1800s. Almost nothing from this period remains, however, because on June 11, 1863, a force of mostly African American Union troops burned Darien's homes and warehouses to the ground (the incident was portrayed in the movie *Glory*).

In the pre-interstate highway days, U.S. 17 was the main route south to booming Florida. McIntosh County got a bad reputation for "clip joints," which would fleece gullible travelers with a variety of illegal schemes. This period is recounted in the best-seller *Praying for Sheetrock* by Melissa Fay Greene.

Sights
SMALLEST CHURCH IN NORTH AMERICA

While several other churches claim that title, fans of the devout and of roadside kitsch alike will enjoy the tiny and charming little **Memory Park Christ Chapel** (U.S. 17, daily 24 hours). The original 12-seat chapel was built in 1949 by local grocer Agnes Harper, when the church was intended as a round-the-clock travelers' sanctuary on what was then the main coastal road, U.S. 17. Upon her death, Harper simply willed the church to Jesus Christ. Sadly, in 2015 an arsonist burned Mrs. Harper's church to the ground. A community effort, however, rebuilt it as closely as possible.

EXCURSIONS
THE GOLDEN ISLES

Clockwise from top left: Gould Cemetery at Harris Neck National Wildlife Refuge; the Smallest Church in North America; re-enactors at Fort King George State Historic Site.

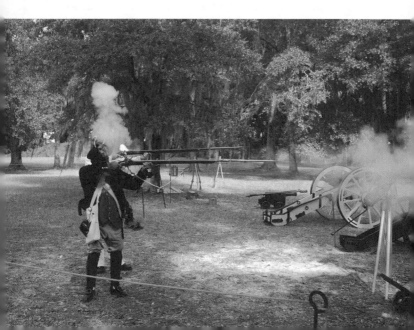

Get there by taking I-95 exit 67 and going south a short way on U.S. 17; the church is on the east side of the road.

★ HARRIS NECK NATIONAL WILDLIFE REFUGE

Literally a stone's throw from the "Smallest Church" is the turnoff onto the seven-mile Harris Neck Road leading east to the **Harris Neck National Wildlife Refuge** (912/832-4608, www.fws.gov/harrisneck, daily dawn-dusk, free). In addition to being one of the single best sites in the South from which to view wading birds and waterfowl in their natural habitat, Harris Neck also has something of a poignant backstory. For generations after the Civil War, an African American community descended from the area's original enslaved population quietly struggled to eke out a living here by fishing and farming.

The settlers' land was taken by the federal government during World War II to build a U.S. Army Air Force base. Now a nearly 3,000-acre nationally protected refuge, Harris Neck gets about 50,000 visitors a year to experience its mix of marsh, woods, and grassland ecosystems and for its nearly matchless bird-watching. Most visitors use the four-mile "wildlife drive" to travel through the refuge, stopping occasionally for hiking or bird-watching.

Kayaks and canoes can put in at the public boat ramp on the Barbour River. Near the landing is the **Gould Cemetery,** an old African American cemetery that is publicly accessible. Charming handmade tombstones evoke the post-Civil War era of Harris Neck before the displacement of local citizens to build the airfield.

To get here, take I-95 exit 67 and go south on U.S. 17 about one mile, then east on Harris Neck Road (Hwy. 131) for seven miles to the entrance gate on the left.

SHELLMAN BLUFF

Just northeast of Darien is the old oystering community of **Shellman Bluff.** It's notable not only for the stunning views from the high bluff, but also for fresh seafood. Go to **Shellman's Fish Camp** (1058 River Rd., 912/832-4331, call ahead) to put in for a kayak or canoe ride. Save room for a meal; there are some great seafood places here.

FORT KING GEORGE STATE HISTORIC SITE

The oldest English settlement in what would become Georgia, **Fort King George State Historic Site** (1600 Wayne St., 912/437-4770, www.gastateparks.org/fortkinggeorge, Tues.-Sun. 9am-5pm, $7.50 adults, $4.50 children) for a short time protected the Carolinas from attack, from its establishment in 1721 to its abandonment in 1727. Walking onto the site, with its restored 40-foot-tall cypress blockhouse fort, instantly reveals why this place was so important: It guards a key bend in the wide Altamaha River, vital to any attempt to establish transportation and trade in the area.

Altamaha Coastal Tours (229 Ft. King George Rd., 912/437-6010, www.
altamaha.com) is your best bet for taking a guided kayak tour (from $50) or
renting a kayak (from $20 per day) to explore the beautiful Altamaha River.

Restaurants

McIntosh County is a powerhouse in the food department, and as you
might expect, fresh and delicious seafood in a casual atmosphere is the
order of the day here.

The Old School Diner (1080 Jesse Grant Rd. NE, Townsend, 912/832-
2136, http://oldschooldiner.com, Wed.-Fri. 5:30pm-9:30pm, Sat.-Sun. noon-
9:30pm, $15-30, cash only) is located in a whimsical semirural compound
seven miles off U.S. 17, just off Harris Neck Road on the way to the wildlife
refuge. The draw here is succulent fresh seafood in the coastal Georgia tradition. Old School's prices aren't so old school, but keep in mind that the
portions are huge, rich, and filling.

Even farther off the main roads than the Old School Diner, the com-
munity of Shellman Bluff is well worth the drive. Find ★ **Hunters Café**
(Shellman Bluff, 912/832-5771, lunch Mon.-Fri. 11am-2pm, dinner Mon.-
Fri. 5pm-10pm, Sat.-Sun. 7am-10pm, $10-20) and get anything that floats
your boat—it's all fresh and local. Wild Georgia shrimp are a particular
specialty, as is the hearty cream-based crab stew. Take a right off Shellman
Bluff Road onto Sutherland Bluff Drive, then a left onto New Shellman
Road. Take a right onto the unpaved River Road and you can't miss it.

Another Shellman Bluff favorite is ★ **Speed's Kitchen** (Shellman
Bluff, 912/832-4763, Thurs.-Sat. 5pm-close, Sun. noon-close, $10-20), where
people move anything but fast, and the fried fish and crab-stuffed flounder
are out of this world. Take a right off Shellman Bluff Road onto Sutherland
Bluff Drive. Take a right onto Speed's Kitchen Road.

Hotels

If you want to stay in McIntosh County, I recommend booking one of the
five charming guest rooms at ★ **Open Gates Bed and Breakfast** (301
Franklin St., Darien, 912/437-6985, www.opengatesbnb.com, $110-150).
This lovingly restored and reasonably priced historic inn, circa 1876, overlooks relaxing Vernon Square in downtown Darien.

Sapelo Island

One of those amazing, undeveloped Georgia barrier islands that can only
be reached by boat, Sapelo also shares with some of those islands a link to
the Gilded Age.

HISTORY

The Spanish established a Franciscan mission on the north end of the island
in the 1500s. Sapelo didn't become fully integrated into the Lowcountry

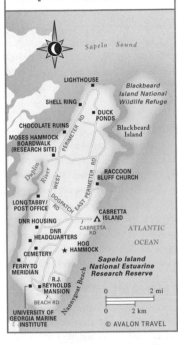

Sapelo Island

LIGHTHOUSE
SHELL RING
CHOCOLATE RUINS
MOSES HAMMOCK BOARDWALK (RESEARCH SITE)
Sapelo Sound
Blackbeard Island National Wildlife Refuge
DUCK PONDS
Blackbeard Island
PERIMETER RD
WEST PERIMETER RD
EAST PERIMETER RD
Duplin River
DOGPATCH RD
RACCOON BLUFF CHURCH
LONG TABBY/ POST OFFICE
CABRETTA RD
CABRETTA ISLAND
DNR HOUSING
DNR HEADQUARTERS
HOG HAMMOCK
ATLANTIC OCEAN
CEMETERY
FERRY TO MERIDIAN
R.J. REYNOLDS MANSION
BEACH RD
UNIVERSITY OF GEORGIA MARINE INSTITUTE
Sapelo Island National Estuarine Research Reserve
Nannygoat Beach
0   2 mi
0   2 km
© AVALON TRAVEL

plantation culture until its purchase by Thomas Spalding in the early 1800s. After the Civil War, many of the nearly 500 formerly enslaved people on the island remained, with a partnership of freedmen buying land as early as 1871.

Hudson Motors mogul Howard Coffin bought all of Sapelo, except for the African American communities, in 1912, building a palatial home and introducing modern infrastructure. Coffin hit hard times in the Great Depression and in 1934 sold Sapelo to tobacco heir R. J. Reynolds, who consolidated the island's African Americans into the single Hog Hammock community. By the mid-1970s the Reynolds family had sold the island to the state, again with the exception of the 430 acres of Hog Hammock, which at the time had slightly more than 100 residents. Today most of the island is administered for marine research purposes under the designation of **Sapelo Island National Estuarine Research Reserve** (www.sapelonerr.org).

SIGHTS

Once on the island, you can take guided tours under the auspices of the Georgia Department of Natural Resources. A tour of the island (Wed. 8:30am-12:30pm) includes the **R. J. Reynolds Mansion** (www.reynoldsonsapelo.com) on the south end as well as Hog Hammock and the Long Tabby ruins. A tour covers the historic **Sapelo Lighthouse** on the north end along with the rest of the island (Sat. 9am-1pm). June-Labor Day there's an extra lighthouse and island tour Friday 8:30am-12:30pm. March-October on the last Tuesday of the month they do an extra-long day trip, 8:30am-3pm. Tours cost $10 adults, $6 children, free under age 6. Call 912/437-3224 for reservations. You can also arrange private tours.

Another key sight on Sapelo is a 4,500-year-old **Native American shell ring** on the north end, one of the oldest and best preserved anywhere. Beach lovers will especially enjoy the unspoiled strands on Sapelo, including the famous **Nannygoat Beach.**

While it's theoretically possible to stay overnight at the **R. J. Reynolds Mansion** (www.reynoldsonsapelo.com), it is limited to groups of at least 16 people. Realistically, to stay overnight on Sapelo you need a reservation with one of the locally owned guesthouses. One recommendation is Cornelia Bailey's six-room **The Wallow** (912/485-2206, call for rates) in historic Hog Hammock. The Baileys also run a small campground, **Comyam's Campground** (912/485-2206, $10 pp). Another option is **The Weekender** (912/485-2277, call for rates).

TRANSPORTATION AND SERVICES

Visitors to Sapelo must embark on the ferry at the **Sapelo Island Visitors Center** (912/437-3224, www.sapelonerr.org, $15 adults, $10 ages 6-18) in little Meridian, Georgia, on Highway 99 north of Darien. The ferry runs three times a day Monday-Saturday, twice on Sunday. The website keeps an up-to-date schedule. The visitors center actually has a nice nature hike of its own as well as an auditorium where you can see an informative video. From here it's a half-hour trip to Sapelo over the Doboy Sound. Keep in mind you must call in advance for reservations before showing up at the visitors center. April-October it's recommended to call at least a week in advance.

CUMBERLAND ISLAND AND ST. MARYS

Actually two islands—Great Cumberland and Little Cumberland—Cumberland Island National Seashore is the largest and one of the oldest of Georgia's barrier islands, and also one of its most remote and least developed. Currently administered by the National Park Service, it's accessible only by ferry or private boat. Most visitors to Cumberland get here from the gateway town of St. Marys, Georgia, a nifty little fishing village.

St. Marys

Much like Brunswick to the north, the fishing town of St. Marys plays mostly a gateway role, in this case to the Cumberland Island National Seashore. During the colonial period, St. Marys was the southernmost U.S. city. In 1812 a British force took over Cumberland Island and St. Marys, with a contingent embarking up the St. Marys River to track down the customs collector.

Unlike towns such as Darien, which was put to the torch by Union troops, St. Marys was saved from destruction in the Civil War. A hotel was built in 1916 (and hosted Marjorie Kinnan Rawlings, author of *The Yearling*), but tourists didn't discover the area until the 1970s. It was also then that the U.S. Navy built the huge nuclear submarine base at Kings Bay, currently the area's largest employer with almost 10,000 workers.

ORIENTATION

Most activity in downtown St. Marys happens up and down Osborne Street, which perhaps not coincidentally is also how you get to the **Cumberland**

Cumberland Island

ATLANTIC
OCEAN

Intracoastal Waterway

Little
Cumberland
Island

Cumberland River

FIRST AFRICAN
BAPTIST CHURCH

Whitney
Lake

Brickhill River

MAIN RD

**Cumberland
Island**

PLUM
ORCHARD ★

★ CUMBERLAND
ISLAND NATIONAL
SEASHORE

MAIN RD

ATLANTIC
OCEAN

Cumberland Sound

GREYFIELD
INN ●

△ SEA CAMP

SEA CAMP
DOCK ■
DUNGENESS ★ ICE HOUSE
DOCK ■ MUSEUM

To
St. Marys

South End
Ponds

Intracoastal Waterway

0   1 mi

0   1 km

© AVALON TRAVEL

Island Visitor Center (113 St. Marys St., 912/882-4335, daily 8am-4:30pm) and from there board the *Cumberland Queen* for the trip to the island. The Cumberland Island Visitor Center and the Cumberland Island Museum are in two different places, about a block apart.

SIGHTS

Tying the past to the present, it's only fitting that the home of the Kings Bay Submarine Base (not open to the public) has a museum dedicated to the "Silent Service." The **St. Marys Submarine Museum** (102 St. Marys St., 912/882-2782, www.stmaryswelcome.com, Tues.-Sat. 10am-5pm, Sun. 1pm-5pm, $5 adults, $3 children) on the riverfront has a variety of exhibits honoring the contribution of American submariners, including a bunch of cool models. There's a neat interactive exhibit where you can look through the genuine sub periscope that sticks out of the roof of the museum.

A block down Osborne Street from the waterfront—and not at the actual Cumberland Island Visitor Center or the actual ferry dock—is the handsome little **Cumberland Island National Seashore Museum** (129 Osborne St., 912/882-4336, www.stmaryswelcome.com, Wed.-Sun. 1pm-4pm, free). It has several very informative exhibits on the natural and human history of Cumberland, as well as a room devoted to the short but fascinating role the island played in the War of 1812.

The most notable historic home in St. Marys is the **Orange Hall House Museum** (311 Osborne St., 912/576-3644, http://orangehallstmarys.org, Mon.-Fri. 11am-3pm, Sat. 10am-3pm, Sun. 1pm-4pm, $5 adults). This beautiful Greek Revival home, circa 1830, survived the Civil War and was the center of town social life during the Roaring '20s.

RESTAURANTS

St. Marys cannot compete in culinary sophistication with Charleston or Savannah, but it does have some of the freshest seafood around. One of the best places to eat seafood on the waterfront in St. Marys is at **Lang's Marina Restaurant** (307 W. St. Marys St., 912/882-4432, lunch Tues.-Fri. 11am-2pm, dinner Wed.-Sat. 5pm-9pm, $15-20). Another pair of good waterfront spots, right next to each other, are **The Shark Bite** (104 W. St. Marys St., 912/576-6993, Tues.-Sat. 11am-9pm, $12-20), which has great burgers and live music, and **Riverside Café** (106 W. St. Marys St., 912/882-3466, Tues.-Sat. 11am-9pm, $15-20), which specializes in Greek favorites.

HOTELS

The most notable lodging for historical as well as economic value is the 18-room **Riverview Hotel** (105 Osborne St., 912/882-3242, www.riverviewhotelstmarys.com, under $100). It was built in the 1920s and has hosted such notables as author Marjorie Rawlings, John Rockefeller, poet Sidney Lanier, and Andrew Carnegie. ★ **Emma's Bed and Breakfast** (300 W. Conyers St., 912/882-4199, www.emmasbedandbreakfast.com, under $200) is situated on four beautiful acres in downtown St. Marys in a grand Southern-style mansion with all the trappings and hospitality you'd expect.

More outdoorsy visitors can stay at cottage, tent, or RV sites at **Crooked River State Park** (6222 Charlie Smith Sr. Hwy., 912/882-5256, www.gastateparks.org). There are 62 tent and RV sites (about $22) and 11 cottages ($85-110) as well as primitive camping ($25).

TRANSPORTATION AND SERVICES

Take I-95 exit 3 for Kingsland-St. Marys Road (Hwy. 40). This becomes Osborne Road, the main drag of St. Marys, as it gets closer to town. The road by the waterfront is St. Marys Street.

The **St. Marys Convention and Visitors Bureau** (406 Osborne St., 912/882-4000, www.stmaryswelcome.com) is a good source of information not only for the town but for Cumberland Island, but keep in mind that this is not actually where you catch the ferry to the island.

★ Cumberland Island National Seashore

Not only one of the richest estuarine and maritime forest environments in the world, **Cumberland Island National Seashore** (912/882-4335, reservations 877/860-6787, www.nps.gov/cuis) is one of the most beautiful places on the planet, as everyone learned when the "it" couple of their day, John F. Kennedy Jr. and Carolyn Bessette, were wed on the island in 1996.

With more than 16 miles of gorgeous beach and an area of over 17,000 acres, there's no shortage of scenery.

Cumberland is far from pristine: It has been used for timbering and cotton, is dotted with evocative abandoned ruins, and hosts a band of beautiful but voracious wild horses. But it is still a remarkable island paradise in a world where those kinds of locations are getting harder and harder to find.

There are two ways to enjoy Cumberland: day trip or overnight stay. An early arrival and departure on the late ferry, combined with bike rental and a tour, still leaves plenty of time for day-trippers to relax. Camping overnight on Cumberland is quite enjoyable, but it's a bit rustic and isn't for novices.

Important note: Distances on the map can be deceiving. Cumberland is very narrow but also very long—about 18 miles tip to tip. You can walk the width of the island in minutes, but you will not be able to hike its length even in a day.

You can have a perfectly enjoyable time on Cumberland just hanging out on the more populated south end, but those who want to explore the island fully should consider renting a bike or booking seats on the new National Park Service van tour around the island.

HISTORY

The indigenous Timucuan people revered this site, visiting it often for shellfish and for sassafras, a medicinal herb common on the island. Cumberland's size and great natural harbor made it a perfect base for Spanish friars, who established the first mission on the island, San Pedro Mocama, in 1587. The first Christian martyr in Georgia was Father Pedro Martinez, killed by indigenous people.

As part of his effort to push the Spanish back into Florida, General James Oglethorpe established Fort William at the south end of Cumberland—the remains of which are now underwater—as well as a hunting lodge named Dungeness, an island place-name that persists today.

Inevitably, the Lowcountry planters' culture made its way down to Cumberland, which was soon the site of 15 thriving plantations and small farms. After the Civil War, Cumberland was set aside as a home for freed African Americans—part of the famous and ill-fated "40 acres and a mule" proposal—but politics intervened: Most of Cumberland's enslaved people were rounded up and taken to Amelia Island, Florida, although some remained and settled at Cumberland's north end (the "Settlement" area today).

As elsewhere on the Georgia coast, the Industrial Revolution came to Cumberland in the form of a vacation getaway for a mega-tycoon, in this case Thomas Carnegie, industrialist and brother of the better-known Andrew Carnegie of Carnegie Library fame. Carnegie built a new, even grander Dungeness, which suffered the same fate as its predecessor in a 1959 fire.

Cumberland Island narrowly avoided becoming the next Hilton

Wild Horses of Cumberland

wild horses near the Dungeness Ruins

Contrary to popular opinion, Cumberland Island's famous wild horses are not direct descendants of the first horses brought to the island by Spanish and English settlers, although feral horses have certainly ranged the island for most of recorded history. The current population of about 140 or so is actually descended from horses brought to the island by the Carnegie family in the 1920s. Responding to overwhelming public opinion, the National Park Service leaves the herd virtually untended and unsupervised. The horses eat, live, fight, grow up, give birth, and die largely without human influence, other than euthanizing animals who are clearly suffering and have no hope of recovery.

You're not guaranteed to see wild horses on Cumberland, but the odds are heavily in your favor. They often congregate to graze around the Dungeness ruins, and indeed any open space. Over the years they've made trails through the forest and sand dunes, and can often be seen cavorting on the windy beach in the late afternoon and early evening.

Each stallion usually acquires a "harem" of dependent mares, and occasionally you might even witness spirited competition between stallions for mares or territory.

Gorgeous and evocative though these magnificent animals are, they have a big appetite for vegetation and frankly are not the best thing for this sensitive barrier island ecosystem. But their beauty and visceral impact on the visitor is undeniable, which means the horses are likely to stay as long as nature will have them.

And yes, these really are *wild* horses, meaning you should never try to feed or pet them, and you certainly won't be riding them.

Head—literally—in 1969, when Hilton Head developer Charles Fraser bought the northern tip of the island and began bulldozing a runway. The dwindling but still influential Carnegies joined with the Georgia Conservancy to broker an agreement that resulted in dubbing Cumberland a National Seashore in 1972, saving it from further development. A $7.5 million gift from the Mellon Foundation enabled the purchase of Fraser's system.

To learn more about Cumberland's fascinating history, visit the **Cumberland Island National Seashore Museum** (129 Osborne St., 912/882-4336, www.stmaryswelcome.com, Wed.-Sun. 1pm-4pm, free) while you're in St. Marys, a block away from the actual ferry docks.

SIGHTS

The ferry typically stops at two docks a short distance from each other, the Sea Camp dock and the Dungeness dock. At 4pm, rangers offer a "dockside" interpretive program at the Sea Camp. A short way farther north at the Dungeness Dock, rangers lead a highly recommended "Dungeness Footsteps Tour" at 10am and 12:45pm, concentrating on the historic sites at the southern end of the island. Also at the Dungeness dock is the little **Ice House Museum** (912/882-4336, daily 9am-5pm, free), containing a range of exhibits on the island's history from Native American times to the present day.

Down near the docks are also where you'll find the stirring, almost spooky **Dungeness Ruins** and the nearby grave marker of Light-Horse Harry Lee. (You're very likely to see some wild horses around this area too.) The cause of the 1866 fire that destroyed the old Dungeness home is still unknown. Another even grander home was built on the same site during the Victorian era, but also fell victim to fire in the 1950s. It's these Victorian ruins you see today.

A very nice addition to the National Park Service offerings is a daily "Lands and Legacies" van tour (reservations 877/860-6787, $15 adults, $12 seniors and children) that takes you all around the island, eliminating the need for lengthy hikes. It's ideal for day-trippers—if a bit long, at six hours—but anyone can take the ride. It leaves from the Sea Camp Ranger Station soon after the first morning ferry arrives. Reservations are strongly advised.

Moving north on the Main Road (Grand Ave.)—a dirt path and the only route for motor vehicles—you come to the **Greyfield Inn** (904/261-6408, www.greyfieldinn.com). Because it is a privately owned hotel, don't trespass through the grounds. A good way farther north, just off the main road, you'll find the restored, rambling 20-room mansion **Plum Orchard** (912/882-4335), another Carnegie legacy. Guided tours (2nd and 4th Sun. of the month, $6 plus ferry fare) of Plum Orchard are available; call to reserve a space.

At the very north end of the island, accessible only by foot or by bicycle, is the former freedmen's community simply known as **The Settlement,** featuring a small cemetery and the now-famous **First African Baptist Church** (daily dawn-dusk)—a 1937 version of the 1893 original—a humble and rustic one-room church made of whitewashed logs and in which the 1996 Kennedy-Bessette wedding took place.

Clockwise from top left: St. Marys Submarine Museum; Folkston Railroad Transportation Museum; an alligator in the Okefenokee Swamp.

There are more than 50 miles of hiking trails all over Cumberland, about 15 miles of nearly isolated beach to comb, and acres of maritime forest to explore—the latter an artifact of Cumberland's unusually old age for a barrier island. Upon arrival, you might want to rent a bicycle at the **Sea Camp dock** (no reservations, arrange rentals on the ferry, adult bikes $16 per day, youth bikes $10, overnight $20). The only catch with the bikes is that you shouldn't plan on taking them to the upcountry campsites.

Shell and sharks' teeth collectors might want to explore south of Dungeness Beach as well as between the docks. Unlike some parks, you are allowed to take shells and fossils off the island. Wildlife enthusiasts will be in heaven. More than 300 species of birds have been recorded on the island, which is also a favorite nesting ground for female loggerhead turtles in late summer. Of course, the most iconic image of Cumberland Island is its famous **wild horses,** a free-roaming band of feral equines who traverse the island year-round, grazing as they please.

Cumberland Island is home to some creepy-crawlies, including mosquitoes, gnats, and, yes, ticks, which are especially prevalent throughout the maritime forest as you work your way north. Bring high-strength insect repellent with you, or buy some at the camp store. Rangers recommend you do a frequent "tick check" on yourself and your companions.

HOTELS

The only "civilized" lodging on Cumberland is the 13-room ★ **Greyfield Inn** (Grand Ave., 904/261-6408, www.greyfieldinn.com, $475), ranked by the American Inn Association as one of the country's "Ten Most Romantic Inns." Opened in 1962 as a hotel, the Greyfield was built in 1900 as the home of the Carnegies. The room rates include meals, transportation, tours, and bicycle usage.

Many visitors opt to camp on Cumberland (reservations 877/860-6787, limit of 7 nights, $4) in one of three basic ways: at the **Sea Camp,** which has restrooms and shower facilities and allows fires; the remote but pleasant **Stafford Beach,** a vigorous three-mile hike from the docks and with a basic restroom and shower; and pure wilderness camping farther north at **Hickory Hill, Yankee Paradise,** and **Brickman Bluff,** all of which are a several-mile hike away, do not permit fires, and have no facilities of any kind. Reservations are required for camping. All trash must be packed out on departure, as there are no refuse facilities on the island. Responsible alcohol consumption is limited to those 21 and over. Insect life is abundant: Bring heavy-duty repellent or purchase some at the camp store.

TRANSPORTATION AND SERVICES

The most vital information about Cumberland is how to get ashore in the first place. Most visitors do this by purchasing a ticket on the *Cumberland Queen* at the **Cumberland Island Visitor Center** (113 St. Marys St., St. Marys, 877/860-6787, daily 8am-4:30pm, $20 adults, $18 seniors, $12 under age 13) on the waterfront in St. Marys. I strongly suggest calling ahead. Be aware that there are often long hold times by phone.

The ferry ride is 45 minutes each way. You can call for reservations Monday-Friday 10am-4pm. The ferry does not transport pets, bicycles, kayaks, or cars. However, you can rent bicycles at the Sea Camp dock once you're there. Every visitor to Cumberland over age 16 must pay a $4 entry fee, including campers.

March 1 to November 30, the ferry leaves St. Marys daily at 9am and 11:45am, returning from Cumberland at 10:15am and 4:45pm. March 1 to September 30 Wednesday-Saturday, there's an additional 2:45pm departure from Cumberland back to St. Marys. December 1 to February 28, the ferry operates only Thursday-Monday. Make sure you arrive and check in at least 30 minutes before your ferry leaves.

One of the quirks of Cumberland, resulting from the unusual way in which it passed into federal hands, is the existence of some private property on which you mustn't trespass, except where trails specifically allow it. Also, unlike the general public, these private landowners are allowed to use vehicles. For these reasons, it's best to make sure you have a map of the island, which you can get before you board the ferry at St. Marys or at the ranger station at the Sea Camp dock.

There are no real stores and very few facilities on Cumberland. *Bring whatever you think you'll need,* whether it be food, water, medicine, suntan lotion, insect repellent, toilet paper, or otherwise.

THE OKEFENOKEE SWAMP

Scientists often refer to Okefenokee as an "analogue," an accurate representation of a totally different epoch in the earth's history. In this case it's the Carboniferous Period, about 350 million years ago, when the living plants were lush and green and the dead plants simmered in a slow-decaying peat that would one day end up as the oil that powers our civilization.

But for the casual visitor, Okefenokee might also be simply a wonderful place to get almost completely away from human influence and witness firsthand some of the country's most interesting wildlife in its natural habitat. Despite the enormous wildfires of spring 2007 and summer 2011—some of the largest the Southeast has seen in half a century, so large they were visible from space—the swamp has bounced back, for the most part, and is once again hosting visitors who wish to experience its timeless beauty.

★ Okefenokee National Wildlife Refuge

It's nearly the size of Rhode Island and just a short drive off I-95, but the massive and endlessly fascinating **Okefenokee National Wildlife Refuge** (912/496-7836, www.fws.gov/okefenokee, Mar.-Oct. daily dawn-7:30pm, Nov.-Feb. daily dawn-5:30pm, $5 per vehicle) is one of the lesser-visited national public lands. Is it that very name "swamp" that keeps people away, with its connotations of fetid misery and lurking danger? Or simply its location, out of sight and out of mind in south Georgia?

The Okefenokee Swamp

Waycross

To Valdosta

Laura S Walker State Park

OKEFENOKEE SWAMP PARK (NORTH ENTRANCE)

Cowhouse Island

MAUL HAMMOCK

Big Water Lake

KINGFISHER LANDING (LAUNCH)

OKEFENOKEE NATIONAL WILDLIFE REFUGE

BIG WATER

Territory Prairie

Big Water Prairie

Floyd's Prairie

CRAVEN'S HAMMOCK

Minnie's Island

Floyd's Island

BLUFF LAKE

Pine Island

SUWANNEE RIVER SILL

Stephen C Foster State Park

(WEST ENTRANCE)

CEDAR HAMMOCK

ROUND TOP

Christie Prairie

Billy's Island

CANAL RUN

Suwannee Canal

CHESSER ISLAND OBSERVATION TOWER

SUWANNEE CANAL RECREATION AREA (EAST ENTRANCE)

Buck Prairie

Suwannee River

Honey Island

Bugaboo Island

Okefenokee National Wildlife Refuge

John's Negro Island

REFUGE OFFICE

Chesser Prairie

SUWANNEE RIVER VISITOR CENTER

Fargo

WILDLIFE DRIVE

CHESSER HOMESTEAD

Blackjack Island

Grand Prairie

Soldier's Camp Island

FLORIDA

St. George

Moniac

To I-10

© AVALON TRAVEL

0   6 mi

0   6 km

In any case, while it long ago entered the collective subconscious as a metaphor for the most untamed, darkly dangerous aspects of the American South—as well as the place where Pogo the Possum lived—the Okefenokee remains one of the most intriguing natural areas on the planet.

The Okefenokee Swamp was created by an accident of geology. About 250,000 years ago, the Atlantic Ocean washed ashore about 70 miles farther inland from where it does today. Over time, a massive barrier island formed off this primeval Georgia coastline, running from what is now Jesup, Georgia, south to Starke, Florida. When the ocean level dropped during the Pleistocene Era, this sandy island became a topographical feature known today as the Trail Ridge, its height effectively creating a basin to its west. Approximately 90 percent of the Okefenokee's water comes from rainfall into that basin, which drains slowly via the Suwannee and St. Marys Rivers.

Native Americans used the swamp as a hunting ground and gave us its current name, which means "Land of the Trembling Earth," a reference to the floating peat islands, called "houses," that dominate the landscape.

It's a common mistake to call the Okefenokee "pristine," because like much of the heavily timbered and farmed southeastern coast, it is anything but. The swamp's ancient cypress stands and primordial longleaf pine forests were heavily harvested in the early 20th century. About 200 miles of old rail bed through the swamp remain as a silent testament to the scope of that logging operation. In 1937, President Franklin Roosevelt brought the area within the federal wildlife refuge system.

The state has also opened the **Suwannee River Visitor Center** (912/637-5274, www.gastateparks.org, Wed.-Sun. 9am-5pm), a "green" building featuring an orientation video and exhibits.

SIGHTS

The Okefenokee features a wide variety of ecosystems, including peat bogs, sand hills, and black gum and bay forests. Perhaps most surprising are the wide-open vistas of the swamp's many prairies or extended grasslands, 22 in all. And as you kayak or canoe on one of the water trails or on the old **Suwannee Canal** (a relic of the logging era), you'll notice the water is all very dark. This blackwater is not due to dirt or silt but to natural tannic acid released into the water from the decaying vegetation that gave the swamp its name.

As you'd expect in a national wildlife refuge, the Okefenokee hosts a huge variety of animal life—more than 400 species of vertebrates, including over 200 varieties of birds and more than 60 types of reptiles. Birders get a special treat in late November-early December when sandhill cranes come south to winter in the swamp.

A great way to see the sandhill cranes and other birds of the Okefenokee is to hike the 0.75-mile boardwalk out to the 50-foot **Chesser Island Observation Tower** on the eastern end of the swamp. This boardwalk

was built after the huge 2011 fire; you can see the charred piers of the old
boardwalk as you stroll.

You can get to the tower by driving or biking the eight-mile round-trip **Wildlife Drive,** which also takes you by the old **Chesser Homestead,** the remnants of one of the oldest settlements in the swamp.

TOURING THE REFUGE

For most visitors, the best way to enjoy the Okefenokee is to book a guided tour through **Okefenokee Adventures** (866/843-7926, www.okefeno-keeadventures.com), the designated concessionaire of the refuge. They offer a 90-minute guided boat tour ($18.50 adults, $11.25 children) that leaves each hour, and a 2.5-hour reservation-only sunset tour ($25 adults, $17 children) that takes you to see the gorgeous sunset over Chesser Prairie. Extended or custom tours, including multiday wilderness excursions, are also available. They also rent bikes, canoes, and camping gear, and even run a decent little café where you can either sit down and have a meal or take it to go out on the trail.

Privately owned canoes and boats with motors under 10 hp may put in with no launch fee, but you must sign in and out. No ATVs are allowed on the refuge, and bicycles are allowed only on designated bike trails. Keep in mind that some hunting goes on in the refuge at designated times. Pets must be leashed at all times.

CAMPING

If fire and water levels permit, it's possible to stay the night in the swamp, canoeing to one of the primitive camping "islands" in the middle of the refuge. You need to make reservations up to two months in advance, however, by calling **U.S. Fish and Wildlife** (912/496-3331, Mon.-Fri. 7am-10am). A nonrefundable fee of $10 pp (which also covers your entrance fee) must be received 16 days before you arrive (mailing address: Okefenokee National Wildlife Refuge, Route 2, Box 3330, Folkston, GA 31537). Campfires are allowed only at Canal Run and Floyds Island. A camp stove is required for cooking at all other shelters. Keep in mind that in times of extreme drought or fire threat, boat trips may not be allowed. Always check the website for the latest announcements.

At **Stephen Foster State Park** (17515 Hwy. 177, 912/637-5274, fall-winter daily 7am-7pm, spring-summer daily 6:30am-8:30pm), a.k.a. the **West Entrance,** near Fargo, Georgia, there are 66 tent sites ($24) and nine cottages ($100). This part of the Okefenokee is widely considered the best way to get that "true swamp" experience.

TRANSPORTATION AND SERVICES

For anyone using this guide as a travel resource, the best way to access the Okefenokee—and the one I recommend—is the **East Entrance** (912/496-7836, www.fws.gov/okefenokee, Mar.-Oct. daily dawn-7:30pm, Nov.-Feb. daily dawn-5:30pm, $5 per vehicle), otherwise known as the **Suwannee**

Canal Recreation Area. This is the main U.S. Fish and Wildlife Service entrance and the most convenient way to hike, rent boating and camping gear, and observe nature. The **Richard S. Bolt Visitor Center** (912/496-7836) has some cool nature exhibits and a surround-sound orientation video. Get to the East Entrance by taking I-95 exit 3 for Kingsland onto Highway 40 west. Go through Kingsland and into Folkston until Highway 40 dead-ends. Take a right, and then an immediate left onto Main Street. At the third light, make a left onto Okefenokee Drive (Hwy. 121) south.

Families with kids may want to hit the **North Entrance** at the privately run **Okefenokee Swamp Park** (U.S. 1, 912/283-0583, www.okeswamp. com, daily 9am-5:30pm, $12 adults, $11 ages 3-11) near Waycross, Georgia. (Fans of the old *Pogo* will recall Waycross from the comic strip, and yes, there's a real "Fort Mudge" nearby.) Here you will find a more touristy vibe, with a reconstructed pioneer village, a serpentarium, and animals in captivity. From here you can take various guided tours for an additional fee.

There's camping at the nearby but unaffiliated **Laura S. Walker State Park** (5653 Laura Walker Rd., 800/864-7275, www.gastateparks.org). Be aware the state park is not in the swamp and isn't very swampy, but it does have a nice man-made lake where you can rent canoes. Get to the North Entrance by taking I-95 exit 29 and going west on U.S. 82 about 45 miles to Highway 177 (Laura Walker Rd.). Go south through Laura S. Walker State Park; the Swamp Park is several miles farther.

If you really want that cypress-festooned classic swamp look, take the long way around the Okefenokee to **Stephen Foster State Park** (17515 Hwy. 177, 912/637-5274, fall-winter daily 7am-7pm, spring-summer daily 6:30am-8:30pm), a.k.a. the **West Entrance,** near Fargo, Georgia. Guided tours are available. Get to Stephen Foster State Park by taking I-95 exit 3 and following the signs to Folkston. Get on Highway 121 south to St. George, and then go west on Highway 94.

Folkston

The chief attraction in Folkston and its main claim to fame is the viewing depot for the **Folkston Funnel** (912/496-2536, www.folkston.com), a veritable train-watcher's paradise. This is the spot where the big CSX double-track rail line—following the top of the ancient Trail Ridge—hosts 60 or more trains a day. They say 90 percent of all freight trains to and from Florida use this track.

Railroad buffs from all over the South congregate here, anticipating the next train by listening to their scanners. The first Saturday each April brings buffs together for the all-day Folkston RailWatch.

The old Atlantic Coast Line depot across the track from the viewing platform has been converted into the very interesting **Folkston Railroad Transportation Museum** (3795 Main St., 912/496-2536, www.charlton-countyga.us, Mon.-Fri. 9am-5pm, Sat. 10am-3pm, free), with lots of history, maps, and technical stuff for the hard-core rail buff and novice alike.

To fuel up in Folkston for your trek in the swamp, go no farther than the friendly ★ **Okefenokee Restaurant** (1507 Third St., 912/496-3263, daily 11am-8pm, $10-20), across from the handsome county courthouse. Their huge buffet is a steal at under $10; come on Friday nights for a massive seafood buffet (mostly fried) for under $20 pp. In any case don't miss the fried catfish, featured at both buffets. It's some of the best I've had anywhere in the South.

HOTELS

For a bit of luxury in town, right outside the refuge's East Entrance is the excellent ★ **Inn at Folkston Bed and Breakfast** (509 W. Main St., 888/509-6246, www.innatfolkston.com, $120-170). There is nothing like coming back to its cozy Victorian charms after a long day out in the swamp. The four-room inn boasts an absolutely outstanding breakfast, an extensive reading library, and a whirlpool tub.

Background

The Landscape

GEOGRAPHY

The area covered by this guide falls within the **Coastal Plain** region of the southeastern United States, which contains some of the most unique ecosystems in North America. It's a place where water is never far away and features large in the daily lives, economy, and folkways of the region's people.

Although it's hundreds of miles away, the Appalachian mountain chain has a major influence on the southeastern coast. It's in Appalachia where so much of the coast's freshwater—in the form of rain—comes together and flows southeast—in the form of rivers—to the Atlantic Ocean. Moving east, the next level down from the Appalachians is the hilly **Piedmont** region, the eroded remains of an ancient mountain chain.

At the Piedmont's eastern edge is the **fall line,** so named because it's where rivers make a drop toward the sea, generally becoming navigable. Around the fall line zone in the **Upper Coastal Plain** you can sometimes spot **sand hills,** usually only a few feet in elevation, generally thought to be the vestigial remains of primordial sand dunes and offshore sandbars. Well beyond the fall line and the sometimes nearly invisible sand hills lies the **Lower Coastal Plain,** gradually built up over a 150-million-year span by sedimentary runoff from the Appalachian Mountains, which at that time were as high or even higher than the modern-day Himalayas.

The Coastal Plain was sea bottom for much of the earth's history, and in some eroded areas you can see dramatic proof of this in the form of pre-historic shells, shark's teeth, and fossilized whale bones and oyster beds, often many miles inland. Sea level has fluctuated wildly with climate and geological changes through the eons. At various times over the last 50 million years, the Coastal Plain has submerged, surfaced, and submerged again. At the height of the last major ice age, when global sea levels were very low, the east coast of North America extended out nearly 100 miles farther than the present shoreline. (We now call this former coastal region the **continental shelf.**) The Coastal Plain has been roughly in its current form for about the last 15,000 years.

Rivers

Visitors from drier climates are sometimes shocked to see how huge the rivers can get in coastal Georgia. Wide and voluminous as they saunter to the sea, their seemingly slow speed belies the massive power they contain. Georgia's big **alluvial,** or sediment-bearing, rivers originate in the region of the Appalachian mountain chain.

Previous: Reynolds Square; azaleas in the spring.

The headwaters of the Savannah River, for example, are near Tallulah Gorge in extreme north Georgia. Some rivers form out of the confluence of smaller rivers, such as Georgia's mighty Altamaha River, actually the child of the Ocmulgee and Oconee Rivers in the middle of the state. Others, like the Ashley and Cooper Rivers in South Carolina, originate much closer to the coast in the Piedmont.

The **blackwater river** is a particularly interesting Southern phenomenon, duplicated only in South America and in one example each in New York and Michigan. While alluvial rivers generally originate in highlands and carry with them a large amount of sediment, blackwater rivers originate in low-lying areas and move slowly toward the sea, carrying with them very little sediment. Rather, their dark tea color comes from the tannic acid of decaying vegetation all along their banks, washed out by the slow, inexorable movement of the river toward the sea. Blackwater courses featured prominently in this guide are Ebenezer Creek near Savannah and Georgia's Suwannee River, which originates in the Okefenokee Swamp and empties into the Gulf of Mexico. Georgia's Altamaha River is a hybrid of sorts because it is partially fed by the blackwater Ohoopee River.

The Intracoastal Waterway

You'll often see its acronym, ICW, on signs—and sadly you'll probably hear the locals mispronounce it "intercoastal"—but the casual visitor might actually find the Intracoastal Waterway difficult to spot. Relying on a natural network of interconnected estuaries and channels, combined with artificial **cuts,** the ICW often blends in rather subtly with the region's already extensive network of creeks and rivers.

Mandated by Congress in 1919 and maintained by the U.S. Army Corps of Engineers, the Atlantic portion of the ICW runs from Key West, Florida, to Boston, Massachusetts, and carries recreational and barge traffic away from the perils of offshore currents and weather. Even if they don't use it specifically, kayakers and boaters often find themselves on it at some point during their nautical adventures.

Estuaries

Most biologists will tell you that the Coastal Plain is where things get interesting. The place where a river interfaces with the ocean is called an estuary, and it's perhaps the most interesting place of all. Estuaries are heavily tidal in nature (indeed, the word derives from *aestus,* Latin for "tide") and feature brackish water and heavy silt content. This portion of the U.S. coast typically has about a 6- to 8-foot tidal range, and the coastal ecosystem depends on this steady ebb and flow for life. At high tide, shellfish open and feed. At low tide, they literally clam up, keeping saltwater inside their shells until the next tide comes. Waterbirds and small mammals feed on shellfish and other animals at low tide, when their prey is exposed. High tide brings an influx of fish and nutrients from the sea, in turn drawing predators like dolphins, who often come into tidal creeks to feed. In the region covered

Salt Marsh

All this water action in both directions—freshwater coming from inland, saltwater encroaching from the Atlantic—results in the phenomenon of the salt marsh, the single most recognizable and iconic geographic feature of the Georgia and South Carolina coast, also known simply as "wetlands." (Freshwater marshes are rarer, with Florida's Everglades being perhaps the premier example.) Far more than just a transitional zone between land and water, marsh is also nature's nursery. Plant and animal life in marshes not only tends to be diverse but encompasses multitudes.

You may not see its denizens easily, but on close inspection you'll find the marsh absolutely teeming with creatures. Visually, the main identifying feature of a salt marsh is its distinctive, reedlike marsh grasses, adapted to survive in brackish water. Like estuaries, marshes and all life in them are heavily influenced by the tides, which bring in nutrients.

The marsh has also played a key role in human history as well, for it was here that the massive rice and indigo plantations grew their signature crops, aided by the natural ebb and flow of the tides. While most marsh you see will look quite undisturbed, very little of it could be called pristine. In the heyday of the rice plantations, much of the coastal salt marsh was criss-crossed by the canal-and-dike system of the paddy fields.

You can still see evidence almost everywhere in this area if you look hard enough (the best time to look is right after takeoff or before land-ing in an airplane, since many approaches to regional airports take you over wetlands). Anytime you see a low, straight ridge running through a marsh, that's likely the eroded, overgrown remnant of an old paddy field dike. Kayakers occasionally find old wooden sluice gates on their paddles.

In the Lowcountry, you'll often hear the term **pluff mud.** This refers to the area's distinctive variety of soft, dark mud in the salt marsh, which often has an equally distinctive odor that locals love but some visitors have a hard time getting used to. Extraordinarily rich in nutrients, pluff mud helped make rice such a successful crop in the marshes of the Lowcountry.

In addition to their vital role as wildlife incubators and sanctuaries, wet-lands are also one of the most important natural protectors of the health of the coastal region. They serve as natural filters, cleansing runoff from the land of toxins and pollutants before it hits the ocean. They also help humans by serving as natural hurricane barriers, their porous nature help-ing to ease the brunt of the damaging storm surge.

Beaches and Barrier Islands

The beautiful, broad beaches of Georgia and South Carolina are almost all situated on barrier islands, long islands parallel to the shoreline and separated from the mainland by a sheltered body of water. Because they're formed from the deposit of sediment by offshore currents, they change shape over the years, with the general pattern of deposit going from north to south (meaning the northern end will begin eroding first). Most of the barrier islands are geologically quite young, only having formed within the last 25,000 years or so. Natural erosion by currents and by storms, combined with the accelerating effects of dredging for local port activity, has quickened the decline of many barrier islands. Many beaches in the area are subject to a mitigation of erosion called **beach renourishment,** which generally involves redistributing dredged material closely offshore so that it will wash up on and around the beach.

As the name indicates, barrier islands are another of nature's safeguards against hurricane damage. Historically, the barrier islands have borne the vast bulk of the damage done by hurricanes in the region. Tybee Island near Savannah was completely under water in the hurricane of 1898. More recently, Sullivan's Island near Charleston was submerged by 1989's Hurricane Hugo, and parts of it were again submerged due to 2017's Hurricane Irma. Like the marshes, barrier islands also help protect the mainland by absorbing the brunt of the storm's wind and surging water.

Though barrier islands are ephemeral by nature, they have played an important role in the area's geography from the beginning of time. In fact, nearly every major settlement on the Georgia coast today—including Savannah, Darien, and Brunswick—is built on the vestiges of massive barrier islands that once guarded a primordial shoreline many miles inland from the present one. By far the largest of these ancient barrier islands, now on dry land, is the fabled **Trail Ridge,** which runs from Jesup, Georgia, to Starke, Florida. The Trail Ridge's height all along its distance made it a favorite route first for Native Americans and then for railroads, which still run along its crest today. The Trail Ridge is such a dominant geographical feature even today that it's actually responsible for the formation of the Okefenokee Swamp. The ridge effectively acts as a levee on the swamp's eastern side, preventing its drainage to the sea.

CLIMATE

One word comes to mind when one thinks about Southern climate: *hot.* That's the first word that occurs to Southerners as well, but virtually every survey of why residents are attracted to the area puts the climate at the top of the list. Go figure. How hot is hot? The average high for July, the region's hottest month, is about 92°F. While that's nothing compared to Tucson or Death Valley, when coupled with the region's notoriously high **humidity** it can have an altogether miserable effect.

Heat aside, there's no doubt that one of the most difficult things for an outsider to adjust to in the South is the humidity. The average annual humidity in Savannah is about 55 percent in the afternoons and a whopping 85 percent in the mornings. The most humid months are August and September. There is no real antidote to humidity—other than air conditioning, that is—although many film crews and other outside workers swear by

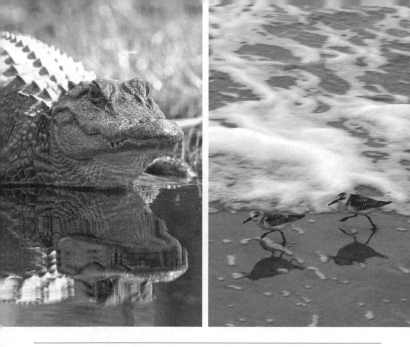

Clockwise from top left: alligator in Okefenokee Swamp; waterfowl along the coast; boat docks along a grass marsh.

the use of Sea Breeze astringent. If you and your traveling companions can deal with the strong minty odor, dampen a hand towel with the astringent, drape it across the back of your neck, and go about your business.

Don't assume that because it's humid you shouldn't drink fluids. Just as in any hot climate, you should drink lots of water if you're going to be out in the Southern heat.

August and September are by far the wettest months in terms of rainfall, with averages well over six inches for each of those months. July is also quite wet, coming in at over five inches on average.

Winters here are pretty mild but can seem much colder than they actually are because of the dampness in the air. The coldest month is January, with a high of about 58°F for the month and 42°F the average low. You're highly unlikely to encounter snow in the area, but if you do, it will likely be only skimpy flurries that a resident of the Great Lakes region wouldn't even notice as snow. But don't let this lull you into a false sense of security.

If such a tiny flurry were to hit, be aware that most people down here have no clue how to drive in rough weather and will not be prepared for even such a small amount of snowfall. Visitors from snow country are often surprised, sometimes bordering on shocked, by how completely a Southern city will shut down when that once-in-a-decade few tenths of an inch of snow finally hits.

Hurricanes

The major weather phenomenon of concern for residents and visitors alike is the mighty hurricane. These massive storms, with counterclockwise-rotating bands of clouds and winds that can push 200 mph, are an ever-present danger to the southeast coast June-November each year.

As most everyone is aware of now, hurricanes are not to be trifled with. Old-fashioned drunken "hurricane parties" are a thing of the past for the most part, the images of cataclysmic destruction everyone has seen on TV having long since eliminated any lingering romanticism about riding out the storm.

Tornadoes—especially those that come in the "back door" through the Gulf of Mexico and overland to the Georgia or Carolina coast—are a very present danger with hurricanes. As hurricanes die out over land, they can spawn dozens of tornadoes, which in many cases prove more destructive than the hurricanes that produced them.

Local TV, websites, and print media can be counted on to give more than ample warning in the event a hurricane is approaching the area during your visit. Whatever you do, do not discount the warnings; it's not worth it. If the locals are preparing to leave, you should too. Typically when a storm is likely to hit the area, there will first be a suggested evacuation. But if authorities determine there's an overwhelming likelihood of imminent hurricane damage, they will issue a **mandatory evacuation order.** What this means in practice is that if you do choose to stay behind, you cannot count on any type of emergency services or help whatsoever.

Generally speaking, the most lethal element of a hurricane is not the wind but the **storm surge,** the wall of ocean water that the winds drive before them onto the coast. During 1989's Hurricane Hugo, Charleston's Battery was inundated with a storm surge of over 12 feet, with an amazing 20 feet reported farther north at Cape Romain.

In the wake of such devastation, local governments have dramatically improved their once tepid disaster-response plans. For example, the large red traffic barriers you see stowed in their ready positions at many exits along I-16 in Georgia are a direct result of the chaos of the botched evacuation during Hurricane Floyd in 1999. Learning from that lesson, Georgia officials decided to make all four lanes of I-16 westbound in the event of a major evacuation, and those red barriers are there today to reroute traffic should they ever be needed.

ENVIRONMENTAL ISSUES

The coast of Georgia is currently experiencing a double whammy, environmentally speaking: Not only are its distinctive wetlands extraordinarily sensitive to human interference, this is one of the most rapidly developing parts of the country. New and often poorly planned subdivisions and resort communities are popping up all over the place. Vastly increased port activity is also taking a devastating toll on the salt marsh and surrounding barrier islands. Combine all that with the South's often skeptical attitude toward environmental activism and you have a recipe for potential ecological disaster.

Thankfully, there are some bright spots. More and more communities are seeing the value of responsible planning and not green-lighting every new development sight unseen. Land trusts and other conservation organizations are growing in size, number, funding, and influence. The large number of marine biologists in these areas at various research and educational institutions means there's a wealth of education and talent available to advise local governments and citizens on how best to conserve the area's natural beauty.

Here's a closer look at some of the most urgent environmental issues facing the region today.

Marsh Dieback

The dominant species of marsh grass, *Spartina alterniflora* (pronounced spar-TINE-uh) and *Juncus roemerianus,* thrive in the typically brackish water of the coastal marsh estuaries, their structural presence helping to stem erosion of banks and dunes. While drought and blight have taken their toll on the grass, increased coastal development and continued channel deepening have also led to a steady creep of ocean saltwater farther and farther into remaining marsh stands.

Effects of Dredging

When General James Oglethorpe first sailed up the Savannah River, it was less than 20 feet deep. Today the Savannah River has been dredged to an average depth of 42 feet—and another deepening is planned, to nearly 50 feet.

Port activity is economically vital—and becoming more so—to the coastal cities. The downside of such large-scale industrial dredging is threefold:

- The deeper the channel, the farther upstream salty ocean water is able to infiltrate. This destroys freshwater and brackish habitats such as the salt marsh.

- Deepening the channel increases both the volume and the velocity of the river, quickening erosion of the riverbanks.

- Too much dredging risks the intrusion of ocean saltwater into underground freshwater aquifers that provide drinking water to millions of people in the area.

Currently the debate over harbor deepening has hit home in Savannah, one of the country's busiest ports. As of this writing the state of Georgia is pursuing deepening at the city's port, much to the consternation of local environmentalists.

The Paper Industry

Early in the 20th century, the Southeast's abundance of cheap undeveloped land and plentiful free water led to the establishment of massive pine tree farms to feed coastal pulp and paper mills. Chances are, if you used a paper grocery bag recently, it was made in a paper mill in the South.

But in addition to making a whole lot of paper bags and providing lots of employment for residents through the decades, the paper industry also gave the area lots of air and water pollution, stressed local rivers (it takes a lot of freshwater to make paper from trees), and took away natural species diversity from the area by devoting so much acreage to a single crop, pine trees.

When driving near rivers in this region, anytime you see a large industrial facility on the riverside it's probably a paper mill. The rotten egg smell that comes next is from the sulfurous discharge from its smokestacks.

Aquifers

Unlike parts of the western United States, where individuals can enforce private property rights to water, the South has generally held that the region's water is a publicly held resource. The upside of this is that everybody has equal claim to drinking water without regard to status or income or how long they've lived here. The downside is that industry also has the same free claim to the water that citizens do—and they use a heck of a lot more of it.

Currently most of coastal region gets its water from aquifers, which are basically huge underground caverns made of limestone. Receiving **groundwater** drip by drip, century after century, from rainfall farther inland, the aquifers essentially act as massive sterile warehouses for freshwater, accessible through wells.

The aquifers have human benefit only if their water remains fresh. Once saltwater from the ocean begins intruding into an aquifer, it doesn't take much to render all of it unfit for human consumption—forever. What keeps that freshwater fresh is natural water pressure, keeping the ocean at bay.

But nearly a century ago, paper mills began pumping millions and millions of gallons of water out of coastal aquifers. Combined with the dramatic rise in coastal residential development and a continuing push to deepen existing shipping channels, the natural water pressure of the aquifers has decreased, leading to measurable saltwater intrusion at several points under the coast.

Currently, local and state governments in both states are increasing their reliance on **surface water** (treated water from rivers and creeks) to relieve the strain on the underground aquifer system. But it's too soon to tell if that has contained the threat from saltwater intrusion.

Air Pollution

Despite growing awareness of the issue, air pollution is still a big problem in the coastal region. Paper mills still operate, putting out their distinctive rotten-eggs odor, and auto emissions standards are notoriously lax. The biggest culprits, though, are coal-powered electric plants, which are the norm throughout the region and which continue to pour large amounts of toxins into the atmosphere.

Plants and Animals

PLANTS

Probably the most iconic plant life of the coastal region is the **Southern live oak** (*Quercus virginiana*), the official state tree of Georgia. Named because of its evergreen nature, a live oak is technically any of a number of evergreens in the *Quercus* genus, many of which reside on the coast, but in local practice almost always refers to the Southern live oak.

Capable of living over 1,000 years and possessing wood of legendary resilience, the Southern live oak is one of nature's most magnificent creations. The timber value of live oaks has been well known since the earliest days of the American shipbuilding industry—when the oak dominated the entire coast inland of the marsh—but their value as a canopy tree has finally been widely recognized.

However, much of the current canopy in the coastal region was deliberately planted in the late Victorian era, and many of the specimens are nearing the end of their natural lifespans. In most situations, they aren't being replanted at an equivalent rate.

Fittingly, the other iconic plant life of the coastal region grows on the branches of the live oak. Contrary to popular opinion, **Spanish moss** (*Tillandsia usneoides*) is neither Spanish nor moss. It's an air plant, a wholly indigenous cousin to the pineapple. Also contrary to folklore, Spanish moss is not a parasite nor does it harbor parasites while living on an oak tree—although it can after it has already fallen to the ground.

Also growing on the bark of a live oak, especially right after a rain shower, is the **resurrection fern** (*Polypodium polypodioides*), which can stay dormant for amazingly long periods of time, only to spring back to life with the introduction of a little water. You can find live oak, Spanish moss, and resurrection fern anywhere in the **maritime forest** ecosystem of coastal Georgia and South Carolina, a zone generally behind the **interdune meadows,** which is right behind the beach zone.

The oak may be Georgia's state tree, but far and away its most important commercial tree is the pine, used for paper, lumber, and turpentine. Rarely seen in the wild today due to tree farming, which has covered most of southern Georgia, the dominant species is now the **slash pine** (*Pinus elliottii*), often seen in long rows on either side of rural highways. Before the introduction of large-scale monoculture tree farming, however, a rich variety of native pines flourished in the **upland forest** inland from the maritime forest, including **longleaf** (*Pinus palustris*) and **loblolly** (*Pinus taeda*) pines.

Right up there with live oaks and Spanish moss in terms of instant recognition would have to be the colorful, ubiquitous **azalea,** a flowering shrub of the *Rhododendron* genus. Over 10,000 varieties have been cultivated through the centuries, with quite a wide range of them on display during blooming season, March-April, on the coast.

The area's other great floral display comes from the **camellia** (*Camellia japonica*), a large, cold-hardy evergreen shrub that generally blooms in late winter (Jan.-Mar.). An import from Asia, the southeastern coast's camellias are close cousins to *Camellia sinensis*, also an import and the plant from which tea is made.

Other colorful ornamentals of the area include the ancient and beautiful **Southern magnolia** (*Magnolia grandiflora*), a native plant with distinctive large white flowers that evolved before the advent of bees; and the **flowering dogwood** (*Cornus florida*), which, despite its very hard wood—great for daggers, hence its original name "dagwood"—is actually quite fragile. An ornamental imported from Asia that has now become quite obnoxious in its aggressive invasiveness is the **mimosa** (*Albizia julibrissin*), which blooms March-August.

Moving into watery areas, you'll find the remarkable **bald cypress** (*Taxodium distichum*), a flood-resistant conifer recognizable by its tufted top, its great height (up to 130 feet), and its distinctive "knees," parts of the root that project above the waterline and which are believed to help stabilize the tree in lowland areas. Much prized for its beautiful pest-resistant wood, great stands of ancient cypress once dominated the marsh along the coast; sadly, overharvesting and destruction of wetlands have made the magnificent sight of this ancient, dignified species much less common. The acres of **smooth cordgrass** for which the Golden Isles are named are plants of the *Spartina alterniflora* species. (A cultivated cousin, *Spartina anglica,* is considered invasive.) Besides its simple natural beauty, *Spartina* is also a key food source for marsh denizens. Playing a key environmental role on the coast are **sea oats** (*Uniola paniculata*). This wispy, fast-growing perennial grass anchors sand dunes and hence is a protected species on the Georgia coast (it's a misdemeanor to pick them).

Palm varieties are not as common up here as in Florida, but you'll definitely encounter several types along the coast. The **cabbage palm** (*Sabal palmetto*) is the largest variety, up to 50-60 feet tall. Its "heart of palm" is an edible delicacy, which coastal Native Americans boiled in bear fat to make porridge. In dunes and sand hills you'll find clumps of the low-lying **saw palmetto** (*Serenoa repens*). The **bush palmetto** (*Sabal minor*) has distinctive fan-shaped branches. The common **Spanish bayonet** (*Yucca aloifolia*) looks like a palm, but it's actually a member of the agave family.

ANIMALS
On the Land

Perhaps the most iconic land animal—or semi-land animal, anyway—of this coastal region is the legendary **American alligator** (*Alligator mississippiensis*), the only species of crocodilian native to the area. Contrary to their fierce reputation, these massive reptiles, 6-12 feet long as adults, are quite shy. If you come in the colder months, you won't see them at all, since alligators require an outdoor temperature over 70°F to become active and feed (indeed, the appearance of alligators was once a well-known symbol of spring in the area).

Often all you'll see is a couple of eyebrow ridges sticking out of the water, and a gator lying still in a shallow creek can easily be mistaken for a floating log. But should you see one or more gators basking in the sun—a favorite activity on warm days for these cold-blooded creatures—it's best to admire them from afar. A mother alligator, in particular, will destroy anything that comes near her nest. Despite the alligator's short, stubby legs, it can run amazingly fast on land—faster than you, in fact.

If you're driving on a country road at night, be on the lookout for **white-tailed deer** (*Odocoileus virginianus*), which, besides being quite beautiful, also pose a serious road hazard. Because coastal development has dramatically reduced the habitat—and therefore the numbers—of their natural predators, deer are very plentiful throughout the area, and as you read this they are hard at work devouring vast tracts of valuable vegetation. No one wants to hurt poor little Bambi, but the truth is that area hunters perform a valuable service by culling the local deer population, which is in no danger of extinction anytime soon.

The coast hosts fairly large populations of playful **river otters** (*Lontra canadensis*). Not to be confused with the larger sea otters of the West Coast, these fast-swimming members of the weasel family inhabit inland waterways and marshy areas, with dominant males sometimes ranging as much as 50 miles within a single waterway. While you're unlikely to encounter an otter, if you're camping you might easily run into the **raccoon** (*Procyon lotor*), an exceedingly intelligent and crafty relative of the bear, sharing that larger animal's resourcefulness in stealing your food. Though nocturnal, raccoons will feed whenever food is available. Rabies is prevalent in the raccoon population, and you should always, always keep your distance.

Another common campsite nuisance, the **opossum** (*Didelphis virginiana*) is a shy, primitive creature that is much more easily discouraged. It's North America's only marsupial, and an opossum's usual "defense" against predators is to play dead. That said, however, they have an immunity to snake venom and often feed on the reptiles, even the most poisonous ones.

While you're unlikely to actually see a **red fox** (*Vulpes vulpes*), you might very well see their distinctive footprints in the mud of a marsh at low tide. These nocturnal hunters, a nonnative species introduced by European settlers, range the coast seeking mice, squirrels, and rabbits.

Once fairly common in this region, the **black bear** (*Ursus americanus*) has suffered from hunting and habitat destruction. Of the regions in this guide, the Okefenokee Swamp area is the only place in which you'll be close to one.

In the Water

Without a doubt the most magnificent denizen—if only part-time—of the southeastern coast is the **North Atlantic right whale** (*Eubalaena glacialis*), which can approach 60 feet in length. Each year December-March the mothers give birth to their calves and nurse them in the warm waters off the Georgia coast in an eons-old ritual. (In the summer they like to hang around the rich fishing grounds off the New England coast, although biologists still can't account for their whereabouts at other times of the year.) Their numbers were so abundant in past centuries that the Spanish name for Jekyll Island, Georgia, was Isla de las Ballenas (Island of the Whales). Whaling and encounters with ship propellers have taken their toll, and numbers of this endangered species are dwindling fast now, with fewer than 500 estimated left in the world.

Another of humankind's aquatic cousins, the **bottlenose dolphin** (*Tursiops truncatus*) is a well-known and frequent visitor to the coast, coming far upstream into creeks and rivers to feed. Children, adults, and experienced sailors alike all delight in encounters with the mammals, sociable creatures who travel in family units. They gather near boats, surfacing often with the distinctive chuffing sound of air coming from their blowholes. Occasionally they'll even lift their heads out of the water to have a look at you; consider yourself lucky indeed to have such a close encounter. Don't be fooled by their cuteness, however. Dolphins live life with gusto and aren't scared of much. They're voracious eaters of fish, energetic lovers, and will take on an encroaching shark in a heartbeat.

Another beloved part-time marine creature of the barrier islands is the **loggerhead turtle** (*Caretta caretta*). Though the species prefers to stay well offshore most of the year, females weighing up to 300 pounds come out of the sea each May-July to dig a shallow hole in the dunes and lay more than 100 leathery eggs, returning to the ocean and leaving the eggs to hatch on their own after two months.

Interestingly, the mothers prefer to nest at the same spot on the same island year after year. After hatching, the baby turtles then make a dramatic, extremely dangerous (and extremely slow) trek to the safety of the waves, at the mercy of various predators. Dedicated research and conservation efforts, like the Caretta Project based on Wassaw Island, Georgia, are working hard to protect the loggerheads' traditional nursery grounds to ensure survival of this fascinating, loveable, and threatened species.

Of course, the coastal waters and rivers are chockablock with fish. The most abundant and sought-after recreational species in the area is the **spotted sea trout** (*Cynoscion nebulosus*), followed by the **red drum** (*Sciaenops ocellatus*). Local anglers also pursue many varieties of **bass, bream, sheepshead,** and **crappie.** It may sound strange to some accustomed to considering it a "trash" fish, but many types of **catfish** are not only plentiful here but are a common and well-regarded food source. Many species of **flounder** inhabit the silty bottoms of estuaries all along the coast. Farther offshore are game and sport fish like **marlin, swordfish, shark, grouper,** and **tuna.**

Each March, anglers jockey for position on coastal rivers for the yearly running of the **American shad** (*Alosa sapidissima*) upstream to spawn. This large (up to eight pounds) catfish-like species is a regional delicacy as a seasonal entrée as well as for its tasty roe. There's a catch limit of eight shad per person per season. One of the more interesting fish species in the area is the endangered **shortnose sturgeon** (*Acipenser brevirostrum*). A fantastically ancient species that has evolved little in hundreds of millions of years, this small freshwater fish is known to exist in the Altamaha, Savannah, and Ogeechee Rivers of Georgia. Traveling upriver to spawn in the winter, the sturgeons remain around the mouths of waterways the rest of the year, venturing near the ocean only sparingly.

Crustaceans and shellfish have been a key food staple in the area for thousands of years, with the massive shell middens of the coast being testament to Native Americans' healthy appetite for them. The beds of the local variant, the **eastern oyster** (*Crassostrea virginica*), aren't what they used to be due to overharvesting, water pollution, and disruption of habitat. In truth, these days most local restaurants import the little filter-feeders from the Gulf of Mexico. Oysters spawn May-August, hence the old folk wisdom about eating oysters only in months with the letter *r* so as not to disrupt the breeding cycle.

Each year April-January, shrimp boats up and down the southeastern coast trawl for **shrimp,** most commercially viable in two local species, the white shrimp (*Litopenaeus setiferus*) and the brown shrimp (*Farfantepenaeus aztecus*). Shrimp are the most popular seafood item in the United States and bring hundreds of millions of dollars in revenue into the coastal economy. While consumption won't slow down anytime soon, the region's shrimping industry is facing serious threats, from species decline due to pollution and overfishing as well as from competition from shrimp farms and the Asian shrimp industry.

Another important commercial crop is the **blue crab** (*Callinectes sapidus*), the species used in such Lowcountry delicacies as crab cakes. You'll often see floating markers bobbing up and down in rivers throughout the region. These signal the presence directly below of a crab trap, often of an amateur crabber.

A true living link to primordial times, the alien-looking **horseshoe crab** (*Limulus polyphemus*) is frequently found on beaches of the coast during the spring mating season (it lives in deeper water the rest of the year). More closely related to scorpions and spiders than crabs, the horseshoe has evolved hardly a lick in hundreds of millions of years.

Any trip to a local salt marsh at low tide will likely uncover hundreds of **fiddler crabs** (*Uca pugilator* and *Uca pugnax*), so-named for the way the males wave their single enlarged claw in the air to attract mates. (Their other, smaller claw is the one they actually eat with.) The fiddlers make distinctive burrows in the pluff mud for sanctuary during high tide, recognizable by the little balls of sediment at the entrances (the crabs spit out the balls after sifting through the sand for food).

One charming beach inhabitant, the **sand dollar** (*Mellita quinquiesperforata*), has seen its numbers decline drastically due to being entirely too charming for its own good. Beachcombers are now asked to enjoy these flat little cousins to the sea urchin in their natural habitat and to refrain from taking them home. Besides, they start to smell bad when they dry out.

The **sea nettle** (*Chrysaora quinquecirrha*), a less-than-charming beach inhabitant, is a jellyfish that stings thousands of people on the coast each year (although only for those with severe allergies are the stings potentially life-threatening). Stinging their prey before transporting it into their waiting mouths, the jellyfish also sting when disturbed or frightened. Most often, people are stung by stepping on the bodies of jellyfish washed up on the sand. If you're stung by a jellyfish, don't panic. You'll probably experience a stinging rash for about half an hour. Locals say applying a little baking soda or vinegar helps cut the sting. (Some also swear fresh urine will do the trick, and I pass that tip along to you purely in the interest of thoroughness.)

In the Air

When enjoying the marshlands of the coast, consider yourself fortunate to see a **wood stork** (*Mycteria americana*), very recently taken off the endangered species list. The only storks to breed in North America, these graceful long-lived birds (routinely living over 10 years) are usually seen on a low flight path across the marsh, although at some birding spots beginning in late summer you can find them at a **roost,** sometimes numbering over 100 birds. Resting at high tide, they fan out over the marsh to feed at simply "the preacher."

Often confused with the wood stork is the gorgeous **white ibis** (*Eudocimus albus*), distinguishable by its orange bill and black wingtips. Like the wood stork, the ibis is a communal bird that roosts in colonies.

Other similar-looking coastal denizens are the white-feathered **great egret** (*Ardea alba*) and **snowy egret** (*Egretta thula*), the former distinguishable by its yellow bill and the latter by its black bill and the tuft of plumes on the back of its head. Egrets are in the same family as herons.

The most magnificent in that family is the **great blue heron** (*Ardea herodias*). Despite their imposing height—up to four feet tall—these waders are shy. Often you hear them rather than see them, as a loud shriek of alarm echoes over the marsh.

So how to tell the difference between all these wading birds at a glance? It's actually easiest when they're in flight. Egrets and herons fly with their necks tucked in, while storks and ibis fly with their necks extended.

Dozens of species of shorebirds comb the beaches, including **sandpipers, plovers,** and the wonderful and rare **American oystercatcher** (*Haematopus palliatus*), instantly recognizable for its prancing walk, dark-brown back, stark white underside, and long bright-orange bill. **Gulls** and **terns** also hang out wherever there's water. They can frequently be seen swarming around incoming shrimp boats, attracted by the catch of little crustaceans.

The chief raptor of the salt marsh is the fish-eating **osprey** (*Pandion haliaetus*). These large grayish birds of prey are similar to eagles but are adapted to a maritime environment, with a reversible outer toe on each talon (the better for catching wriggly fish) and closable nostrils so they can dive into the water after prey. Very common all along the coast, they like to build big nests on top of buoys and channel markers in addition to trees.

The **bald eagle** (*Haliaeetus leucocephalus*) is making a comeback in the area thanks to increased federal regulation and better education of trigger-happy locals. Apparently not as all-American as their bumper stickers might sometimes indicate, local farmers would often regard the national symbol as more of a nuisance and fire away anytime they saw one. Of course, as we all should have learned in school, the bald eagle is not actually bald but has a head adorned with white feathers. Like the osprey, bald eagles prefer fish, but unlike the osprey will settle for rodents and rabbits.

Inland among the pines you'll find the most common area woodpecker, the huge **pileated woodpecker** (*Dryocopus pileatus*) with its large crest. Less common is the smaller, more subtly marked **red-cockaded woodpecker** (*Picoides borealis*). Once common in the vast primordial pine forests of the Southeast, the species is now endangered, its last real refuge being the big tracts of relatively undisturbed land on military bases.

Insects

Down here they say that God invented bugs to keep the Yankees from

completely taking over the South. And insects are probably the most unpleasant fact of life in the southeastern coastal region. The list of annoying
indigenous insects must begin with the infamous **sand gnat** (*Culicoides
furens*). This tiny and persistent nuisance, a member of the midge family,
lacks the precision of the mosquito with its long proboscis. No, the sand
gnat is more torture master than surgeon, brutally gouging and digging
away its victim's skin until it hits a source of blood. Most prevalent in the
spring and fall, the sand gnat is drawn to its prey by the carbon dioxide trail
of its breath. While long sleeves and long pants are one way to keep gnats
at bay, the only real antidote to the sand gnat's assault—other than never
breathing—is the Avon skin-care product Skin So Soft, which has taken
on a new and wholly unplanned life as the South's favorite anti-gnat lotion.
In calmer moments, grow to appreciate the great contribution sand gnats
make to the salt marsh ecosystem—as food for birds and bats.

Running a close second to the sand gnat are the over three dozen species
of the highly aggressive **mosquito,** which breeds anywhere a few drops of
water lie stagnant. Not surprisingly, massive populations blossom in the
rainiest months, in late spring and late summer, feeding in the morning and
late afternoon. Like the gnat, the mosquito—the biters are always female—
homes in on its victim by trailing the plume of carbon dioxide exhaled in
the breath. More than just a biting nuisance, mosquitoes are now carrying
West Nile disease to the Lowcountry and Georgia coast, signaling a possibly dire threat to public health. Alas, Skin So Soft has little effect on the
mosquito. Try over-the-counter sprays, anything smelling of citronella, and
wearing long sleeves and long pants when weather permits.

But undoubtedly the most viscerally loathed of all pests on the
Lowcountry and Georgia coasts is the so-called "palmetto bug," or
American cockroach (*Periplaneta americana*). These black, shiny, and
sometimes grotesquely massive insects—up to two inches long—are living fossils, virtually unchanged over hundreds of millions of years. And
perfectly adapted as they are to life in and among wet, decaying vegetation,
they're unlikely to change a bit in 100 million more years. While they spend
most of their time crawling around, usually under rotting leaves and tree
bark, American cockroaches can indeed fly—sort of. There are few more
hilarious sights than a room full of people frantically trying to dodge a
palmetto bug that has just clumsily launched itself off a high point on the
wall. Because the cockroach doesn't know any better than you do where
it's going, it can be a particularly bracing event—though the insect does
not bite and poses few real health hazards.

Popular regional use of the term *palmetto bug* undoubtedly has its roots
in a desire for polite Southern society to avoid using the ugly word *roach*
and its connotations of filth and unclean environments. But the colloqui-
alism actually has a basis in reality. Contrary to what anyone tells you, the
natural habitat of the American cockroach—unlike its kitchen-dwelling,
much-smaller cousin the German cockroach—is outdoors, often up in
trees. They only come inside human dwellings when it's especially hot,

especially cold, or especially dry outside. Like you, the palmetto bug is easily driven indoors by extreme temperatures and by thirst.

Other than visiting the Southeast during the winter, when the roaches go dormant, there's no convenient antidote for their presence. The best way to keep them out of your life is to stay away from decaying vegetation and keep doors and windows closed on especially hot nights.

History

BEFORE THE EUROPEANS

Based on artifacts found throughout the state, anthropologists know the first humans arrived on the coasts of South Carolina and Georgia at least 13,000 years ago, at the tail end of the last ice age. During this **Paleo-Indian period,** sea levels were over 200 feet lower than present levels, and large mammals such as woolly mammoths, horses, and camels were hunted for food and skins. However, rapidly increasing temperatures, rising sea levels, and efficient hunting techniques combined to quickly kill off these large mammals, relics of the Pleistocene era, ushering in the **Archaic period.** Still hunter-gatherers, Archaic period inhabitants began turning to small game such as deer, bears, and turkeys, supplemented with fruit and nuts. The latter part of the Archaic period saw more habitation on the coasts, with an increasing reliance on fish and shellfish. It's to this time that the great **shell middens** of the coastal region trace their origins. Basically serving as trash heaps for discarded oyster shells, as the middens grew in size they also took on a ceremonial status, often being used as sites for important rituals and meetings. Such sites are often called **shell rings,** and the largest yet found was over nine feet high and 300 feet in diameter.

The introduction of agriculture and improved pottery techniques about 3,000 years ago led to the **Woodland period** of Native American settlement. Extended clan groups were much less migratory, establishing year-round communities of up to 50 people, who began the practice of clearing land to grow crops. The ancient shell middens of their ancestors were not abandoned, however, and were continually added onto. Native Americans had been cremating or burying their dead for years, a practice that eventually gave rise to the construction of the first **mounds** during the Woodland period. Essentially built-up earthworks sometimes marked with spiritual symbols, often in the form of animal shapes, mounds contained not only the remains of the deceased but items like pottery to accompany the deceased into the afterlife.

Increased agriculture led to increased population, and with that population growth came competition over resources and a more formal notion of warfare. This period, about AD 800-1600, is termed the **Mississippian period.** It was the Mississippians who would be the first Native Americans in what's now the continental United States to encounter

European explorers and settlers after Columbus. The Native Americans who would later be called **Creek Indians** were the direct descendants of the Mississippians in lineage, language, and lifestyle. Native American social structure north of Mexico reached its apex with the Mississippians, who were not only prodigious mound builders but constructed elaborate wooden villages and evolved a top-down class system. The defensive palisades surrounding some of the villages attest to the increasingly martial nature of the groups and their chieftains, or *micos*.

Described by later European accounts as a tall, proud people, the Mississippians often wore elaborate body art and, like the indigenous inhabitants of Central and South America, used the practice of **head shaping,** whereby an infant's skull was deliberately deformed into an elongated shape by tying the baby's head to a board for about a year.

THE SPANISH ARRIVE

The first known contact by Europeans on the southeastern coast came in 1521, roughly concurrent with Cortés's conquest of Mexico. A party of Spanish slavers ventured into what's now Port Royal Sound, South Carolina, from Santo Domingo in the Caribbean. Naming the area Santa Elena, they kidnapped a few Indian slaves and left, ranging as far north as the Cape Fear River in present-day North Carolina.

The first serious exploration of the coast came in 1526, when Lucas Vázquez de Ayllón and about 600 colonists made landfall at Winyah Bay in South Carolina, near present-day Georgetown. They didn't stay long, however, immediately moving down the coast and trying to set down roots in the St. Catherine's Sound area of modern-day Liberty County, Georgia.

That colony—called San Miguel de Gualdape—was the first European settlement in North America since the Vikings (the continent's oldest continuously occupied settlement, St. Augustine, Florida, wasn't founded until 1565). The colony also brought with it the seed of a future nation's dissolution: slaves from Africa. While San Miguel lasted only six weeks due to political tension and a slave uprising, artifacts from its brief life have been discovered in the area.

Hernando de Soto's ill-fated trek of 1539-1543 from Florida through Georgia to Alabama (where De Soto died of a fever) did not find the gold he anticipated, nor did it enter the coastal region covered in this guide. But De Soto's legacy was indeed soon felt there and throughout the Southeast in the form of various diseases for which the Mississippian people had no immunity whatsoever: smallpox, typhus, influenza, measles, yellow fever, whooping cough, diphtheria, tuberculosis, and bubonic plague.

While the cruelties of the Spanish certainly took their toll, these deadly diseases were far more damaging to a population totally unprepared for them. Within a few years, the Mississippian people—already in a state of internal decline—were losing a huge percentage of their population to disease, echoing what had already happened on a massive scale to the indigenous people of the Caribbean after Christopher Columbus's expeditions.

As the viruses they introduced ran rampant, the Europeans themselves stayed away for a couple of decades after the ignominious end of De Soto's fruitless quest.

During that quarter-century, the once-proud Mississippian culture continued to disintegrate, dwindling into a shadow of its former greatness. In all, disease would claim the lives of at least 80 percent of all indigenous inhabitants of the Western Hemisphere.

THE FRENCH MISADVENTURE

The next European presence on the Georgia and South Carolina coast was another ill-fated attempt, the establishment of Charlesfort in 1562 by French Huguenots under Jean Ribault on present-day Parris Island, South Carolina. Part of a covert effort by the Protestant French admiral Gaspard II de Coligny to send Huguenot colonists around the globe, Ribault's crew of 150 first explored the mouth of the St. Johns River near present-day Jacksonville, Florida, before heading north.

After establishing Charlesfort, Ribault returned to France for supplies. In his absence, religious war had broken out in his home country. Ribault sought sanctuary in England but was clapped in irons anyway. Meanwhile, most of Charlesfort's colonists grew so demoralized they joined another French expedition led by René Laudonnière at Fort Caroline on the St. Johns River. The remaining 27 built a ship to sail from Charlesfort back to France; 20 of them survived the journey, which was cut short in the English Channel when they had to be rescued.

Ribault himself was dispatched to reinforce Fort Caroline, but was headed off by a contingent from the new Spanish settlement at St. Augustine. The fate of the French presence on the southeast coast was sealed when not only did the Spanish take Fort Caroline but a storm destroyed Ribault's reinforcing fleet; Ribault and all survivors were killed as soon as they came ashore. To keep the French away for good and cement Spain's hold on this northernmost part of their province of La Florida, the Spanish built the fort of Santa Elena directly on top of Charlesfort. Both layers are currently being excavated and studied.

THE MISSION ERA

With Spanish dominance of the region ensured for the near future, the lengthy mission era began. It's rarely mentioned as a key part of U.S. history, but the Spanish missionary presence on the Georgia coast was longer and more comprehensive than its much more widely known counterpart in California. St. Augustine's governor, Pedro Menéndez de Avilés—sharing "biscuits with honey" on the beach at St. Catherine's Island with a local *mico*—negotiated for the right to establish a system of Jesuit missions in two coastal chiefdoms: the Mocama on and around Cumberland Island, and the Guale (pronounced "wallie") to the north. Those early missions, the first north of Mexico, were largely unsuccessful. But a renewed, organized effort by the Franciscan Order came to fruition during the 1580s.

Henry Woodward, Colonial Indiana Jones

He's virtually unsung in the history books, and there are no movies made about him, but Dr. Henry Woodward, the first English settler in South Carolina, lived a life that is the stuff of novels and screenplays. Educated in medicine in London, Woodward first tried his hand in the colony of Barbados. Still in his teens, Woodward left Barbados in Captain Robert Sandford's 1664 expedition to Carolina. In 1666, in what is perhaps the New World's first "cultural exchange program," Woodward volunteered to stay behind while the rest of the expedition returned to England.

Woodward learned the local language and established relations with Native Americans, actions for which the Lords Proprietors granted him temporary "formall possession of the whole Country to hold as Tennant att Will." The Spanish kidnapped the young Englishman, taking him to the Spanish stronghold of St. Augustine in Florida. Woodward was popular and treated well. During that time, he studied Spanish government, commerce, and culture, with the same diligence with which he had studied the Indians a year earlier. In 1668, Woodward was "rescued" by English pirates under the command of Robert Searle. Woodward's sojourn with the pirates would last two years, during which he was kept on board as ship's surgeon.

In 1670 Woodward was rescued when the pirates shipwrecked on the Caribbean island of Nevis. His rescuers were none other than settlers on their way to found Charles Towne. Woodward used his previous experience

Starting with Santa Catalina de Guale on St. Catherine's Island, missions were established all along the Georgia coast.

The looming invasion threat to St. Augustine from English adventurer and privateer Sir Francis Drake was a harbinger of trouble to come, as was a Guale uprising in 1597. The Spanish consolidated their positions near St. Augustine, and Santa Elena was abandoned. As Spanish power waned, in 1629 Charles I of England laid formal claim to what is now the Carolinas, Georgia, and much of Florida but made no effort to colonize the area. Largely left to their own devices and facing an indigenous population dying from disease, the missions in the Georgia interior nonetheless carried on. A devastating Indian raid in 1661 on a mission at the mouth of the Altamaha River, possibly aided by the English, persuaded the Spanish to pull the mission effort to the barrier islands. But even as late as 1667, right before the founding of Charles Towne far to the north, there were 70 missions still extant in the old Guale kingdom.

Pirate raids and slave uprisings finished off the Georgia missions for good by 1684. By 1706 the Spanish mission effort in the Southeast had fully retreated to St. Augustine. In an interesting postscript, 89 Native Americans—the only surviving descendants of Spain's Georgia missions—evacuated to Cuba with the final Spanish exodus from Florida in 1763.

to direct the colonists to an area of less Spanish influence. That same year he began a series of expeditions to contact Native Americans in the Carolina interior—the first non-Spanish European to set foot in the area. Using information gained from the Spanish, Woodward's goal was to jump-start the trade in deerskins that would be the bulwark of the Charles Towne colony. Woodward's 1674 alliance with the aggressive Westo people was instrumental in this burgeoning trade. As if all this weren't enough, in 1680 Woodward, now with property of his own on Johns Island, would introduce local farmers to a certain crop recently imported from Madagascar: rice.

Woodward made enemies of settlers who were envious of his growing affluence and suspicious of his friendship with the Westo. His outspoken disgust with the spread of Indian slavery brought a charge against him of undermining the interests of the crown. But Woodward, by now a celebrity of sorts, returned to England to plead his case directly to the Lords Proprietors. They not only pardoned him but made him their official Indian agent—with a 20 percent share of the profits.

Woodward returned to the American colonies to trek inland, making alliances with groups of Creek Indians in Spanish-held territory. Hounded by Spanish troops, Woodward fell ill of a fever somewhere in the Savannah River valley. He made it to Charleston and safety but never fully recovered and died around 1690.

ENTER THE ENGLISH

With the native populations in steep decline due to disease and a wholesale retrenchment by European powers, a sort of vacuum came to the southeastern coast. Into the vacuum came the first English-speaking settlers of South Carolina. The first attempt was an expedition by a Barbadian colonist, William Hilton, in 1663. While he didn't establish a new colony, he did leave his name on the most notable geographic feature he saw—Hilton Head Island.

In 1665 King Charles II gave a charter to eight **Lords Proprietors** to establish a colony, generously to be named Carolina after the monarch himself. Remarkably, none of the Proprietors ever set foot in the colony they established for their own profit. Before their colony was even set up, the Proprietors themselves set the stage for the vast human disaster that would eventually befall it. They encouraged slavery by promising that each colonist would receive 20 acres of land for every black male slave and 10 acres for every black female slave brought to the colony within the first year.

In 1666 explorer Robert Sandford officially claimed Carolina for the king. The Proprietors then sent out a fleet of three ships from England, only one of which, the *Carolina*, would make it the whole way. After stops in the thriving English colonies of Barbados and Bermuda, the ship landed in Port Royal. The settlers were greeted without violence, but the fact that the local indigenous people spoke Spanish led the colonists to conclude that perhaps the site was too close for comfort to Spain's sphere of influence.

A Kiawah chief, eager for allies against the fierce, slave-trading Westo people, invited the colonists north to settle instead. So the colonists—148 of them, including three African slaves—moved 80 miles up the coast and in 1670 pitched camp on the Ashley River at a place they dubbed Albemarle Point after one of their lost ships. Living within the palisades of the camp, the colonists farmed 10-acre plots outside the walls.

A few years later some colonists from Barbados, which was beginning to suffer the effects of overpopulation, joined the Carolinians. The Barbadian influence, with an emphasis on large-scale slave labor and a caste system, would have an indelible imprint on the colony. Indeed, within a generation a majority of settlers in the new colony would be African slaves.

By 1680, however, Albemarle Point was feeling growing pains as well, and the Proprietors ordered the site moved to Oyster Point at the confluence of the Ashley and Cooper Rivers (the present-day Battery). Within a year Albemarle Point was abandoned, and the walls of Charles Towne were built a few hundred yards up from Oyster Point on the banks of the Cooper River.

The original Anglican settlers were quickly joined by various **Dissenters,** among them French Huguenots, Quakers, Congregationalists, and Jews. A group of Scottish Presbyterians established the short-lived Stuart Town near Port Royal in 1684. Recognizing this diversity, the colony in 1697 granted religious liberty to all "except Papists," meaning Catholics. The Anglicans attempted a crackdown on Dissenters in 1704, but two years later Queen Anne stepped in and ensured religious freedom for all Carolinians (again with the exception of Catholics, who wouldn't be a factor in the colony until after the American Revolution).

THE YAMASEE WAR

Within 20 years the English presence had expanded throughout the Lowcountry to include Port Royal and Beaufort. Charles Towne became a thriving commercial center, dealing in deerskins with traders in the interior and with foreign concerns from England to South America. Its success was not without a backlash, as the local **Yamasee** people became increasingly disgruntled at the settlers' growing monopolies on deerskin and the trade in Native American slaves.

As rumors of war spread, on Good Friday, 1715, a delegation of six Carolinians went to the Yamasee village of Pocataligo to address some of the Native Americans' grievances in the hopes of forestalling violence. Their effort was in vain, however, as warriors murdered four of them in their sleep; the remaining two escaped to sound the alarm.

The treacherous attack signaled the beginning of the two-year Yamasee War, which would claim the lives of nearly 10 percent of the colony's population and an unknown number of Native Americans—making it one of the bloodiest conflicts fought on American soil.

Energized and ready for war, the Yamasee attacked Charles Towne itself and killed almost all the white traders in the interior, effectively ending commerce in the area. As Charles Towne began to swell with refugees from the hinterland, water and supplies ran low, and the colony's very existence was in peril.

After an initially poor performance by the Carolina militia, a professional army—including armed African slaves—was raised. Well trained and well led, the new army more than held its own despite being outnumbered. A key alliance with local Cherokees was all the advantage the colonists needed to turn the tide. While the Cherokee never received the overt military backing from the settlers that they sought, they did garner enough supplies and influence to convince their Creek rivals, the Yamasee, to begin the peace process. The war-weary settlers, eager to get back to life and to business, were anxious to negotiate with them, offering goods as a sign of their earnest intent. By 1717 the Yamasee threat had subsided and trade in the region began flourishing anew.

No sooner had the Yamasee War ended, however, than a new threat emerged: the dreaded pirate Edward Teach, aka Blackbeard. Entering Charleston harbor in May 1718 with his flagship *Queen Anne's Revenge* and three other vessels, he promptly plundered five ships and began a full-scale blockade of the entire settlement. He took a number of prominent citizens hostage before finally departing northward.

SLAVERY

For the colonists, the Blackbeard episode was the final straw. Already disgusted by the lack of support from the Lords Proprietors during the Yamasee War, the humiliation of the pirate blockade was too much to take. To almost universal agreement in the colony, the settlers threw off the rule of the Proprietors and lobbied in 1719 to become a crown colony, an effort that came to final fruition in 1729.

While this outward-looking and energetic Charleston was originally built on the backs of merchants, with the introduction of the rice and indigo crops in the early 1700s it would increasingly be built on the backs of slaves. For all the wealth gained through the planting of rice and cotton seeds, another seed was sown by the Lowcountry plantation culture. The area's total dependence on slave labor would ultimately lead to a disastrous war, a conflict signaled for decades to those smart enough to read the signs.

By the early 18th century Savannah and Charleston were firmly established as the key American ports for the importation of African slaves, with about 40 percent of the trade centered in Charleston alone. As a result, the black population of the coast outnumbered the white population by more than three to one, and much more than that in some areas. The fear of violent slave uprisings had great influence over not only politics but day-to-day affairs.

These fears were eventually realized in the **Stono Rebellion** on September 9, 1739. Twenty African American slaves led by an Angolan known only as Jemmy met near the Stono River near Charleston. Marching with a banner that read "Liberty," they seized guns with the plan of marching all the way to Spanish Florida and finding sanctuary in the wilderness. On the way they burned seven plantations and killed 20 more whites. A militia eventually caught up with them, killing 44 escaped slaves while losing 20 of their own. The prisoners were decapitated and had their heads spiked on every milepost between the spot of that final battle and Charleston. Inspired by the rebellion, at least two other uprisings would take place over the next two years in South Carolina and Georgia.

OGLETHORPE'S VISION

In 1729, Carolina was divided into north and south. In 1731, a colony to be known as Georgia, after the new English king, was carved out of the southern part of the Carolina land grant. A young general, aristocrat, and humanitarian named James Edward Oglethorpe gathered together a group of Trustees—similar to Carolina's Lords Proprietors—to take advantage.

While Oglethorpe would go on to found Georgia, his wasn't the first English presence in the area. A garrison built Fort King George in modern-day Darien, Georgia, in 1721, which you can visit today. A cypress blockhouse surrounded by palisaded earthworks, the fort defended the southern reaches of England's claim for seven years before being abandoned in 1728.

On February 12, 1733, after stops in Beaufort and Charleston, the ship *Anne* with its 114 passengers made its way to the highest bluff on the Savannah River. The area was controlled by the peaceful Yamacraw people, who had been encouraged by the powers-that-be in Charleston to settle on this vacant land 12 miles up the Savannah River to serve as a buffer for the Spanish. Led by an elderly chief, or *mico,* named Tomochichi, the Yamacraw enjoyed the area's natural bounty of shellfish, fruit, nuts, and small game.

A deft politician, Oglethorpe struck up a treaty and eventually a genuine friendship with Tomochichi. To the Yamacraw, Oglethorpe was a rare bird—a white man who behaved with honor and was true to his word. The Native Americans reciprocated by helping the settlers and pledging fealty to the crown. Oglethorpe reported to the Trustees that Tomochichi personally requested "that we would Love and Protect their little Families."

In negotiations with local tribes using Mary Musgrove, a Creek-English settler in the area, as translator, the persuasive Oglethorpe convinced the coastal Creek to cede to the crown all Georgia land to the Altamaha River. Oglethorpe's impact was soon felt farther down the Georgia coast, as St. Simons Island, Jekyll Island, Darien, and Brunswick were settled in rapid succession, and with them the entrenchment of the plantation system and slave labor.

While the Trustees' utopian vision was largely economic in nature, like Carolina the Georgia colony also emphasized religious freedom. While to modern ears Charleston's antipathy toward "papists" and Oglethorpe's original ban of Catholics from Georgia might seem incompatible with

Clockwise from top left: a horse on the grounds of the Coastal Discovery Museum at Honey Horn; the Savannah Cotton Exchange; Fort Pulaski.

this goal, the reason was a coldly pragmatic one for the time: England's two main global rivals, France and Spain, were both staunchly Catholic countries.

SPAIN VANQUISHED

Things heated up on the coast in 1739 with the so-called **War of Jenkins' Ear,** which despite its seemingly trivial beginnings over the humiliation of a British captain by Spanish privateers was actually a proxy struggle emblematic of changes in the European balance of power. A year later Oglethorpe cobbled together a force of settlers, Indian allies, and Carolinians to reduce the Spanish fortress at St. Augustine, Florida. The siege failed, and Oglethorpe retreated to St. Simons Island to await the inevitable counterattack. In 1742, a Spanish force invaded the island but was eventually turned back for good at the **Battle of Bloody Marsh.** That clash marked the end of Spanish overtures on England's colonies in what is now the United States.

Though Oglethorpe returned to England a national hero, things fell apart in Savannah. The settlers became envious of the success of Charleston's slave-based rice economy and began wondering aloud why they couldn't also make use of free labor. With Oglethorpe otherwise occupied in England, the Trustees of Georgia—distant in more ways than just geographically from the new colony—bowed to public pressure and relaxed the restrictions on slavery and rum. By 1753 the Trustees voted to return their charter to the crown, officially making Georgia the 13th and final colony of England in America. With first the French and then the Spanish effectively shut off from the American East Coast, the stage was set for an internal battle between England and its burgeoning colonies across the Atlantic.

REVOLUTION AND INDEPENDENCE

The population of the colonies swelled in the mid-1700s, not only from an influx of slaves but a corresponding flood of European immigrants. The interior began filling up with Germans, Swiss, Scottish, and Irish settlers. Their subsequent demands for political representation led to tension between them and the coastal inhabitants, typically depicted through the years as an Upcountry versus Lowcountry competition. It is a persistent but inaccurate myth that the affluent elite on the southeastern coast were reluctant to break ties with England. While the Lowcountry's cultural and economic ties to England were certainly strong, the **Stamp Act** and the **Townshend Acts** combined to turn public sentiment against the mother country here as elsewhere in the colonies.

South Carolinian planters like Christopher Gadsden, Henry Laurens, John Rutledge, and Arthur Middleton were early leaders in the movement for independence. Planters in what would be called Liberty County, Georgia, also strongly agitated for the cause. War broke out between the colonists and the British in New England and soon made its way southward. The British failed to take Charleston—the fourth-largest city in the colonies—in June 1776, an episode that gave South Carolina its "Palmetto State" moniker when redcoat cannonballs bounced off the palm tree-lined walls of Fort Moultrie. The British under General Sir Henry Clinton successfully took the city in 1780, however, occupying it until 1782.

The British, under General Archibald Campbell, took Savannah in 1778. Royal Governor Sir James Wright returned from exile to Georgia to reclaim it for the crown, the only one of the colonies to be subsumed again into the British Empire. A polyglot force of colonists, Haitians, and Hessians attacked the British fortifications on the west side of Savannah in 1779 but were repulsed with heavy losses. Although the area's two major cities had fallen to the British, the war raged on throughout the surrounding area.

Indeed, throughout the Lowcountry, fighting was as vicious as anything yet seen on the North American continent. With over 130 known military engagements occurring there, South Carolina sacrificed more men during the war than any other colony—including Massachusetts, the "Cradle of the Revolution."

The struggle became a guerrilla war of colonists versus the British as well as a civil war between patriots and loyalists, or **Tories.** Committing what would today undoubtedly be called war crimes, the British routinely burned homes, churches, and fields and massacred civilians. Using Daufuskie Island as a base, British soldiers staged raids on Hilton Head plantations.

In response, patriots of the Lowcountry bred a group of deadly guerrilla soldiers under legendary leaders such as Francis Marion, "the Swamp Fox," and Thomas Sumter, "the Gamecock," who attacked the British in daring hit-and-run raids staged from swamps and marshes. A covert group of patriots called the **Sons of Liberty** met clandestinely throughout the Lowcountry, plotting revolution over pints of ale. Sometimes their efforts transcended talk, however, and atrocities were committed against area loyalists.

In all, four South Carolinians signed the Declaration of Independence (Thomas Heyward Jr., Thomas Lynch Jr., Arthur Middleton, and Edward Rutledge), as did three Georgians (Button Gwinnett, Lyman Hall, and George Walton).

HIGH COTTON

True to form, the new nation wasted no time in asserting its economic strength. Rice planters from Georgetown north of Charleston on down to the Altamaha River in Georgia built on their already impressive wealth, becoming the new nation's richest men by far—with fortunes built on the backs of the slaves working in their fields.

In 1786, a new crop was introduced that would only enhance the financial clout of the coastal region: cotton. A former loyalist colonel, Roger Kelsal, sent some seed from the West Indies to his friend James Spaulding, owner of a plantation on St. Simons Island, Georgia. This crop, soon to be known as **Sea Island cotton** and considered the best in the world, would supplant rice as the crop of choice for coastal plantations. At the height of

Nathanael Greene and Mulberry Grove

Nathanael Greene's time in Savannah was short and mostly unfortunate. One of the American Revolution's greatest heroes, Greene rose from the rank of private in the Continental Army to become George Washington's right-hand man. As a brigadier general in the Rhode Island militia, Greene's innate military prowess caught Washington's eye during the siege of Boston, whereupon the future president gave Greene command of the entire Southern theater of the fight for independence. Greene's guerrilla tactics forced the English contingent to divide and hence weaken itself. It was Greene who sent General "Mad Anthony" Wayne in 1782 to free Savannah from the British. Greene insisted that no revenge be taken on Savannah's loyalists, instead welcoming them into the new nation as partners. For his service, Washington granted Greene a large estate on the banks of the Savannah River known as Mulberry Grove, known to history as the place where Eli Whitney would later invent the cotton gin while serving as tutor to the Greene children.

Mulberry Grove was less productive for Greene, who as a lifelong abolitionist refused to use slave labor on the plantation, and hence paid a steep financial price. The 44-year-old Greene had spent less than a year at Mulberry Grove, mostly worrying about finances, when he caught sunstroke on a particularly brutal June day in 1786 and died shortly thereafter.

At some point Greene's remains were said to have been lost after a family vault in Colonial Cemetery was vandalized by Union troops. Then in 1900 the Society of the Cincinnati of Rhode Island appointed a search committee to find and properly inter the general's long-lost remains. The remains were indeed found—right in the vault in Colonial Cemetery where they were supposed to have been, which you can see to this day. However, they were underneath someone else: After removing the coffin of one Robert Scott, excavators found "a mass of rotten wood and human bones mixed with sand," along with a rusty coffin plate reading, "Nathanael Greene / Obit June 19, 1786 / Aetat [Age] 44 Years." In 1902, Greene's remains were put to rest under his monument in Johnson Square—dedicated to him by the Marquis de Lafayette in 1825.

All buildings at Mulberry Grove were razed by Sherman's troops in 1864. The area entered industrial use in 1975 and is currently occupied by the Georgia Ports Authority. No full-scale archaeological dig has ever been done at the site, although the nonprofit Mulberry Grove Foundation (www.mulberrygrove.org) is working toward that as well as a plan to make part of the 2,200-acre parcel a wildlife preserve.

the Southern cotton boom in the early 1800s, a single Sea Island cotton harvest on a single plantation might go for $100,000—in 1820 dollars. While Charleston was still by far the largest, most powerful, and most influential city on the southeastern coast of the United States, at the peak of the cotton craze Savannah was actually doing more business—a fact that grated to no end on the Holy City's elite. Unlike Charleston, where the planters themselves dominated city life, in Savannah it was cotton brokers called **factors** who were the city's leading class. During this time most of the grand homes of downtown Savannah's historic district were built. This boom period, fueled largely by cotton exports, was perhaps most iconically represented by the historic sailing of the SS *Savannah* from Savannah to Liverpool in 29 days, the first transatlantic voyage by a steamship.

During the prosperous antebellum period, the economy of Charleston, Savannah, and surrounding areas was completely dependent on slave labor, but the cities themselves boasted large numbers of African Americans who were active in business and agriculture. For example, the vending stalls at the City Markets of both Savannah and Charleston were predominantly staffed by African American workers, some of them free.

SECESSION

Much of the lead-in to the Civil War focused on whether slavery would be allowed in the newest U.S. territories in the West, but there's no doubt that all figurative roads eventually led to South Carolina. During Andrew Jackson's presidency in the 1820s, his vice president, South Carolina's John C. Calhoun, became a thorn in Jackson's side with his aggressive advocacy for **nullification.** In a nutshell, Calhoun said that if a state decided the federal government wasn't treating it fairly—in this case with regard to tariffs that were hurting the cotton trade in the Palmetto State—it could simply nullify the federal law, superseding it with law of its own.

As the abolition movement gained steam and tensions over slavery rose, South Carolina congressman Preston Brooks took things to the next level. On May 22, 1856, he beat fellow senator Charles Sumner of Massachusetts nearly to death with his walking cane on the Senate floor. Sumner had just given a speech criticizing pro-slavery forces—including a relative of Brooks—and called slavery "a harlot." (In a show of support, South Carolinians sent Brooks dozens of new canes to replace the one he broke over Sumner's head.)

In 1860, the national convention of the Democratic Party, then the dominant force in U.S. politics, was held in—where else?—Charleston. Rancor over slavery and states' rights was so high that they couldn't agree on a single candidate to run to replace President James Buchanan. Reconvening in Maryland, the party split along sectional lines, with the Northern wing backing Stephen A. Douglas. The Southern wing, fervently desiring secession, deliberately chose its own candidate, John Breckinridge, in order to split the Democratic vote and throw the election to Republican Abraham Lincoln, an outspoken opponent of the expansion of slavery. During that so-called **Secession Winter** before Lincoln took office, seven states seceded from the union, first among them the Palmetto State, followed by Mississippi, Florida, Alabama, Georgia, Louisiana, and Texas.

CIVIL WAR

Five days after South Carolina's secession on December 21, 1860, U.S. Army major Robert Anderson moved his garrison from Fort Moultrie on Sullivan's Island to nearby Fort Sumter in Charleston Harbor. Over the

Robert E. Lee and Savannah

Before reluctantly surrendering his commission to serve the Confederacy, Robert E. Lee was a bright up-and-comer with the U.S. Army Corps of Engineers. As a 22-year-old lieutenant, the talented Virginian spent a year and a half in and around Savannah overseeing the construction of Fort Pulaski, named for the brave Polish count who lost his life in 1779's Siege of Savannah. On Lee's arrival in Savannah, construction was on hiatus due to the stifling summer heat. The handsome and dashing young man made the most of his time off, making significant inroads into downtown Savannah's high society. He was heartily welcomed into the home of his old West Point roommate John Mackay, whose three daughters adored him. The same was true of the two Minis daughters who lived nearby and also frequently had the young lieutenant over (and all this while Lee was conducting a long-distance courtship with his future wife back home in Virginia).

Construction of the fort on Cockspur Island began in 1829 under Major Samuel Babcock, whose health problems soon forced Lee to take over. Most of Lee's work focused on draining and diking the marshy island and its blue clay soil, and much of his handiwork remains functional today. After Lee was reassigned in 1831, Lieutenant Joseph Mansfield completed construction of the fort in 1847. A mix of slave labor and paid artisans lived in a sprawling construction camp. Today only Fort Pulaski's brick structures remain.

Five years after the war, Robert E. Lee paid a final visit to Savannah at age 63, accompanied by his daughter Agnes, to see his old comrade-in-arms General Joseph E. Johnston, who lived at 105 East Oglethorpe Avenue. During his stay in town, Lee slept at the Andrew Low House (Andrew's wife, Mary, was Jack Mackay's niece). Lee died six months later.

Fort Pulaski National Monument is currently administered by the National Park Service, which maintains an excellent website (www.nps.gov) detailing the rich history and fascinating archaeology of this, one of Savannah's great must-see sights.

next few months and into the spring, Anderson would ignore many calls to surrender, and Confederate forces would prevent any Union resupply or reinforcement. The stalemate was broken and the Confederates finally got their *casus belli* when a Union supply ship successfully ran the blockade and docked at Fort Sumter. Shortly before dawn on April 12, 1861, Confederate batteries around Charleston—ironically none of which were at the famous Battery itself—opened fire on Fort Sumter for 34 straight hours, until Anderson surrendered on April 13.

In a classic example of why you should always be careful what you wish for, the secessionists had been too clever by half in pushing for Lincoln. Far from prodding the North to sue for peace, the fall of Fort Sumter instead caused the remaining states in the Union to rally around the previously unpopular tall man from Illinois. Lincoln's skillful management of the Fort Sumter standoff meant that from then on, the South would bear history's blame for initiating the conflict that would claim over half a million American lives.

After Fort Sumter, four more Southern states—Virginia, Arkansas,

Old Dominion was the real prize for the secessionists, as Virginia had the South's only ironworks and by far the largest manufacturing base.

In November 1861, a massive Union invasion armada landed in Port Royal Sound in South Carolina, effectively taking the entire Lowcountry out of the war. Hilton Head was a Union encampment, and Beaufort became a major hospital center for the U.S. Army. The coast of Georgia was also blockaded, with Union forces using new rifled cannons in 1862 to quickly reduce Fort Pulaski at the mouth of the Savannah River. Charleston, however, did host two battles in the conflict. The **Battle of Secessionville** came in June 1862, when a Union force attempting to take Charleston was repulsed on James Island with heavy casualties.

The next battle, an unsuccessful Union landing on Morris Island in July 1863, was immortalized by the movie *Glory*. The 54th Massachusetts Regiment, an African American unit with white commanders, performed so gallantly in its failed assault on the Confederate **Battery Wagner** that it inspired the North and was cited by abolitionists as further proof that African Americans should be given freedom and full citizenship rights. Another invasion attempt on Charleston would not come, but the city was besieged and bombarded for nearly two more years (devastation made even worse by a massive fire, unrelated to the shelling, that destroyed much of the city in 1861).

Otherwise, the coast grew quiet. From Charleston to Brunswick, white Southerners evacuated the coastal cities and plantations for the hinterland, leaving behind only slaves to fend for themselves. In many coastal areas, African Americans and Union garrison troops settled into an awkward but peaceful coexistence. Many islands under Union control, such as Cockspur Island, where Fort Pulaski sat, became endpoints in the Underground Railroad.

General William Sherman concluded his **March to the Sea** in Savannah in 1864, famously giving the city to Lincoln as a Christmas present. While staunch Confederates, city fathers were wise enough to know what would happen to their accumulated wealth and fine homes should they be foolhardy enough to resist Sherman's army of war-hardened veterans.

The only military uncertainty left was in how badly Charleston, the "cradle of secession," would suffer for its sins. Historians and local wags have long debated why Sherman spared Charleston, the hated epicenter of the Civil War. Did he fall in love with the city during his brief posting there as a young lieutenant? Did he literally fall in love there, with one of the city's legendarily beautiful and delicate local belles? We may never know for sure, but it's likely that the Lowcountry's marshy, mucky terrain simply made it too difficult to move large numbers of men and supplies. So Sherman turned his army inland toward the state capital, Columbia, which would not be so lucky.

For the African American population of Savannah and Charleston, however, it was not a time of sadness but the great Day of Jubilee. Soon after

BACKGROUND HISTORY

the Confederate surrender, black Charlestonians held one of the largest parades the city has ever seen, with one of the floats being a coffin bearing the sign, "Slavery is dead."

As for the place where it all began, a plucky Confederate garrison remained underground at Fort Sumter throughout the war, as the walls above them were literally pounded into dust by the long Union siege. The garrison quietly left the fort under cover of night on February 17, 1865. Major Robert Anderson, who surrendered the fort at war's beginning, returned to Sumter in April 1865 to raise the same flag he'd lowered exactly four years earlier. Three thousand African Americans attended the ceremonies. Later that same night, Abraham Lincoln was assassinated in Washington DC.

RECONSTRUCTION

A case could be made that slavery need not have led the United States into Civil War. The U.S. government had banned the importation of slaves long before, in 1808. The great powers of Europe would soon ban slavery altogether (Spain in 1811, France in 1826, and Britain in 1833). Visiting foreign dignitaries in the mid-1800s were often shocked to find the practice in full swing in the American South. Even Brazil, the world center of slavery, where four out of every 10 slaves taken from Africa were brought (less than 5 percent came to the United States), would ban slavery in 1888, suggesting that slavery in the United States would have died a natural death. Still, the die was cast, the war was fought, and everyone had to deal with the aftermath.

For a brief time, Sherman's benevolent dictatorship on the coast held promise for an orderly postwar future. In 1865 he issued his sweeping "40 acres and a mule" order seeking dramatic economic restitution for coastal Georgia's free blacks. Politics reared its ugly head in the wake of Lincoln's assassination, however, and the order was rescinded, ushering in the chaotic Reconstruction era, echoes of which linger to this day.

Even as the trade in cotton and naval stores resumed to even greater heights than before, urban life and racial tension became more and more problematic. Urban populations swelled as freed blacks from all over the depressed countryside rushed into the cities. As one of them, his name lost to history, famously said: "Freedom was freer in Charleston."

RECONCILIATION

The opening of the exclusive Jekyll Island Club in 1886 marked the coming of the effects of the Industrial Revolution to the Deep South and the rejuvenation of regional economies. In Savannah, the Telfair Academy of Arts and Sciences, the South's first art museum, opened that same year. The cotton trade built back up to antebellum levels, and the South was on the long road to recovery.

The Spanish-American War of 1898 was a major turning point for the South, the first time since the Civil War that Americans were joined in patriotic unity. The southeastern coast felt this in particular, as it was a staging area for the invasion of Cuba. President William McKinley addressed the troops bivouacked in Savannah's Daffin Park, and Charlestonians cheered the exploits of their namesake heavy cruiser the USS *Charleston,* which played a key role in forcing the Spanish surrender of Guam.

Charleston would elect its first Irish American mayor, John Grace, in 1911, who would serve until 1923 (with a break 1915-1919). Although it wouldn't open until 1929, the first Cooper River Bridge joining Charleston with Mount Pleasant was the child of the Grace administration, credited today for modernizing the Holy City's infrastructure.

The arrival of the tiny but devastating boll weevil all but wiped out the cotton trade on the coast after the turn of the century, forcing the economy to diversify. Naval stores and lumbering were the order of the day at the advent of World War I, the combined patriotic effort for which did wonders in repairing the wounds of the Civil War, still vivid in many local memories. A major legacy of World War I that still greatly influences life in the Lowcountry is the Marine Corps Recruit Depot Parris Island, which began life as a small Marine camp in 1919.

RENAISSANCE AND DEPRESSION

In the Roaring '20s, that boom period following World War I, both Savannah and Charleston entered the world stage and made some of their most significant cultural contributions to American life. It was also the era of Prohibition. Savannah became notorious as a major import center for illegal rum from the Bahamas.

As elsewhere in the country, Prohibition ironically brought out a new appreciation for the arts and just plain having fun. The "Charleston" dance, originated on the streets of the Holy City and popularized in New York, would sweep the world. The Jenkins Orphanage Band, credited with the dance, traveled the world, even playing at President William Howard Taft's inauguration.

In the visual arts, the "Charleston Renaissance" took off, specifically intended to introduce the Holy City to a wider audience. Key work included the Asian-influenced art of self-taught painter Alice Ravenel Huger Smith and the etchings of Elizabeth O'Neill Verner. Edward Hopper was a visitor to Charleston during that time and produced several noted watercolors. The Gibbes Art Gallery, now the Gibbes Museum of Art, opened in 1905. Recognizing the cultural importance of the city and its history, in 1920 socialite Susan Pringle Frost and other concerned Charlestonians formed the Preservation Society of Charleston, the oldest community-based historic preservation organization in the country.

In 1924, lauded Charleston author DuBose Heyward wrote the locally set novel *Porgy.* With Heyward's cooperation, the book would soon be turned into the first American opera, *Porgy and Bess,* by George Gershwin, who labored over the composition in a cottage on Folly Beach. Ironically, *Porgy and Bess,* which premiered with an African American cast in New York in 1935, wouldn't be performed in its actual setting until 1970 because of segregation laws.

In Savannah, the Roaring '20s coincided with the rise of Johnny Mercer, who began his theater career locally in the Town Theater Group. In 1925, Flannery O'Connor was born in Savannah, and the quirky, Gothic nature of the city would mark her later writing indelibly.

The Depression hit the South hard, but since wages and industry were already behind the national average, the economic damage wasn't as bad as elsewhere in the country. As elsewhere in the South, the public works programs of President Franklin D. Roosevelt's New Deal not only helped to keep locals employed but contributed greatly to the cultural and archaeological record of the region. The Civilian Conservation Corps built much of the modern state park system in the area.

WORLD WAR II AND THE POSTWAR BOOM

With the attack on Pearl Harbor and the coming of World War II, life on the southeastern coast would never be the same. Military funding and facilities swarmed into the area, and populations and long-depressed living standards rose as a result. In many outlying Sea Islands of Georgia and South Carolina, electricity came for the first time.

The "Mighty Eighth" Air Force was founded and based in Savannah, and Camp Stewart, later Fort Stewart, was built in nearby Hinesville. In shipyards in Savannah and Brunswick, hundreds of Liberty ships were built to transport cargo to the citizens and allied armies of Europe.

The postwar U.S. infatuation with the automobile—and its troublesome child, the suburb—brought exponential growth to the great cities of the coast. The first bridge to Hilton Head Island was built in 1956, leading to the first of many resort developments, Sea Pines, in 1961. With rising coastal populations came pressure to demolish more and more fine old buildings to put parking lots and high-rises in their place. A backlash grew among the elite, aghast at the destruction of so much history.

The immediate postwar era brought about the formation of both the Historic Charleston Foundation and the Historic Savannah Foundation, which began the financially and politically difficult work of protecting historic districts from the wrecking ball. They weren't always successful, but the work of these organizations—mostly older women from the upper crust—laid the foundation for the successful coastal tourist industry to come and preserved important American history for the ages.

CIVIL RIGHTS

The ugly racial violence that plagued much of the country during the civil rights era rarely visited the Georgia coast. Whether due to the laid-back ambience or the fact that African Americans were simply too numerous there to be denied, cities like Savannah experienced little real unrest during that time.

Contrary to popular opinion, the civil rights era wasn't just a blip in the 1960s. The gains of that decade were the fruits of efforts begun decades earlier. Many of the exertions involved efforts to expand black suffrage. Though African Americans had secured the nominal right to vote years before, primary contests were not under the jurisdiction of federal law. As a result, Democratic Party primary elections—the de facto general elections because of that party's total dominance in the South at the time—were effectively closed to African American voters.

Savannah was at the forefront of expanding black suffrage, and Ralph Mark Gilbert, pastor of the historic First African Baptist Church, launched one of the first black voter registration drives in the South. In Charleston, the Democratic primary was opened to African Americans for the first time in 1947. In 1955, a successful black realtor, J. Arthur Brown, became head of the Charleston chapter of the NAACP and membership soared, bringing an increase in activism. In 1960, the Charleston Municipal Golf Course voluntarily integrated to avoid a court battle.

Martin Luther King Jr. visited South Carolina in the late 1960s, speaking in Charleston in 1967 and helping reestablish the Penn Center on St. Helena Island as not only a cultural center but a center of political activism as well. The hundred-day strike of hospital workers at the Medical University of South Carolina in 1969—right after King's assassination—got national attention and was the culmination of Charleston's struggle for civil rights. By the end of the 1960s, the city councils of Savannah and Charleston had elected their first black aldermen, and the next phase in local history began.

A COAST REBORN

The decade of the 1970s brought the seeds of the future success of the coastal region. Influential and long-serving mayor John P. Rousakis was elected. The Greek American would break precedents and forge key alliances, reviving the local economy.

In the years 1970-1976, Rousakis renovated the then-seedy riverfront district, making it the centerpiece of the city's burgeoning tourist trade. The Savannah College of Art and Design (SCAD) opened in 1979 and began the process of renovating dozens of the city's historic buildings, a process that continues today.

The coast's combination of beautiful scenery and cheap labor proved irresistible to the movie and TV industry, which would begin filming many series and films in the area in the 1970s and continuing to this day.

The economic boom of the 1990s was particularly good to Savannah, whose port saw a huge dividend from increasing globalization. Also in the 1990s came the *Midnight in the Garden of Good and Evil* phenomenon, which would put Savannah—already on the upswing—on the tourist map for good. Although not a Savannah native, the iconic Paula Deen brought a new national focus on the city through her long presence on the Food Network and through her local restaurant, The Lady and Sons, which continues to pack in visitors.

Today Savannah's tourism business is healthier than ever. Attracted by the coastal region, artists, writers, and entrepreneurs continue to flock, increasing the economic and social diversity of the area and taking it to new heights of livability. With that has come the usual struggles with growth vs. quality of life, as Savannah is coping with an influx of Airbnb-style short-term vacation rentals in its historic district.

People and Culture

Contrary to how the region is portrayed in the media, the coast from Charleston down to the Georgia-Florida border is hardly exclusive to natives with thick, flowery accents who still obsess over the Civil War and eat grits three meals a day. As you will quickly discover, the entire coastal area is heavily populated with transplants from other parts of the country, and in some areas you can actually go quite a long time without hearing even one of those Scarlett O'Hara accents. Some of this is due to the region's increasing attractiveness to professionals and artists, drawn by the temperate climate, natural beauty, and business-friendly environment. Part of it is due to its increasing attractiveness to retirees, most of them from the frigid Northeast. Indeed, in some places, chief among them Hilton Head, the most common accent is a New York or New Jersey one, and a Southern accent is rare.

In any case, don't make the common mistake of assuming you're coming to a place where footwear is optional and electricity is a recent development (though it's true that many of the islands didn't get electricity until the 1950s and 1960s). Because so much new construction has gone on in the South in the last quarter-century or so, you might find some aspects of the infrastructure—specifically the roads and the electrical utilities—actually superior to where you came from.

POPULATION

The Savannah Metropolitan Statistical Area (MSA), which includes Chatham, Bryan, and Effingham Counties, numbered about 347,000 people in the 2010 census. The city of Savannah itself has a population of about 136,000. The Hilton Head-Beaufort MSA includes Beaufort and Jasper Counties and comprised about 180,000 people in the 2010 census. The town of Hilton Head had about 37,000 residents in 2010, and Beaufort had about 13,000. The Brunswick MSA includes Brantley, Glynn, and McIntosh Counties and has about 100,000 people.

Racial Makeup

Its legacy as the center of the U.S. slave trade and plantation culture means that the Savannah region has a large African American population. The Savannah MSA is about 35 percent black. In the city proper, the black population percentage is higher, nearly 60 percent.

Voodoo and Hoodoo

BACKGROUND
PEOPLE AND CULTURE

The spiritual system called voodoo—the word is a corruption of various West African spellings—came to the Western Hemisphere with the importation of slaves. Voodoo is a clearly defined religion and is the dominant religion of millions of West Africans.

Like many ancient belief systems, voodoo is based on the veneration of ancestors and the possibility of continued communication with them. Up until fairly recently the African American Gullah and Geechee populations of the South Carolina and Georgia Sea Islands still had a common belief that the older slaves who were born in Africa could actually fly in spirit form to the continent of their birth and back again.

While voodoo has always been unfairly sensationalized—a notable recent example being the "voodoo priestess" Minerva in *Midnight in the Garden of Good and Evil*—it's not necessarily as malevolent in actual practice as in the overactive imaginations of writers and directors. The stereotypical practice of sticking pins in dolls to bring pain to a living person actually has its roots in European and Native American folklore.

Much of what the layperson thinks is voodoo is actually hoodoo, a body of folklore—not a religion—indigenous to the American South. Hoodoo combines elements of voodoo (communicating with the dead) and fundamentalist Christianity (extensive scriptural references). In the United States, most African American voodoo tradition was long ago subsumed within Protestant Christianity, but the Gullah populations of the Sea Islands of South Carolina and Georgia still keep alive the old ways. In the Gullah and Geechee areas of the Georgia and Carolina Sea Islands, the word *conjure* is generally the preferred terminology for this hybrid belief system, which has good sides and bad sides and borrows liberally from African lore and Christian folkways.

The old Southern practice of painting shutters and doors blue to ward off evil comes from hoodoo, where the belief in ghosts, or "haints," is largely a byproduct of poorly understood Christianity (Mediterranean countries also use blue to keep evil at bay, and the word *haint* is of Scots-Irish origin). You can still see this particular shade of "haint blue" on rural and vernacular structures throughout the Lowcountry.

Another element of hoodoo that you can still encounter today is the role of the "root doctor," an expert at folk remedies who blends together various indigenous herbs and plants in order to produce a desired effect or result. In *Midnight in the Garden of Good and Evil*, this role belongs to the fabled Dr. Buzzard, who teaches Minerva everything she knows about "conjure work." However, a root doctor is not to be confused with a "gifted reader," a fortune-teller born with the talent to tell the future. From the no-doubt embellished account in John Berendt's *Midnight*, scholars would put the late Minerva squarely into the category of root doctor or "conjurer" rather than the undeniably more compelling "voodoo priestess."

The Hispanic population, as elsewhere in the United States, is growing rapidly, but statistics can be misleading. Though Hispanics are growing at a triple-digit clip in the region, they still remain less than 3 percent of Georgia's population. Bilingual signage is becoming more common but is still quite rare.

RELIGION

This area is unusual in the Deep South for its wide variety of religious faiths. While Georgia remains overwhelmingly Protestant—at least three-quarters of all Christians in Georgia are members of some Protestant denomination, chief among them Southern Baptist and Methodist—Savannah's cosmopolitan, polyglot history has made it a real melting pot of faith.

Savannah was originally dominated by the Episcopal Church (known as the Anglican Church in other countries), but from early on it was also a haven for those of other faiths. Various types of Protestant offshoots soon arrived, including the Scottish Presbyterians and German Salzburger Lutherans. The seeds of Methodism and the "Great Awakening" were planted along the coast from Savannah up to Charleston.

Owing to vestigial prejudice from the European realpolitik of the founding era, the Roman Catholic presence on the coast was late in arriving, but once it came it was there to stay. Savannah has quite a large Roman Catholic population by Southern standards, mostly due to the influx of Irish in the mid-1800s.

But most unusually of all for the Deep South, Savannah and Charleston not only have large Jewish populations but ones that have been key participants in the cities from the very first days of settlement. Sephardic Jews of primarily Portuguese descent were among the first settlers of both Savannah and Charleston, and they kept up an energetic trade between the two cities for centuries afterward, continuing to the present day.

MANNERS

The prevalence and importance of good manners is the main thing to keep in mind about the South. While it's tempting for folks from more outwardly assertive parts of the world to take this as a sign of weakness, that would be a major mistake. Southerners use manners, courtesy, and chivalry as a system of social interaction with one goal above all: to maintain the established order during times of stress. A relic from a time of extreme class stratification, etiquette and chivalry are ways to make sure that the elites are never threatened—and, on the other hand, that even those on the lowest rungs of society are afforded at least a basic amount of dignity. But as a practical matter, it's also true that Southerners of all classes, races, and backgrounds rely on the observation of manners as a way to sum up people quickly. To any Southerner, regardless of class or race, your use or neglect of basic manners and proper respect indicates how seriously they should take you—not in a socioeconomic sense, but in the big picture overall.

The typical Southern sense of humor—equal parts irony, self-deprecation, and good-natured teasing—is part of the code. Southerners are loath to criticize another individual directly, so often they'll instead take the opportunity to make an ironic joke. Self-deprecating humor is also much more common in the South than in other areas of the country. Because of this, conversely you're also expected to be able to take a joke yourself without being too sensitive.

Sephardic Jews in the South

Two of the oldest cities in the Anglo-Saxon Protestant South have rich and early histories of an active Jewish presence—specifically, **Sephardic Jews** (those with a Spanish or Portuguese background). Jews and Muslims on the Iberian Peninsula got along quite well while the Islamic Moors of North Africa dominated the area. But after Ferdinand and Isabella's completion of the Reconquista in 1492, the Jews of Spain went from being respected citizens to persecuted pariahs nearly overnight. Five years later, Portugal followed suit, expelling all Jews on pain of death unless they became "New Christians," or *conversos*. A sizable proportion of *conversos*, however, were actually so-called crypto-Jews, who publicly practiced Roman Catholicism while secretly remaining devout Jews. Many synagogues of Sephardic origin today have their floors covered in sand to remember that dark time when Jewish congregations practiced their faith in basements covered with sand to muffle the sounds of their feet.

The diaspora of the Sephardic Jews, ironically, contributed greatly to the health of the global Jewish community, as skilled tradesmen, doctors, and men of letters spread out to Spanish, Portuguese, English, and Dutch colonies where the Inquisition had little sway. It was primarily from the ranks of this Sephardic diaspora that the Jewish settlers of the Lowcountry and Georgia coast came.

Savannah wasn't the first colonial town to host Jewish settlers, but the group of 42 Sephardic Jews that arrived five months after Oglethorpe's landing in 1733 was by far the largest contingent to travel to North America up to that time. All but eight of this core group were Spanish and Portuguese Jews who immigrated to London after spending years as crypto-Jews in their home countries. Accepted without question by Oglethorpe, the Jews of Savannah quickly rose in power and influence. In fact, the first white male child born in Georgia was a Jewish boy, Philip "Uri" Minis.

The assimilation of the Jews into Southern society was so complete that the Secretary of State of the Confederate States of America, Judah Benjamin, was a practicing Jew of Sephardic origin. This assimilation also had a flip side, in that the Sephardic Jews were generally just as enthusiastic about owning slaves as any other white citizens of the area. In 1830 about 83 percent of Jewish households in Charleston had slaves, compared to an almost-identical percentage of 87 percent of white Christian Charlestonians.

In Savannah, the key Judaic attraction is **Temple Mickve Israel** (20 E. Gordon St., 912/233-1547, www.mickveisrael.org, 30-minute tours Mon.-Fri. 10am-12:30pm and 2pm-3:30pm, $6 suggested donation), the only Gothic synagogue in the country and the third-oldest Jewish congregation in North America.

Another key element in Southern manners is the discussion of money—or rather, the nondiscussion. Unlike some parts of the United States, in the South it's considered the height of rudeness to ask someone what their salary is or how much they paid for their house. Not that the subject is entirely taboo—far from it; you just have to know the code. For example, rather than brag about how much or how little they paid for their home, a Southern head of household will instead take you on a guided tour of the grounds. Along the way they'll make sure to detail: (a) all the work that

Walter Edgar's Journal

He's originally from Alabama, but you could call University of South Carolina (USC) professor Walter Edgar the modern voice of the Palmetto State. From the rich diversity of barbecue to the inner workings of the poultry business and the charms of beach music, Edgar covers the gamut of South Carolina culture and experience on his popular weekly radio show *Walter Edgar's Journal,* airing on South Carolina public radio stations throughout the state.

Currently director of the USC Institute of Southern Studies, the Vietnam vet and certified barbecue contest judge explains the show like this: "On the *Journal* we look at current events in a broader perspective, trying to provide context that is often missing in the mainstream media." More specifically, Edgar devotes each one-hour show to a single guest, usually a South Carolinian—by birth or by choice—with a unique perspective on some aspect of state culture, business, arts, or folkways. By the time the interview ends, you have a much deeper understanding not only of the topic of the show but of the interviewee as well. And because of Edgar's unique way of tying strands of his own vast knowledge and experience into every interview, you also leave with a deeper understanding of South Carolina itself.

In these days of media saturation, a public radio show might sound like a rather insignificant perch from which to influence an entire state. But remember that South Carolina is a small, close-knit place, a state of Main Street towns rather than impersonal metro areas. During any given show, many listeners in Edgar's audience will know his guests on a personal basis. And by the end of the show, the rest of the listeners will feel as if they do.

Listen to "Walter Edgar's Journal" each Friday at noon on South Carolina public radio, with a repeat each Sunday at 4pm. Hear podcasts of previous editions at www.scetv.org.

was done; (b) how grueling and unexpected it all was; and (c) how hard it was to get the contractors to show up.

Depending on the circumstances, in the first segment, (a), you were just told either that the head of the house is made of money and has a lot more of it to spend on renovating than you do, or that they are a brilliant negotiator who got the house for a song. In part (b) you were told that you are not messing around with a lazy deadbeat here, but with someone who knows how to take care of themselves and can handle adversity with aplomb. And with part (c) you were told that the head of the house knows the best contractors in town and can pay enough for them to actually show up, and if you play your cards right, they might pass on their phone numbers to you with a personal recommendation. See? Breaking the code is easy once you get the hang of it.

Etiquette

As we've seen, it's rude here to inquire about personal finances, along with the usual no-go areas of religion and politics. Here are some other specific etiquette tips:

- **Basics:** Be liberal with "please" and "thank you," or conversely, "no thank you" if you want to decline a request or offering.

- **Eye contact:** With the exception of very elderly African Americans, eye contact is not only accepted in the South, it's encouraged. In fact, to avoid eye contact in the South means you're likely a shady character.

- **Handshake:** Men should always shake hands with a *very* firm, confident grip and appropriate eye contact. It's OK for women to offer a handshake in professional circles, but otherwise not required.

- **Chivalry:** When men open doors for women here—and they will—it is not thought of as a patronizing gesture but as a sign of respect. Accept graciously and walk through the door.

- **The elderly:** Senior citizens—or really anyone obviously older than you—should be called "sir" or "ma'am." Again, this is not a patronizing gesture in the South but is considered a sign of respect. Also, in any situation where you're dealing with someone in the service industry, addressing them as "sir" or "ma'am" regardless of their age will get you far.

- **Bodily contact:** Interestingly, though public displays of affection by romantic couples are generally frowned upon here, Southerners are otherwise pretty touchy-feely once they get to know you. Southerners who are well acquainted often say hello or goodbye with a hug.

- **Driving:** With the exception of the interstate perimeter highways around the larger cities, drivers in the South are generally less aggressive than in other regions. Cutting sharply in front of someone in traffic is taken as a personal offense. If you need to cut in front of someone, poke the nose of your car a little bit in that direction and wait for a car to slow down and wave you in front. Don't forget to wave back as a thank-you. Similarly, using a car horn can also be taken as a personal affront, so use your horn sparingly, if at all. In rural areas, don't be surprised to see the driver of an oncoming car offer a little wave. This is an old custom, sadly dying out. Just give a little wave back; they're trying to be friendly.

THE GUN CULTURE

One of the most misunderstood aspects of the South is the value the region places on the personal possession of firearms. No doubt, the 2nd Amendment to the U.S. Constitution ("A well regulated Militia, being necessary to the security of a free State, the right of the people to keep and bear Arms, shall not be infringed") is well known here and fiercely protected, at the governmental and at the grassroots levels.

State laws do tend to be significantly more accommodating of gun owners here than in much of the rest of the country. It is legal to carry a concealed handgun in South Carolina and Georgia with the proper permit, and you need no permit at all to possess a weapon in your house or car for self-defense. However, there are regulations regarding how a handgun must be conveyed in automobiles.

Both states now have so-called (and controversial) "stand your ground" laws, whereby if you're in imminent lethal danger, you do not have to first try to run away before resorting to deadly force to defend yourself.

In 2014, Georgia passed what is widely considered to be the most permissive new gun law in the country, allowing those with the proper license to carry an open or concealed handgun into a bar (though if you do, you're not supposed to drink alcohol). You can now even take your handgun into a church service in Georgia unless the church specifically prohibits it.

Essentials

Transportation

AIR

Savannah is served by the fairly efficient **Savannah/Hilton Head International Airport** (SAV, 400 Airways Ave., 912/964-0514, www.savannahairport.com), directly off I-95 at exit 104. The airport is about 20 minutes from downtown Savannah and 45 minutes from Hilton Head Island. Airlines with routes to SAV include American (www.aa.com), Allegiant (www.allegiant.com), Delta (www.delta.com), JetBlue (www.jetblue.com), Sun Country (www.suncountry.com), and United (www.ual.com).

Taxis and rideshare operators provide transportation into Savannah. The maximum cab fare for destinations in the historic district is $28.

CAR

Savannah is the eastern terminus of I-16, and that interstate is the most common entrance to the city. However, most travelers get to I-16 via I-95, taking the exit for downtown Savannah (Historic District). Once on I-16, the most common entry points into Savannah proper are via the Gwinnett Street exit, which puts you near the southern edge of the Historic District near Forsyth Park, or, more commonly, the Montgomery Street exit farther into the heart of downtown.

Paralleling I-95 is the old coastal highway, now U.S. 17, which goes through Savannah. U.S. 80 is Victory Drive for most of its length through town; after you pass through Thunderbolt on your way to the islands area, however, it reverts to U.S. 80, the only route to and from Tybee Island.

In Savannah, for quick access to the south, take the one-way streets Price (on the east side of downtown) or Whitaker (on the west side of downtown). Conversely, if you want to make a quick trip north into downtown, three one-way streets taking you there are East Broad, Lincoln, and Drayton.

When you're driving downtown and come to a square, the law says traffic within the square *always* has the right of way. In other words, if you haven't yet entered the square, you must yield to any vehicles already in the square.

Car Rentals

The majority of rental car facilities are at the Savannah/Hilton Head International Airport, including **Avis** (800/831-2847), **Budget** (800/527-0700), **Dollar** (912/964-9001), **Enterprise** (800/736-8222), **Hertz** (800/654-3131), **National** (800/227-7368), and **Thrifty** (800/367-2277). Rental locations away from the airport are **Avis** (7810 Abercorn St.,

---

Previous: the ferry to Cumberland Island; Savannah tram.

912/354-4718), **Budget** (7070 Abercorn St., 912/355-0805), and **Enterprise**
(3028 Skidaway Rd., 912/352-1424; 9505 Abercorn St., 912/925-0060; 11506-A Abercorn Expressway, 912/920-1093; 7510 White Bluff Rd., 912/355-6622).

PARKING

Parking is at a premium in downtown Savannah. Traditional coin-operated meter parking is available throughout the city, but more and more the city is going to self-pay kiosks, which accept debit and credit cards. There is also a free app to pay on your phone, called ParkSavannah. Bottom line: Be sure to pay for all parking weekdays and Saturday 8:30am-8pm. The rate is $2 per hour north of Liberty Street to the Savannah River, $1 per hour elsewhere.

The city operates several parking garages at various rates and hours: the **Bryan Street Garage** (100 E. Bryan St.), the **Robinson Garage** (132 Montgomery St.), the **State Street Garage** (100 E. State St.), the **Liberty Street Garage** (401 W. Liberty St.), and the new **Whitaker Street Garage,** underneath revitalized Ellis Square.

Tybee Island has paid parking year-round daily 8am-8pm.

TAXI

Taxi services in Georgia tend to be less regulated than in other states, but service is plentiful in Savannah and is generally reasonable. The chief local provider is **Yellow Cab** (866/319-9646, www.savannahyellowcab.com). For wheelchair accessibility, request cab number 14. Other providers include **Adam Cab** (912/927-7466), **Magikal Taxi Service** (912/897-8294), and **Sunshine Cab** (912/272-0971).

If you're not in a big hurry, it's always fun to take a **Savannah Pedicab** (912/232-7900, www.savannahpedicab.com) for quick trips around downtown, or with the competing company **Royal Bike Taxi** (912/341-3944, www.royalbiketaxi.com). In both cases your friendly driver will pedal one or two passengers anywhere within the historic district, and you essentially pay what you think is fair (I recommend $5 pp minimum).

RIDE SHARING

Uber and Lyft are widely available in Savannah and will serve you well at just about any time of day or night. The other areas covered in this book have significantly less population density, so don't depend on these services there.

TRAIN

Savannah is on the New York-Miami *Silver Service* of **Amtrak** (2611 Seaboard Coastline Dr., 912/234-2611, www.amtrak.com). To get to the station on the west side of town, take I-16 west and then I-516 north. Immediately take the Gwinnett Street-Railroad Station exit and follow the Amtrak signs.

BUS

Chatham Area Transit (www.catchacat.org, Mon.-Sat. 5:30am-11:30pm, Sun. 7am-9pm, $1.50, includes one transfer, free for children under 41 inches tall, exact change only), Savannah's publicly supported bus system, is quite thorough and efficient considering Savannah's relatively small size. Plenty of routes crisscross the entire area.

Of primary interest to visitors is the free and recently expanded **Dot Express Shuttle** (Mon.-Fri. 7am-7pm, Sat. 10am-7pm, Sun. 10am-6pm, www.connectonthedot.com), which travels a continuous circuit route through the historic district with 24 stops at hotels, historic sites, and the Savannah Visitors Center. It comes around roughly every 10 minutes and is wheelchair accessible. It's a great option.

Travel Tips

TRAVELING WITH CHILDREN

The Lowcountry and Georgia coast are very kid-friendly, with the possible exception of some B&Bs that are clearly not designed for younger children. If you have any doubts about this, feel free to inquire. Otherwise, there are no special precautions unique to this area. There are no zoos per se in the region, but animal lovers of all ages will enjoy the **Oatland Island Wildlife Center** in Savannah. Better still, take the kids on nature outings to the amazing national wildlife refuges in the area.

ACCESS FOR TRAVELERS WITH DISABILITIES

While the vast majority of attractions and accommodations make every effort to comply with federal law regarding those with disabilities, as they're obliged to do, the very historic nature of this region means that some structures simply cannot be retrofitted for maximum accessibility. This is something you'll need to find out on a case-by-case basis, so call ahead. The sites administered by the National Park Service in this guide (Fort Pulaski, Fort Frederica, and Cumberland Island National Seashore) are as wheelchair-accessible as possible.

Some special shuttles are available. In Savannah, Chatham Area Transit (www.catchacat.org) runs a **Teleride** service (912/354-6900). For the visually impaired, there's the **Savannah Association for the Blind** (214 Drayton St., 912/236-4473).

ALTERNATIVE LODGING

The sharing economy is in full swing in Savannah, with Airbnb and various Vacation Rental by Owner facilities available online. The city is currently embroiled in an ongoing effort to determine, whether politically or through the courts, how much if any regulation they can assert over Airbnb operations.

As of this writing, Airbnbs are widely available in the Savannah Historic District and most areas north of Victory Drive. This area includes most tourist-frequented areas covered in this book. In other parts of town, however, it is currently illegal by city ordinance.

LGBTQ TRAVELERS

Visitors often find Savannah to be surprisingly cosmopolitan and diverse for a Deep South city, and nowhere is this truer than in its sizeable and influential gay and lesbian community. In line with typical Southern protocol, the community is largely apolitical and more concerned with integration than provocation. But they're still very much aware of their growing impact on the local economy and are major players in art and commerce.

The **Savannah Pride Festival** is held every autumn at various venues in town. Top-flight dance-oriented musical acts perform, restaurants show off their creativity, and activists staff information booths. The chief resource for local gay and lesbian information and concerns is the **First City Network,** whose main website (www.firstcitynetwork.net) features many useful links. Another great Internet networking resource is **Gay Savannah** (www.gaysavannah.com).

SENIOR TRAVELERS

Both because of the large proportion of retirees in the region and because of Southerners' traditional respect for the elderly, the area is quite friendly to senior citizens. Many accommodations and attractions offer a slight senior discount, which can add up over the course of a trip. Always inquire about such discounts before making a reservation, however, as checkout time is too late to do so.

TRAVELING WITH PETS

While the United States is very pet friendly, that friendliness rarely extends to restaurants and other indoor locations. More and more accommodations are allowing pet owners to bring pets, often for an added fee, but inquire before you arrive. In any case, keep your dog on a leash at all times. Some beaches in the area permit dog walking at certain times of the year, but as a general rule, keep dogs off of beaches unless you see signage saying otherwise.

CRIME

While crime rates are indeed above national averages in many of the areas covered in this guide, incidents of crime in the more heavily trafficked tourist areas are no more common than anywhere else. In fact, these areas might be safer because of the amount of foot traffic and police attention.

By far the most common crime against visitors here is simple theft, primarily from cars. (Pickpocketing, thankfully, is rare in the United States.) Always lock your car doors. Conversely, only leave them unlocked if you're absolutely comfortable living without whatever's inside at the time. As a general rule, I try to lock valuables—such as CDs, a recent purchase, or my wife's purse—in the trunk. (Just make sure the "valet" button, allowing the trunk to be opened from the driver's area, is disabled.)

For emergencies, always call 911.

POLICE

If you are the victim of a crime, *always call the police.* Law enforcement wants more information, not less, and at very least you'll have an incident report in case you need to make an insurance claim for lost or stolen property.

The Savannah Police Department has jurisdiction throughout the city of Savannah. For unincorporated Chatham County, the Chatham County Police Department has jurisdiction. Other municipalities, such as Tybee Island and Pooler, have their own city departments. For nonemergencies in Savannah, call 912/651-6675; for emergencies, call 911.

AUTO ACCIDENTS

If you're in an auto accident where there's injury or damage to one or both cars, you must at minimum exchange insurance information with the other driver. It's always prudent to wait for police. Unless there is personal injury involved, you should move your car just enough to clear the way for other traffic if able to do so.

Since it's illegal to drive in these states without auto insurance, I'll assume you have some. And because you're insured, the best course of action in a minor accident, where injuries are unlikely, is to wait for the police and give them your side of the story. After that, let the insurance companies deal with it; that's what they're there for. If you suspect any injuries, call 911 immediately.

ILLEGAL DRUGS

Marijuana, heroin, methamphetamine, and cocaine and all its derivatives are illegal in states covered by this guide. The use of ecstasy and similar mood-elevators is also illegal. The penalties for illegal drug possession and use are quite severe.

ALCOHOL

The drinking age in the United States is 21. Most restaurants that serve alcoholic beverages allow those under 21 inside. Generally speaking, if only those over 21 are allowed inside, you will be greeted at the door by someone asking to see identification. These people are often poorly trained and anything other than a state driver's license may confuse them, so be forewarned.

Drunk driving is a problem on the highways of the United States, and South Carolina and Georgia are no exceptions. Always drive defensively, especially late at night, and obey all posted speed limits and road signs—and never assume the other driver will do the same. You may never drive with an open alcoholic beverage in the car, even if it belongs to a passenger.

As far as retail purchase goes, in most parts of Georgia, no alcoholic beverages are sold at the retail level on Sunday, other than in restaurants that also sell food. In South Carolina you may buy only beer and wine, not hard liquor, on Sundays.

MEDICAL SERVICES

Unlike most developed nations, the United States has no comprehensive national health care system. Visitors from other countries who need non-emergency medical attention are best served by going to freestanding medical clinics. The level of care is typically very good, but unfortunately you'll be paying out of pocket for the service. For emergencies, however, do not hesitate to go to the closest hospital emergency room, where the level of care is generally also quite good, especially for trauma. Worry about payment later; emergency rooms in the United States are required to take true emergency cases whether or not the patient can pay for services. Call 911 for ambulance service.

Hospitals

Savannah has two very good hospital systems. Centrally located near midtown, **Memorial Health University Hospital** (4700 Waters Ave., 912/350-8000, www.memorialhealth.com) is the region's only Level-1 trauma center and is one of the best in the nation. The St. Joseph's-Candler Hospital System (www.sjchs.org) has two units, **St. Joseph's Hospital** (11705 Mercy Blvd., 912/819-4100) on the extreme south side and **Candler Hospital** (5401 Paulsen St., 912/819-6000), closer to midtown.

Pharmaceuticals

Unlike many other nations, antibiotics are available in the United States only on a prescription basis and are not available over the counter. Most cold, flu, and allergy remedies are available over the counter, though some require you to provide ID in order to purchase to thwart purchases for illegal drug manufacture. While homeopathic remedies are gaining popularity in the United States, they are nowhere near as prevalent as in Europe.

Drugs with the active ingredient ephedrine are available in the

United States without a prescription, but their purchase is tightly regulated to cut down on the use of these products to make the illegal drug methamphetamine.

STAYING HEALTHY
Vaccinations

As of this writing, there are no vaccination requirements to enter the United States. Contact your embassy before coming to confirm this before arrival, however. In the autumn, at the beginning of flu season, preventive influenza vaccinations, simply called "flu shots," often become available at easily accessible locations like clinics, health departments, and even supermarkets.

Humidity, Heat, and Sun

There is only one way to fight the South's high heat and humidity, and that's to drink lots of fluids. A surprising number of people each year refuse to take this advice and find themselves in various states of dehydration, some of which can land you in a hospital. Remember: If you're thirsty, you're already suffering from dehydration. The thing to do is keep drinking fluids *before* you're thirsty as a preventative action rather than a reaction.

Always use sunscreen, even on a cloudy day. If you do get a sunburn, get a pain-relief product with aloe vera as an active ingredient. On extraordinarily sunny and hot summer days, don't even go outside between the hours of 10am and 2pm.

HAZARDS
Insects

Because of the recent increase in the mosquito-borne West Nile virus, the most important step to take in staying healthy in the Lowcountry and Georgia coast—especially if you have small children—is to keep **mosquito bites** to a minimum. Do this with a combination of mosquito repellent and long sleeves and long pants, if possible. Not every mosquito bite will give you the virus; in fact, chances are quite slim that one will. But don't take the chance if you don't have to.

The second major step in avoiding insect nastiness is to steer clear of **fire ants,** whose large gray or brown dirt nests are quite common in this area. They attack instantly and in great numbers, with little or no provocation. They don't just bite; they inject you with poison from their stingers. In short, fire ants are not to be trifled with. While the only real remedy is the preventative one of never coming in contact with them, should you find yourself being bitten by fire ants, the first thing to do is to stay calm. Take off your shoes and socks and get as many of the ants off you as you can. Unless you've had a truly large number of bites—in which case you should seek medical help immediately—the best thing to do next is wash the area to get any venom off, and then disinfect with alcohol if you have any handy. Then a topical treatment such as calamine lotion or hydrocortisone is advised. A fire ant bite will leave a red pustule that lasts about a week. Try your best not to scratch it so that it won't get infected.

Outdoor activity, especially in woodsy, undeveloped areas, may bring you in contact with another unpleasant indigenous creature, the tiny but obnoxious **chigger,** sometimes called the redbug. The bite of a chigger can't be felt, but the enzymes it leaves behind can lead to a very itchy little red spot. Contrary to folklore, putting fingernail polish on the itchy bite will not "suffocate" the chigger, because by this point the chigger itself is long gone. All you can do is get some topical itch or pain relief and go on with your life. The itching will eventually subside.

Threats in the Water

While enjoying area beaches, a lot of visitors become inordinately worried about **shark attacks.** Every couple of summers there's a lot of hysteria about this, but the truth is that you're much more likely to slip and fall in a bathroom than you are to even come close to being bitten by a shark in these shallow Atlantic waters.

A far more common fate for area swimmers is to get stung by a **jellyfish,** or sea nettle. They can sting you in the water, but most often beachcombers are stung by stepping on beached jellyfish stranded on the sand by the tide. If you get stung, don't panic; wash the area with saltwater, not freshwater, and apply vinegar or baking soda. A product called Jellyfish Squish is also available and seems to work well.

Lightning

The southeastern United States is home to vicious fast-moving thunderstorms, often with an amazing amount of electrical activity. Death by lightning strike occurs often in this region and is something that should be taken quite seriously. The general rule of thumb is that if you're in the water, whether at the beach or in a swimming pool, and hear thunder, get out of the water immediately until the storm passes. If you're on dry land and see lightning flash a distance away, that's your cue to seek safety indoors. Whatever you do, do not play sports outside when lightning threatens.

Information and Services

VISITOR INFORMATION
Savannah

The main clearinghouse for visitor information is the downtown **Savannah Visitors Center** (301 MLK Jr. Blvd., 912/944-0455, daily 9am-5:30pm). The newly revitalized Ellis Square features a small visitors kiosk (daily from 10am) at the northwest corner of the square, with public restrooms and elevators to the underground parking garage beneath the square.

Other visitors centers in the area include the **River Street Hospitality**

Center (1 River St., 912/651-6662, daily 9am-8pm), the **Tybee Island Visitor Center** (S. Campbell Ave. and U.S. 80, 912/786-5444, daily 9am-5:30pm), and the **Savannah Airport Visitor Center** (464 Airways Ave., 912/964-1109, daily 8:30am-midnight).

Visit Savannah (101 E. Bay St., 877/728-2662, www.visitsavannah.com), the local convention and visitors bureau, maintains a list of lodgings and visitors centers on its website.

Hilton Head Island

In Hilton Head, get information, book a room, or secure a tee time just as you come onto the island at the **Hilton Head Island Chamber of Commerce Welcome Center** (100 William Hilton Pkwy., 843/785-3673, www.hiltonheadisland.org, daily 9am-6pm).

The Golden Isles

The **Brunswick-Golden Isles Visitor Center** (2000 Glynn Ave., 912/264-5337, daily 9am-5pm) is at the intersection of U.S. 17 and the Torras Causeway to St. Simons Island. A downtown information station is in **Old City Hall**, at the corner of Mansfield and Newcastle Streets (912/262-6934, daily 8am-5pm).

The **Jekyll Island Visitor Center** (901 Downing Musgrove Causeway, 912/635-3636, daily 9am-5pm) is before you get to the island, on the long causeway along the marsh. The **St. Simons Visitor Center** (530-B Beachview Dr., 912/638-9014, www.bgivb.com, daily 9am-5pm) is in the St. Simons Casino building near Neptune Park and the Village.

The **Darien Welcome Center** is at the corner of U.S. 17 and Fort King George Drive (912/437-6684, Mon.-Sat. 9am-5pm). The **Sapelo Island Visitors Center** (912/437-3224, www.sapelonerr.org, Tues.-Fri. 7:30am-5:30pm, Sat. 8am-5:30pm, Sun. 1:30pm-5pm) is actually not on Sapelo but at the dock where you take the ferry, in Meridian, Georgia, on Highway 99 from Darien.

The **St. Marys Visitor Center** is located at 406 Osborne Street (912/882-4000, www.stmaryswelcome.com, Mon.-Sat. 9am-5pm, Sun. noon-5pm). The **Cumberland Island Visitors Center** is at 113 St. Marys Street (912/882-4336, daily 8am-6pm).

There are several entrances to the Okefenokee Swamp, with the closest thing to a visitors center being the U.S. Fish and Wildlife Service's **Richard S. Bolt Visitor Center** (912/496-7836, daily 9am-5pm) at the eastern entrance near Folkston, Georgia.

LIBRARIES

The **Live Oak Public Library** (www.liveoakpl.org) is the umbrella organization for the libraries of Chatham, Effingham, and Liberty Counties. By far the largest branch is south of downtown Savannah, the **Bull Street Branch** (222 Bull St., 912/652-3600, Mon.-Tues. 9am-8pm, Wed.-Fri. 9am-6pm, Sun. 2pm-6pm). Farthest downtown and tucked away on Upper

Factor's Walk is the charming little **Ola Wyeth Branch** (4 E. Bay St., 912/232-5488, Mon.-Fri. noon-3pm). In midtown Savannah is the historic **Carnegie Branch** (537 E. Henry St., 912/231-9921, Mon. 10am-8pm, Tues. Thurs. 10am-6pm, Fri. 2pm-6pm, Sat. 10am-6am).

The **Georgia Historical Society** (501 Whitaker St., 912/651-2128, www.georgiahistory.com, Tues.-Sat. 10am-5pm) has an extensive collection of clippings, photos, maps, and other archival material at its headquarters at the corner of Forsyth Park in Hodgson Hall. Their website has been extensively revamped and is now one of the Southeast's best online resources for Georgia history information.

The **Jen Library** (201 E. Broughton St., 912/525-4700, www.scad.edu, Mon.-Fri. 7:30am-1am, Sat. 10am-1am, Sun. 11am-1am, shorter hours during school breaks), run by the Savannah College of Art and Design, has a cavernous 85,000-square-foot space. Its main claim to fame is the remarkable variety of art periodicals to which it subscribes, nearly 1,000 at last count. It was built for the school's 7,000-plus art students, but the public can enter and use it as well with photo ID (you just can't check anything out).

MEDIA AND COMMUNICATIONS
Internet Access
Visitors from Europe and Asia are likely to be disappointed at the quality of Internet access in the United States, particularly the area covered in this guide. Fiber-optic lines are still a rarity, and while many hotels and B&Bs now offer in-room Internet access—some charge, some don't, so make sure to ask ahead—the quality and speed of the connection might prove poor. Wireless (Wi-Fi) networks are also less than impressive, but that situation continues to improve on a daily basis in coffeehouses, hotels, and airports. Unfortunately, many hotspots in private establishments charge fees.

Phones
Generally speaking, the United States is behind Europe and much of Asia in terms of cell phone technology. Unlike Europe, where "pay as you go" refills are easy to find, most American cell phone users pay for monthly plans through a handful of providers. Still, you should have no problem with cell phone coverage in urban areas. Where it gets much less dependable is in rural areas and on beaches. Bottom line: Don't depend on having cell service everywhere you go.

As with a regular landline, any time you face an emergency, call 911 on your cell phone.

All phone numbers in the United States are seven digits preceded by a three-digit area code. You may have to dial "1" before a phone number if it's a long-distance call, even within the same area code. The area code for the part of South Carolina covered in this guide is 843. The area code for the part of Georgia covered in this guide is 912.

Newspapers

The daily newspaper of record is the *Savannah Morning News* (912/525-0796, www.savannahnow.com). It puts out an entertainment insert, called "Do," on Thursday. The free weekly newspaper in town is *Connect Savannah* (912/721-4350, www.connectsavannah.com), hitting stands each Wednesday. Look to it for culture and music coverage as well as an alternative take on local politics and issues.

Two glossy magazines compete: the hipper *The South* magazine (912/236-5501, www.thesouthmag.com) and the more establishment *Savannah* magazine (912/652-0293, www.savannahmagazine.com).

Radio

The National Public Radio affiliate is the Georgia Public Broadcasting station WSVH (91.1 FM). Savannah State University offers jazz, reggae, and Latin music on WHCJ (90.3 FM). Georgia Public Broadcasting is on WVAN. The local NBC affiliate is WSAV, the CBS affiliate is WTOC, the ABC affiliate is WJCL, and the Fox affiliate is WTGS.

Post Offices

The main post office of note for most visitors to Savannah is the **Telfair Square Station** (118 Barnard St., Mon.-Fri. 8am-5pm).

MONEY

Automated teller machines (ATMs) are available in all urban areas covered in this guide. Be aware that if the ATM is not owned by your bank, not only will that ATM likely charge you a service fee, but your bank may charge you one as well. While ATMs have made traveler's checks less essential, traveler's checks do have the important advantage of accessibility, as some rural and less-developed areas covered in this guide have few or no ATMs. You can purchase traveler's checks at just about any bank.

Establishments in the United States only accept the national currency, the U.S. dollar. To exchange foreign money, go to any bank.

Generally, establishments that accept credit cards will feature stickers on the front entrance with the logo of the particular cards they accept, although this is not a legal requirement. The use of debit cards has dramatically increased in the United States. Most retail establishments and many fast-food chains are now accepting them. Make sure you get a receipt whenever you use a credit card or a debit card.

Resources

Suggested Reading

NONFICTION

Aberjhani and Sandra West. *Encyclopedia of the Harlem Renaissance*. New York: Checkmark Books, 2003. A brilliantly researched account of the great African American diaspora out of the South that eventually gave birth to the Charleston dance craze of the 1920s.

Calonius, Erik. *The Wanderer: The Last American Slave Ship and the Conspiracy That Set Its Sails*. New York: St. Martin's Press, 2006. A page-turning tale of the last illegal slave shipment to land in the United States, on Jekyll Island, Georgia.

Fraser, Walter J. Jr. *Savannah in the Old South*. Athens, GA: University of Georgia Press, 2005. An insightful and balanced history of Georgia's first city, from founding through Reconstruction.

Georgia Writers Project. *Drums and Shadows: Survival Studies among the Georgia Coastal Negroes*. Athens, GA: University of Georgia Press, 1986. Arising from a government-funded research project during the Depression, this still ranks as one of the best oral histories ever assembled, using firsthand accounts from African American residents of Georgia's Sea Islands to paint a picture of a lifestyle gone by.

Greene, Melissa Fay. *Praying for Sheetrock*. New York: Ballantine, 1992. In this modern classic, Greene explores the racism and corruption endemic in McIntosh County, Georgia, during the era of the civil rights movement.

Kemble, Fanny. *Journal of a Residence on a Georgian Plantation in 1838-1839*. Athens, GA: University of Georgia Press, 1984. A famed English actress's groundbreaking antislavery account of her stay on a rice plantation in McIntosh County, Georgia.

Lewis, Lloyd. *Sherman: Fighting Prophet*. Lincoln, NE: University of Nebraska Press, 1993. Though first published in 1932, this remains the most thorough, insightful, and well-written biography of General William Sherman in existence.

Morgan, Philip, ed. *African American Life in the Georgia Lowcountry: The Atlantic World and the Gullah Geechee.* Athens, GA: University of Georgia Press, 2010. The best book I've come by on the history and folkways of Georgia's Gullah or Geechee people. Balanced, scholarly, yet still readable in the extreme.

Seabrook, Charles. *Cumberland Island: Strong Women, Wild Horses.* Winston-Salem, NC: John F. Blair, 2002. An even-handed, journalistic look inside the tension between environmentalists and the residents of Cumberland Island.

Williams, Robin B. *Buildings of Savannah.* Charlottesville, VA: University of Virginia Press, 2016. The best and most practical single source for personally exploring the wide variety of architectural styles in Savannah, from colonial times through the Victorian streetcar era to Modernist examples.

Wood, Betty, ed. *Mary Telfair to Mary Few: Selected Letters, 1802-1844.* Athens, GA: University of Georgia Press, 2007. The revealing, chatty letters of a great arts patron and member of a major Savannah slave-owning family, to her best friend who left the city and moved north because of her abolitionist leanings. We know that Mary Few replied, but her letters remain undiscovered.

FICTION

Berendt, John. *Midnight in the Garden of Good and Evil.* New York: Vintage, 1999. Well, not exactly fiction, but far from completely true, nonetheless this modern classic definitely reads like a novel while remaining one of the unique and readable travelogues of recent times.

Caskey, James. *Haunted Savannah: The Official Guidebook to Savannah Haunted History Tour.* Savannah: Bonaventture Books, 2012. The author may quibble with this being in the "fiction" section, but this is an entertaining and also quite educating look at Savannah's various paranormal tales.

Hervey, Harry. *The Damned Don't Cry.* Marietta, GA: Cherokee Publishing, 2003. The original *Midnight,* this bawdy 1939 potboiler takes you into the streets, shanties, drawing rooms, and boudoirs of real Savannahians during the Depression.

O'Connor, Flannery. *Flannery O'Connor: Collected Works.* New York: Library of America, 1988. For a look into Savannah's conflicted, paradoxical soul, read anything by this native-born writer, so grounded in tradition yet so ahead of her time even to this day. This volume includes selected letters, an especially valuable (and entertaining) insight.

TOURISM INFORMATION

Visit Savannah
www.visitsavannah.com
Savannah's Convention & Visitors Bureau is particularly adept at social media.

CUISINE AND ENTERTAINMENT

A Common Connoisseur
www.acommonconnoisseur.com
An insider's look at the Savannah restaurant scene, with an emphasis on new spots.

RECREATION

Georgia Department of Natural Resources
www.gadnr.org
Ditto for this site, which has lots of great information on the wildlife and geology of Georgia's beautiful and largely undeveloped barrier islands.

Savannah Bicycle Campaign
www.bicyclecampaign.org
The clearinghouse for routes and rides by Savannah's most dedicated cyclists.

Georgia State Parks
www.gastateparks.org
Vital historical and visitor information for Georgia's underrated network of historical state park sites along the coast, including camping reservations.

NATURE AND ENVIRONMENT

Ocean Science
http://www.skio.uga.edu/category/blog
A blog by the staff of Savannah's Skidaway Institute of Oceanography, focusing on barrier island ecology and the maritime environment.

HISTORY AND BACKGROUND

New Georgia Encyclopedia
www.georgiaencyclopedia.org
A mother lode of concise, neutral, and well-written information on the natural and human history of Georgia from prehistory to the present.

Restaurants Index

Nightlife Index

Hotels Index

Photo Credits

Advice on where to sleep, eat, and explore

Detailed driving directions including mileage and drive times

Itineraries for a range of timelines

MOON

NEW ENGLAND
Road Trip

BOSTON, ACADIA NATIONAL PARK, WHITE MOUNTAINS, BERKSHIRES, NEWPORT, AND CAPE COD

JEN ROSE SMITH

MOON

PACIFIC NORTHWEST
Road Trip

SEATTLE, VANCOUVER, VICTORIA, THE OLYMPIC PENINSULA, PORTLAND, THE OREGON COAST & MOUNT RAINIER

ALLISON WILLIAMS

MOON

ROUTE 66
Road Trip

MIDPOINT CAFE

CANDACY TAYLOR

MOON

SOUTH FLORIDA & THE KEYS
Road Trip

WITH MIAMI, WALT DISNEY WORLD, TAMPA & THE EVERGLADES

JASON FERGUSON

MOON

SOUTHWEST
Road Trip

LAS VEGAS, ZION & BRYCE, MONUMENT VALLEY, SANTA FE & TAOS, AND THE GRAND CANYON

TIM HULL

MOON

VANCOUVER & CANADIAN ROCKIES
Road Trip

VICTORIA, BANFF, JASPER, CALGARY, THE OKANAGAN, WHISTLER & THE SEA-TO-SKY HIGHWAY

CAROLYN B. HELLER

MAP SYMBOLS

■	**Sights**	◉	National Capital	▲	Mountain	═══	Major Hwy
■	**Restaurants**	◉	State Capital	✚	Natural Feature		Road/Hwy
■	**Nightlife**	○	City/Town	⚐	Waterfall		Pedestrian Friendly
■	**Arts and Culture**	★	Point of Interest	⌀	Park	- - - - -	Trail
■	**Sports and Activities**	•	Accommodation	⬟	Archaeological Site	▪▪▪▪▪	Stairs
■	**Shops**	▼	Restaurant/Bar	❶	Trailhead	··········	Ferry
■	Hotels	▪	Other Location	❷	Parking Area	-·-·-·-	Railroad

CONVERSION TABLES

°FAHRENHEIT   °CELSIUS

WATER BOILS (100°C / 210-220°F)

WATER FREEZES (0°C / 30-40°F)

$$°C = (°F - 32) / 1.8$$
$$°F = (°C \times 1.8) + 32$$

1 inch = 2.54 centimeters (cm)
1 foot = 0.304 meters (m)
1 yard = 0.914 meters
1 mile = 1.6093 kilometers (km)
1 km = 0.6214 miles
1 fathom = 1.8288 m
1 chain = 20.1168 m
1 furlong = 201.168 m
1 acre = 0.4047 hectares
1 sq km = 100 hectares
1 sq mile = 2.59 square km
1 ounce = 28.35 grams
1 pound = 0.4536 kilograms
1 short ton = 0.90718 metric ton
1 short ton = 2,000 pounds
1 long ton = 1.016 metric tons
1 long ton = 2,240 pounds
1 metric ton = 1,000 kilograms
1 quart = 0.94635 liters
1 US gallon = 3.7854 liters
1 Imperial gallon = 4.5459 liters
1 nautical mile = 1.852 km

MOON SAVANNAH

Avalon Travel
Hachette Book Group
1700 Fourth Street
Berkeley, CA 94710, USA
www.moon.com

Editor: Rachel Feldman
Series Manager: Leah Gordon
Copy Editor: Christopher Church
Graphics and Production Coordinator: Suzanne Albertson
Cover Design: Faceout Studios, Charles Brock
Moon Logo: Tim McGrath
Map Editor and Cartographer: Kat Bennett
Indexer: Greg Jewett

ISBN-13: 978-1-64049-302-5

Printing History
1st Edition — 2015
2nd Edition — November 2018
5 4 3 2 1

Front cover photo: River Street © Joe Daniel Price/Getty Images

Back cover photo: detail of fountain in Forsyth Park © Rolf52 | Dreamstime.com

Printed in Canada by Friesens